Database Concepts

Database Concepts

Second Edition

David M. Kroenke
University of Washington

PEARSON

Prentice Hall

Upper Saddle River, New Jersey 07458

Library of Congress Cataloging-in-Publication Data
Kroenke, David.
    Data concepts / David Kroenke – 2nd ed.
        p. cm.
    Includes bibliographical references and index.
    ISBN 0-13-145141-3 (alk. paper)
    1. Database management. 2. Relational databases. I. Title.

QA76.9.D3K736 2004
005.74—dc22   2003068968

Executive Editor, MIS: Robert Horan
Publisher: Natalie E. Anderson
Project Manager (Editorial): Kyle Hannon
Editorial Assistant: Robyn Goldenberg
Media Project Manager: Joan Waxman
Marketing Manager: Sharon M. Koch
Marketing Assistant: Danielle Torio
Managing Editor (Production): John Roberts
Production Editor: Renata Butera
Production Assistant: Joe DeProspero
Manufacturing Buyer: Diane Peirano
Design Manager: Maria Lange
Interior Design: Heather Peres
Cover Design: Bruce Kenselaar
Manager, Print Production: Christy Mahon
Composition/Full-Service Project Management: BookMasters, Inc.
Printer/Binder: VonHoffmann

Credits and acknowledgments borrowed from other sources and reproduced, with permission, in this textbook appear on appropriate page within the text.

Microsoft® and Windows® are registered trademarks of the Microsoft Corporation in the U.S.A. and other countries. Screen shots and icons reprinted with permission from the Microsoft Corporation. This book is not sponsored or endorsed by or affiliated with the Microsoft Corporation.

Pearson Education LTD.   Pearson Education Australia PTY, Limited
Pearson Education Singapore, Pte. Ltd   Pearson Education North Asia Ltd
Pearson Education, Canada, Ltd   Pearson Educación de Mexico, S.A. de C.V.
Pearson Education–Japan   Pearson Education Malaysia, Pte. Ltd

10 9 8 7 6 5 4 3 2 1
ISBN 0-13-145141-3

Brief Contents

Contents

Preface

Colin Johnson is a production supervisor for a small manufacturer in Seattle. Several years ago, Colin wanted to build a database to keep track of components in product packages. At the time, he was using a spreadsheet to perform this task, but he could not get the reports that he needed from the spreadsheet. Colin had heard about Microsoft Access, and he tried to use it to solve his problem. After several days of frustration, he bought several popular Access books and attempted to learn from them. Ultimately, he gave up and hired a consultant who built an application that more or less met Colin's needs. Over time, Colin wanted to change his application, but he did not dare try.

Colin was a successful businessperson who was highly motivated to achieve his goals. A seasoned Windows user, he had been able to teach himself how to use Excel, PowerPoint, and a number of production-oriented application packages. He was flummoxed at his inability to use Access to solve his problem. "I'm sure I could do it, but I just don't have any more time to invest," he thought. This story is even more remarkable because it has occurred tens of thousands of times over the last decade.

Microsoft Corporation, Oracle Corporation, and other database management system (DBMS) vendors are aware of such scenarios and have invested millions of dollars in creating better graphical interfaces, hundreds of multi-panel wizards, and many sample applications. Unfortunately, such efforts treat the symptom and not the cause. In fact, most users have no clear idea of what wizards are doing on their behalf. As soon as these users require changes to database structure or to components such as forms and queries, they drown in a sea of complexity for which they are unprepared. With little understanding of the underlying fundamentals, these users grab at any straw that appears to lead in the direction they want. The consequence is poorly designed databases and applications that fail to meet the users' requirements.

Why can people like Colin learn a word processor or a spreadsheet product, yet fail when trying to learn to use a DBMS product? First, the underlying database concepts are unnatural to most people. Whereas everyone knows what paragraphs and margins are, no one knows what a relation is. Second, it seems like using a DBMS product ought to be easier than it is. "All I want to do is keep track of something. Why is it so hard?" people ask. Without knowledge of the relational model, breaking a sales invoice into five separate tables before storing the data is mystifying to business users.

▶ THE NEED FOR ESSENTIAL CONCEPTS

With today's technology, it is impossible to utilize a DBMS successfully without first learning fundamental concepts. After years of developing databases with business users, I believe that the following database concepts are essential.

> Fundamentals of the relational model
> Structured Query Language (SQL)
> Data modeling

> Database design
> Database administration

Users like Colin—and students who will accept jobs similar to his—need not learn these topics to the same depth as do future information systems professionals. Consequently, this textbook presents only essential concepts—those that are necessary for users like Colin who want to create and use small databases. I have rewritten, simplified, and omitted topics that you will find in my in-depth book on the subject, *Database Processing.*[1] However, in this process, I have endeavored to ensure that the discussions remain accurate and do not mislead. Nothing here will need to be unlearned if students take more advanced database courses.

▶ TEACHING CONCEPTS INDEPENDENT OF DBMS PRODUCTS

This book does not assume that any particular DBMS product will be used by students. Access is introduced in the Appendix, but all of the concepts are presented in a DBMS-agnostic manner. When learned this way, students come to understand that the fundamentals pertain to any database, from the smallest Access database to the largest Oracle or DB2 database.

Moreover, this approach avoids a common pitfall. When concepts and products are taught at the same time, students frequently confound concepts with product features and functions. For example, consider referential integrity constraints. When taught from a conceptual standpoint, students learn that there are times when the values of a column in one table must always be present as values of a column in a second table. Students also will learn how this constraint arises in the context of relationship definition and how either the DBMS or the application must enforce this constraint. If taught in the context of a DBMS—say in the context of Access—students will only learn that in some cases you check a check box, and in other cases you don't. The danger is that the underlying concept will be lost in the product feature.

All of this is not to say that a DBMS should not be used in this class. On the contrary, students can best master these concepts by applying them using a commercial DBMS product. This book was written assuming that you will use a second book or other materials to teach the features and functions of the DBMS that you select for your class. Prentice-Hall provides a number of companion workbooks for Microsoft Access 2003 that may be packaged with this text.

▶ REVIEW QUESTIONS, EXERCISES, AND PROJECTS

Because it is so important for students to apply the concepts they learn, each chapter concludes with sets of review questions, exercises, and three projects that run throughout the book. Students should be able to answer the review questions if they have read and understood the chapter material. The exercises require the students to apply the chapter concepts to a small problem or task.

The first of the projects, Garden Glory, concerns the development and use of a database for a partnership that provides gardening and yard maintenance services to individuals and organizations. The second project, James River Jewelry, addresses the need for a database to support a frequent-buyer program for a retail store, and the third project concerns the scheduling of lab equipment for the chemistry department of a university. These three projects appear in all of the book's chapters. In each instance, students are asked to apply concepts from the chapter to the project. Instructors will find

---

[1]David Kroenke, *Database Processing,* ninth edition (Upper Saddle River, NJ: Prentice Hall, 2004).

more information on the use of these projects in the instructor's manual and can obtain databases and data from the password-protected instructor's portion of our Web site (**www.prenhall.com/kroenke**).

▶ CHANGES FROM THE FIRST EDITION

This text features two major changes from the first edition. First, the discussion of normalization has been altered to provide a prescriptive procedure for normalizing relations. Whereas the first edition described normalization principles but left it to the student to apply those principles, Chapter 2 of this edition presents a four-step process (see page 38) that students can use to normalize. This change will not only make the normalization task easier, it will make normalization principles easier to understand.

Second, a new Chapter 7 presents an overview of the following advanced topics.

> Web database processing
> Database processing with XML
> Distributed database processing
> OLAP and data mining
> Object-relational database management

The goal of these discussions is to introduce the essence of the topic to the student to increase the students' database literacy and to encourage them to continue their studies in this important topic.

▶ BOOK OVERVIEW

This textbook consists of seven chapters and an appendix. Chapter 1 explains why databases are used, what their components are, and how they are developed. Students will learn the purpose of databases and their applications, and how databases differ from and improve on keeping lists in spreadsheets. Chapter 2 introduces the relational model and defines basic relational terminology. It also introduces the fundamental ideas that underlie normalization and describe a normalization process.

Chapter 3 presents fundamental SQL statements. Basic SQL statements for data definition are described, as are SQL SELECT and data modification statements. No attempt is made to present advanced SQL statements; only the essential statements are described.

The next three chapters consider database design and management. Chapter 4 addresses data modeling using the entity-relationship (E-R) model. The need for data modeling is described, basic E-R terms and concepts are introduced, and a short case application of E-R modeling is presented. Chapter 5 describes database design and explains the essentials of normalization. The data model from the case example in Chapter 4 is transformed into a relational design in Chapter 5.

Chapter 6 provides an overview of database administration. It describes the need for database administration and surveys concurrency control, security, and backup and recovery techniques. I believe this topic is important for all databases, even for personal, single-user databases. In fact, in some ways this topic is more important for such databases because no professional database administrator is present to ensure that critical tasks are performed.

Finally, Chapter 7 introduces advanced topics as described previously. Microsoft Access is introduced in the appendix. This brief introduction can be used in conjunction with Access documentation to help students create simple databases and application components.

► ACKNOWLEDGMENTS

I wish to thank the following reviewers for their insightful and helpful comments:

Tina Ashford, Macon State College
Karin Bast, University of Wisconsin–La Crosse
Shoba Chengular-Smith, State University of New York at Albany
Sam Chung, Pacific Lutheran University
Mary Daul, Marian College
Jamie Doll, Foothill College
Deena Engel, New York University
Larry Fudella, Erie Community College
Thanh Giang, Leeward Community College
Constanza Hagmann, Kansas State University
Larry Holt, Rollins College
Peter Johnson, Humboldt State University
Ted Lemser, Oklahoma City Community College
Brian Mennecke, Iowa State University
Anne Nelson, High Point University
Terry Redman, Webster University
Eileen Sikkema, University of Washington
Pat Smith, Temple College
Charles Stout, High Point University
Richard Tibbs, Radford University

In addition, I would like to thank my editor, Bob Horan, and my associate editor, Kyle Hannon, for their continued support, insight, and assistance in the development of this project.

Over the past 30-plus years, I have found the development of databases and database applications to be an enjoyable and rewarding activity. I believe that the number, size, and importance of databases will increase in the future, and that the field will achieve even greater prominence. It is my hope that the concepts, knowledge, and techniques presented in this book will help students participate successfully in database projects now and for many years to come.

David Kroenke
Seattle, Washington

About the Author

David M. Kroenke is one of the pioneers of database technology. In 1971, while working at the Pentagon, he programmed one of the world's first database management system (DBMS) products. In 1974, Grace Hopper appointed him to the CODAYSL EUF committee, and in 1977 he worked as a consultant for Fred Brooks at IBM. Kroenke helped start the Microrim Corporation, where he led the development of the R:base family of DBMS products. In a 1991 article, Wayne Ratliff credited one of Kroenke's textbooks for giving him the idea for the development of d:base. In 1989, Kroenke consulted for Microsoft on the project that led to the development of Microsoft Access. He is also the father of the semantic object model, a data model that many believe is superior to the entity-relationship model.

Kroenke is the author of five computer textbooks. His text *Database Processing* was first published in 1977 and is currently in its ninth edition. In 1990 and 1991, he was the Hanson Professor of Management Science at the University of Washington. In that same year, the International Association for Computer Information Systems named him Computer Educator of the Year. He holds a B.S. in economics from the U.S. Air Force Academy, an M.S. in management science from the University of Southern California, and a Ph.D. from Colorado State University, where he studied linear models under Franklin Graybill. He currently teaches at the University of Washington.

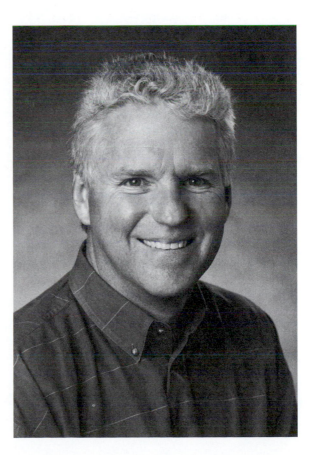

Database
Concepts

PART I

Fundamentals

Part I introduces fundamental concepts and techniques of relational database management. Chapter 1 explains database technology and why databases are used, and describes the components of a database system. Chapter 2 introduces the relational model and defines key relational terms. It also presents basic relational design principles. Finally, Chapter 3 presents Structured Query Language, an international standard for creating and processing relational databases.

Once you have learned this basic technology, we will then turn to database design and management in Part II.

Getting Started

> Identify the purpose and scope of this book
> Know the potential problems with lists
> Understand the reasons for using a database
> Understand how related tables avoid the problems of lists
> Know the components of a database system
> Learn the elements of a database
> Learn the purpose of the database management system (DBMS)
> Understand the functions of a database application

Knowledge of database technology increases in importance every day. Databases are used everywhere: They are key components of e-commerce and other Web-based applications. They lay at the heart of organization-wide operational and decision support applications. Databases also are used by thousands of work groups and millions of individuals. In fact, estimates of the number of active databases in the world today exceed 10 million.

The purpose of this book is to teach you the essential database concepts, technology, and techniques that you will need to begin a career as a database developer. This book does not teach everything of importance in database technology, but it will give you sufficient background to be able to create your own personal databases and to participate as a member of a team in the development of larger, more complicated databases. You will also be able to ask the right questions to learn more on your own.

In this first chapter, we will investigate the reasons for using a database. We begin by describing the problems that can occur when using lists. Using a series of three examples, you will see how sets of related tables avoid those problems. Next we will describe the components of a database system and explain the elements of a database, the purpose of the database management system (DBMS), and the functions of a database application.

► WHY USE A DATABASE?

A database is used to help people keep track of things. You might wonder why we need a special term (and course) for such technology when a simple list could serve the same purpose. In fact, many people do keep track of things using lists, and sometimes such lists are valuable. In other cases, however, simple lists lead to data inconsistencies and other problems.

In this section, we will examine several different lists and show some of these problems. As you will see, we can solve the problems by splitting lists into tables of data. Such tables are the key components of a database. In fact, a majority of this text concerns the design of such tables and techniques for manipulating the data they contain.

Problems with Lists

Figure 1-1 shows a simple list of student data stored in a spreadsheet. For such a simple list, a spreadsheet works well. Even if the list is long, you can sort it alphabetically by name or e-mail address to find any entry you want. You can change the data values, add data for a new student, or delete student data. With a list like the one in Figure 1-1, none of these actions is problematical and a database is unnecessary. Keeping this list in a spreadsheet is just fine.

Suppose, however, we change this list by adding adviser data as shown in Figure 1-2. You can still sort this list any way you want to find an entry, but modifying this list causes problems. Suppose, for example, you want to delete the data for student Marino. If you delete the sixth row, you will remove Marino's data, but you will also remove the fact that there is an adviser named Tran and that professor Tran's e-mail address is **Tran@ourcampus.edu**. See Figure 1-3.

Similarly, updating a value in this list can have unintended consequences. If, for example, you change AdviserEmail in the eighth row, you will have inconsistent data. After the change, the fifth row indicates one e-mail address for professor Taing, and the eighth row indicates a different e-mail address for the same professor. Or is it the same professor? From this list, we cannot tell if there is one professor Taing with two inconsistent e-mail addresses or whether there are two professors named Taing with different e-mail addresses. By making this update, we add confusion and uncertainty to our list.

Finally, what do we do if we want to add data for a professor who has no advisees? Say, for example, Professor Greene has no advisees, but we still want to record his or her e-mail address. As shown in Figure 1-3, we must insert a row with incomplete values, or as they are called in the database field, **null values**. As you will learn in the next chapter, null values are always problematical and we want to avoid them when possible.

FIGURE 1-1

Student List in
Spreadsheet

	A	B
1	Name	Email
2	Andrews, Matthew	MattA@ourcampus.edu
3	Brisbon, Lisa	LisaB@ourcampus.edu
4	Fischer, Douglas	DougF@ourcampus.edu
5	Hwang, Terry	TerryH@ourcampus.edu
6	Marino, Chip	ChipM@myserver.com
7	Lai, Tzu	TzuL@ourcampus.edu
8	Thompson, James	JamesT@myserver.com

FIGURE 1-2

Student List with
Advisers

	A	B	C	D
1	Name	Email	Adviser	AdviserEmail
2	Andrews, Matthew	MattA@ourcampus.edu	Baker	Baker@ourcampus.edu
3	Brisbon, Lisa	LisaB@ourcampus.edu	Valdez	Valdez@ourcampus.edu
4	Fischer, Douglas	DougF@ourcampus.edu	Baker	Baker@ourcampus.edu
5	Hwang, Terry	TerryH@ourcampus.edu	Taing	Taing@ourcampus.edu
6	Marino, Chip	ChipM@myserver.com	Tran	Tran@ourcampus.edu
7	Lai, Tzu	TzuL@ourcampus.edu	Valdez	Valdez@ourcampus.edu
8	Thompson, James	JamesT@myserver.com	Taing	Taing@ourcampus.edu

FIGURE 1-3

Student/Adviser List with Problematic Changes

	A	B	C	D
1	Name	Email	Adviser	AdviserEmail
2	Andrews, Matthew	MattA@ourcampus.edu	Baker	Baker@ourcampus.edu
3	Brisbon, Lisa	LisaB@ourcampus.edu	Valdez	Valdez@ourcampus.edu
4	Fischer, Douglas	DougF@ourcampus.edu	Baker	Baker@ourcampus.edu
5	Hwang, Terry	TerryH@ourcampus.edu	Taing	Taing@ourcampus.edu
6	Marino, Chip	ChipM@myserver.com	Tran	Tran@ourcampus.edu
7	Lai, Tzu	TzuL@ourcampus.edu	Valdez	Valdez@ourcampus.edu
8	Thompson, James	JamesT@myserver.com	Taing	Taing2@ourcampus.edu
9	??	??	Greene	Greene@ourcampus.edu

Deleted row—
Too much lost

Changed row—
Inconsistent data

Inserted row—
Data missing

What happened in these two examples? We had a simple list with two columns, added two more columns to it, and thereby created several problems. It isn't that the list has four columns instead of two. The list in Figure 1-4 has four columns, yet it suffers from none of the problems that the list in Figure 1-3 does. We can delete the data for student Marino and lose only data for that student. No unintended side consequence

FIGURE 1-4

Four-Column Student List with Changes

	A	B	C	D
1	Name	Email	Phone	Dorm
2	Andrews, Matthew	MattA@ourcampus.edu	301.555.1234	McKinley
3	Brisbon, Lisa	LisaB@ourcampus.edu	301.555.3335	Dorsett
4	Fischer, Douglas	DougF@ourcampus.edu	301.555.1688	McKinley
5	Hwang, Terry	TerryH@ourcampus.edu	301.555.1837	McKinley
6	Ingrum, Garret	Garretl@somewhere.com	301.555.3880	Dorsett
7	Marino, Chip	ChipM@myserver.com	301.555.8665	Johnson
8	Lai, Tzu	TzuL@ourcampus.edu	301.555.4139	McKinley
9	Thompson, James	JamesT@myserver.com	301.555.3240	Johnson

Inserted
row

Deleted
row

Changed
row

occurs. Similarly, we can change the value of Dorm for student Lai without introducing any inconsistency. We can add data for student Ingram and not have any null values.

An essential difference exists between the list in Figure 1-3 and that in Figure 1-4. See if you can determine this difference before continuing. The essential difference is that the list in Figure 1-4 is all about a single thing: All of the data in that list concern students. In contrast, the list in Figure 1-3 is about two things: Some of the data concerns students and some of the data concerns advisers. In general, whenever a list has data about two or more different things, modification problems will result.

To reinforce this idea, examine Figure 1-5. This list has data about three different things: students, advisers, and departments. As you can see in the figure, the problems with inserting, updating, and deleting data just get worse. A change in the value of Adviser, for example, might necessitate a change in only AdviserEmail, or it might require a change in AdviserEmail, Department, and Admin. As you can imagine, if this list is long—say it has thousands of rows—and if several people process it, in a short time it will be a mess.

Using Relational Database Tables

The problems of using lists were first identified in the 1960s, and a number of different techniques were developed to solve them. Over time, a methodology called the **relational model** emerged as the leading solution, and today almost every commercial database is based on the relational model. We will examine this model in detail in Chapter 2. Here, however, we will introduce the basic ideas of the relational model by showing how it solves the modification problems of lists.

Remember Mrs. Gazernenplatz, your eighth-grade English teacher? She said that a paragraph should have a single theme. If you have a paragraph with more than one theme, she said to break it up into two or more paragraphs, each with a single theme.

That idea is the foundation of the design of relational databases. A relational database contains a collection of separate tables. In most circumstances, the data in each table concern one and only one theme. If a table has two or more themes, we break it up into two or more tables.

A Relational Design for the Student/Adviser List
The list in Figure 1-2 has two themes: students and advisers. If we put this data into a relational database, we place the student data in one table and the adviser data in a second table. We still want to show which students have which advisers, however, so we leave AdviserName in the

FIGURE 1-5

Student/Adviser/ Department List with Problematic Changes

If changed to Taing, need to change AdviserEmail only.
If changed to Valdez, need to change AdviserEmail, Department, Admin.

	A	B	C	D	E	F
1	Name	Email	Adviser	AdviserEmail	Department	Admin
2	Andrews, Matthew	MattA@ourcampus.edu	Baker	Baker@ourcampus.edu	Accounting	Shawna
3	Brisbon, Lisa	LisaB@ourcampus.edu	Valdez	Valdez@ourcampus.edu	Chemistry	Robin
4	Fischer, Douglas	DougF@ourcampus.edu	Baker	Baker@ourcampus.edu	Accounting	Shawna
5	Hwang, Terry	TerryH@ourcampus.edu	Taing	Taing@ourcampus.edu	Accounting	Shawna
6	Marino, Chip	ChipM@myserver.com	Tran	Tran@ourcampus.edu	Info Systems	Aaron
7	Lai, Tzu	TzuL@ourcampus.edu	Valdez	Valdez@ourcampus.edu	Chemistry	Robin
8	Thompson, James	JamesT@myserver.com	Taing	Taing@ourcampus.edu	Accounting	Shawna
9	??	??	??	??	Biology	Chris

Inserted row— both Student and Adviser data missing

Deleted row— Student, Adviser, Department data lost

FIGURE 1-6

Adviser and Student Tables

ADVISER data linked to STUDENT data via AdviserName

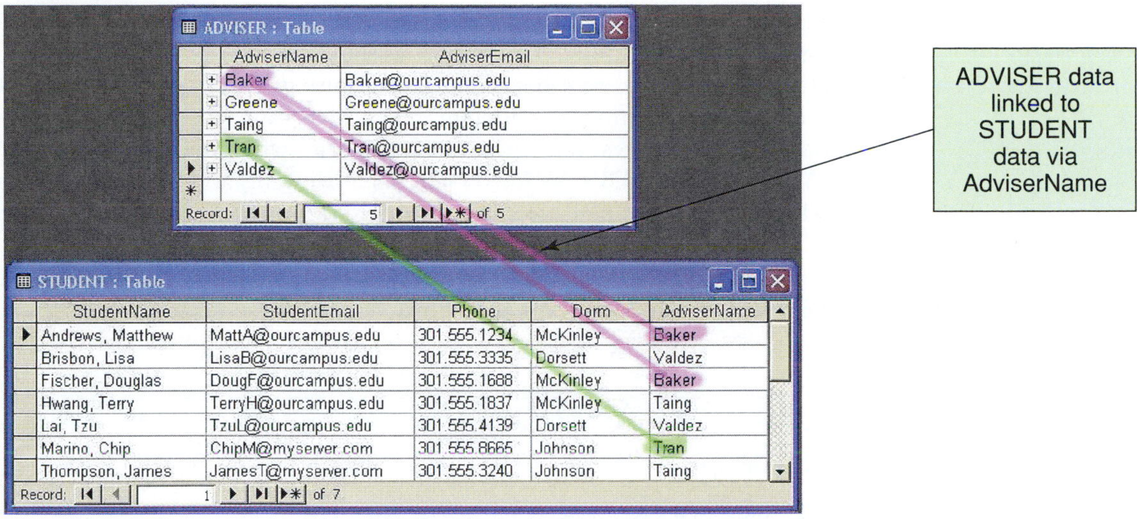

ADVISER table. (In this book, table names will be shown in all capital letters; column names will be shown with initial capitals only.) Figure 1-6 shows the results.

Now consider possible modifications to these tables. As you saw in the last section, three basic modification actions are possible: insert, update, and delete. To evaluate a design, we need to consider each of these three. In Figure 1-7, we can insert the data for Professor Greene with no problem. We just add his or her data to the ADVISER table. No student references Professor Greene, but this is not a problem. Perhaps a student will have Greene as an adviser in the future.

We can also update data values without unintended consequences. In Figure 1-7, the e-mail address for Professor Taing can be changed to **Taing2@ourcampus.edu**, and no inconsistent data will result because Taing's e-mail address is stored just once. Finally,

FIGURE 1-7

Updating the Adviser and Student Tables

Inserted row— No STUDENT data required

Changed row— Data consistent

Deleted row— No ADVISER data lost

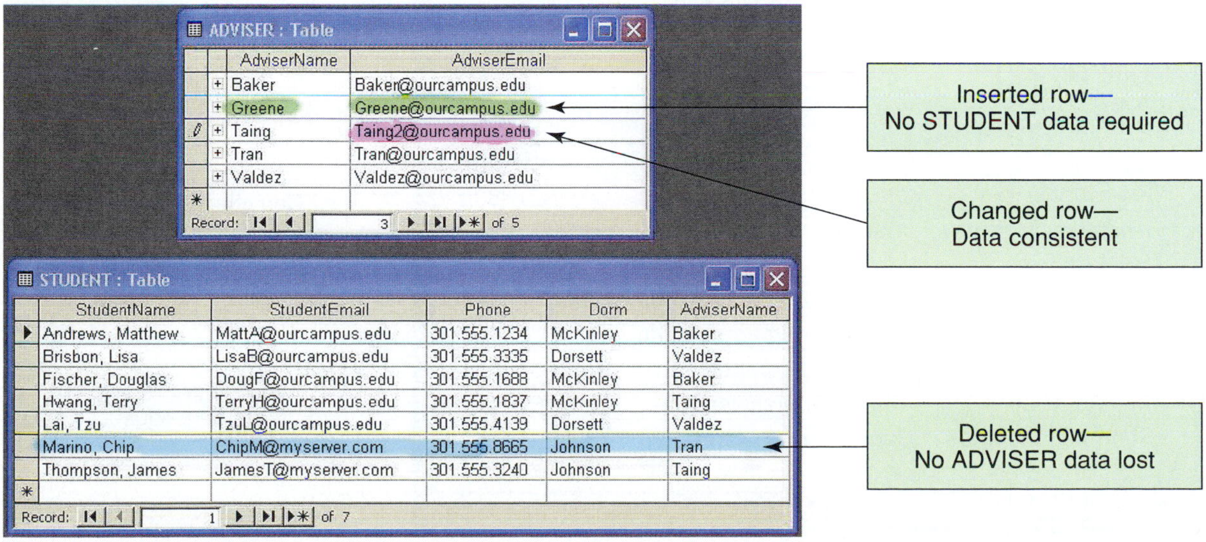

we can delete data without associated consequences. If we delete the data for student Marino, we lose no adviser data.

A Relational Design for the Student/Adviser/Department List

We can use a similar strategy to develop a relational database for the list in Figure 1-5. This list has three themes: students, advisers, and departments. Accordingly, we create three tables, one for each of these three themes as shown in Figure 1-8.

As shown in this figure, we can insert new data without creating null values, we can modify data without creating inconsistencies, and we can delete data without unintended side consequences. Notice in particular that when we add a new row to DEPARTMENT, we can add rows in ADVISORs if we want, and we can add rows in STUDENT for each of the new rows in ADVISOR, if we want. However, all of these actions are independent. None of them leaves the tables in an inconsistent state.

Similarly, when we modify AdviserName of a row in STUDENT, we automatically pick up the correct e-mail and department. If we change AdviserName in the first row of

FIGURE 1-8

Department/Adviser/Student Tables with Changes

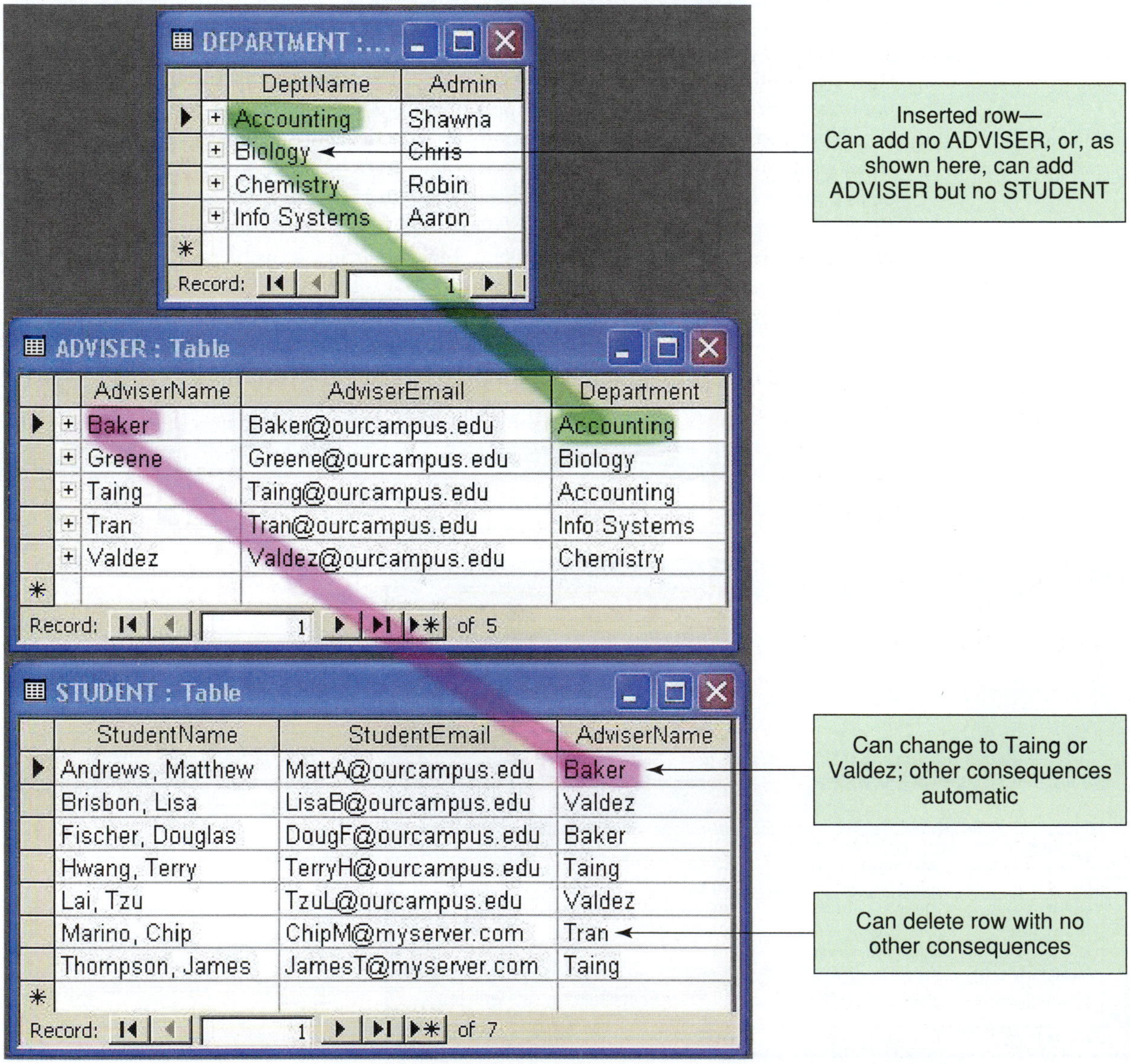

DEPARTMENT : ...

	DeptName	Admin
+	Accounting	Shawna
+	Biology	Chris
+	Chemistry	Robin
+	Info Systems	Aaron

Record: 1

Inserted row—Can add no ADVISER, or, as shown here, can add ADVISER but no STUDENT

ADVISER : Table

	AdviserName	AdviserEmail	Department
+	Baker	Baker@ourcampus.edu	Accounting
+	Greene	Greene@ourcampus.edu	Biology
+	Taing	Taing@ourcampus.edu	Accounting
+	Tran	Tran@ourcampus.edu	Info Systems
+	Valdez	Valdez@ourcampus.edu	Chemistry

Record: 1 of 5

STUDENT : Table

StudentName	StudentEmail	AdviserName
Andrews, Matthew	MattA@ourcampus.edu	Baker
Brisbon, Lisa	LisaB@ourcampus.edu	Valdez
Fischer, Douglas	DougF@ourcampus.edu	Baker
Hwang, Terry	TerryH@ourcampus.edu	Taing
Lai, Tzu	TzuL@ourcampus.edu	Valdez
Marino, Chip	ChipM@myserver.com	Tran
Thompson, James	JamesT@myserver.com	Taing

Record: 1 of 7

Can change to Taing or Valdez; other consequences automatic

Can delete row with no other consequences

STUDENT to Taing, it will be connected to the row that has the correct AdviserEmail and Department values. If we want, we can use the value of Department in ADVISER to obtain the correct DEPARTMENT data, as well. Finally, notice that we can delete the row for student Marino without a problem.

As an aside, the design in Figure 1-8 has removed the problems that occur when modifying a list, but it has also introduced a new problem. Specifically, what happens if we delete the first row in ADVISER? Students Andrews and Fischer would have an invalid value of AdviserName because a Baker would no longer exist in the ADVISER table. To prevent this problem, we can design the database so that a deletion of a row is not allowed if other rows depend on it, or we can design it so that the dependent rows are deleted, as well. We're skipping way ahead of the story, however. We will discuss such issues in later chapters.

A Relational Design for Art Course Enrollments To fix these ideas in your mind, consider the list in Figure 1-9, which is used by an art school that offers art courses to the public. This list has modification problems. For example, suppose we change the value of CourseDate in the first row. This change might mean that the date for the course is changing, in which case the CourseDate values should be changed in other rows, as well. Alternatively, this change could mean that a new Adv Pastel course is being offered. Either is a possibility.

As with the other examples, we can remove the problems and ambiguities by creating a separate table for each theme. However, in this case, the themes are more difficult to determine. Clearly, one of the themes is "customer" and another one is "art course." However, a third theme exists that is more difficult to bring to light. The customer has paid a certain amount toward a course. The amount paid is not a property of the customer because it varies depending on which course the customer is taking. The customer Ariel Johnson, for example, paid $250 for the Adv Pastels class and $350 for the Int Pastels class. Similarly, the amount paid is not a property of the course, because it varies with which customer has taken the course. In fact, the third theme of this list concerns the enrollment of a particular student in a particular class.

Figure 1-10 shows a design of three tables that correspond to these three themes. Notice that this design assigns a unique CustomerNumber to each row of CUSTOMER; this is necessary because some customers might have the same name. Also notice that it assigns a unique CourseNumber to each row of COURSE. This is necessary because some courses have the same name. Finally, notice that the rows of the ENROLLMENT table show the amount paid by a particular customer for a particular course.

FIGURE 1-9

Art Class List with Problematic Changes

	A	B	C	D	E	F
1	Customer	Phone	CourseDate	AmountPaid	Course	Fee
2	Ariel Johnson	206.555.1234	10/1/2003	$250	Adv Pastels	$500
3	Robin Green	312.555.6689	9/15/2003	$350	Beg Oils	$350
4	Charles Jackson	306.555.1488	10/1/2003	$500	Adv Pastels	$500
5	Ariel Johnson	206.555.1234	3/15/2003	$350	Int Pastels	$350
6	Jeffrey Pearson	212.555.8878	10/1/2003	$500	Adv Pastels	$500
7	Miguel Sears	770.555.3289	9/15/2003	$350	Beg Oils	$350
8	Leah Kyle	444.555.3833	11/15/2003	$250	Adv Pastels	$500
9	Lynda Myers	509.555.3303	10/15/2003	$0	Beg Oils	$350

How to enter the fee for a new course?

Consequences of deleting this row?

Consequences of changing this date?

FIGURE 1-10

Art Class Tables with Changes

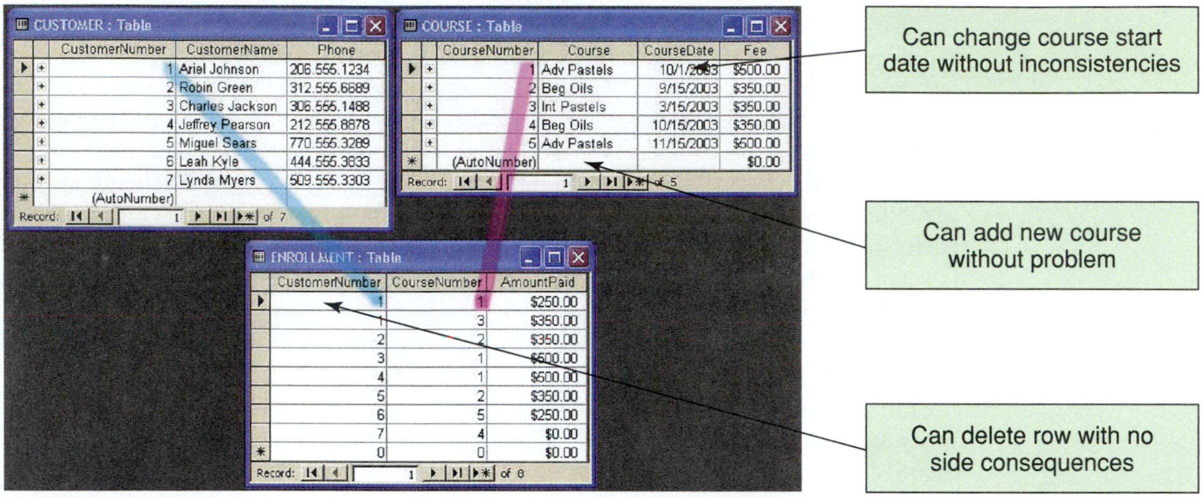
CUSTOMER : Table
COURSE : Table
ENROLLMENT : Table
Can change course start date without inconsistencies
Can add new course without problem
Can delete row with no side consequences

A Relational Design for Parts and Prices Now consider a more complicated example. Figure 1-11 shows a list used by a housing contractor named Carbon River Construction to keep track of the parts that it buys for various construction projects.

Suppose your job is to maintain this list, and your boss tells you that customer Elizabeth Barnaby changed her phone number. How many changes would you need to make to this spreadsheet? For the data in Figure 1-11, you would need to make this change 10 times. Now suppose the spreadsheet has five thousand rows. How many changes might you need to make? The answer could be dozens, and you need to worry not only about the time this will take but also about the possibility of errors—you might miss her name in a row or two.

Consider a second problem with this list. In this business, each supplier agrees to a particular discount for all parts it supplies. For example, in Figure 1-11, supplier NW Electrical has agreed to a 25 percent discount. With this list, every time you enter a new part quotation, you must enter the supplier of that part along with the correct discount. If dozens or hundreds of suppliers are used, there is always the chance that you will enter the wrong discount. Then the list would have more than one discount for one supplier—a situation that is incorrect and confusing.

FIGURE 1-11

Equipment List as a Spreadsheet

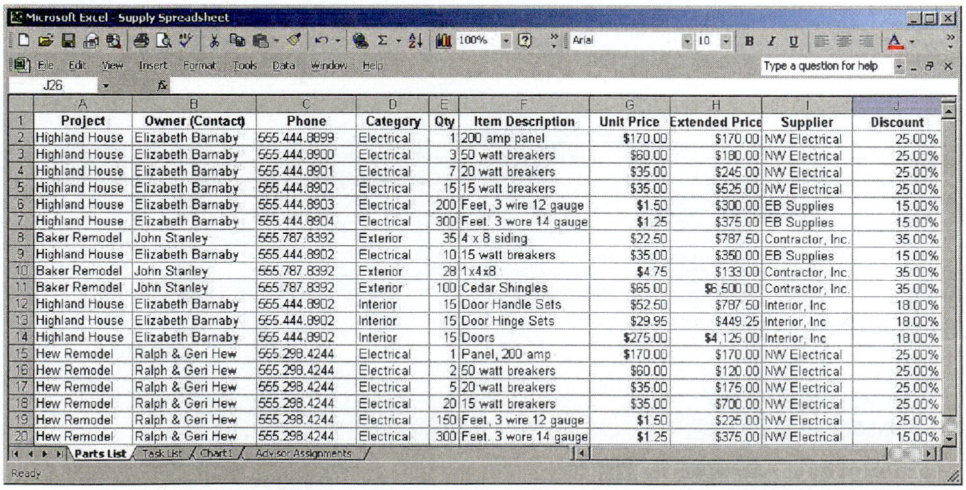

	Project	Owner (Contact)	Phone	Category	Qty	Item Description	Unit Price	Extended Price	Supplier	Discount
2	Highland House	Elizabeth Barnaby	555.444.8899	Electrical	1	200 amp panel	$170.00	$170.00	NW Electrical	25.00%
3	Highland House	Elizabeth Barnaby	555.444.8900	Electrical	3	50 watt breakers	$60.00	$180.00	NW Electrical	25.00%
4	Highland House	Elizabeth Barnaby	555.444.8901	Electrical	7	20 watt breakers	$35.00	$245.00	NW Electrical	25.00%
5	Highland House	Elizabeth Barnaby	555.444.8902	Electrical	15	15 watt breakers	$35.00	$525.00	NW Electrical	25.00%
6	Highland House	Elizabeth Barnaby	555.444.8903	Electrical	200	Feet, 3 wire 12 gauge	$1.50	$300.00	EB Supplies	15.00%
7	Highland House	Elizabeth Barnaby	555.444.8904	Electrical	300	Feet. 3 wore 14 gauge	$1.25	$375.00	EB Supplies	15.00%
8	Baker Remodel	John Stanley	555.787.8392	Exterior	35	4 x 8 siding	$22.50	$787.50	Contractor, Inc.	35.00%
9	Highland House	Elizabeth Barnaby	555.444.8902	Electrical	10	15 watt breakers	$35.00	$350.00	EB Supplies	15.00%
10	Baker Remodel	John Stanley	555.787.8392	Exterior	28	1x4x8	$4.75	$133.00	Contractor, Inc.	35.00%
11	Baker Remodel	John Stanley	555.787.8392	Exterior	100	Cedar Shingles	$65.00	$6,500.00	Contractor, Inc.	35.00%
12	Highland House	Elizabeth Barnaby	555.444.8902	Interior	15	Door Handle Sets	$52.50	$787.50	Interior, Inc	18.00%
13	Highland House	Elizabeth Barnaby	555.444.8902	Interior	15	Door Hinge Sets	$29.95	$449.25	Interior, Inc	18.00%
14	Highland House	Elizabeth Barnaby	555.444.8902	Interior	15	Doors	$275.00	$4,125.00	Interior, Inc	18.00%
15	Hew Remodel	Ralph & Geri Hew	555.298.4244	Electrical	1	Panel, 200 amp	$170.00	$170.00	NW Electrical	25.00%
16	Hew Remodel	Ralph & Geri Hew	555.298.4244	Electrical	2	50 watt breakers	$60.00	$120.00	NW Electrical	25.00%
17	Hew Remodel	Ralph & Geri Hew	555.298.4244	Electrical	5	20 watt breakers	$35.00	$175.00	NW Electrical	25.00%
18	Hew Remodel	Ralph & Geri Hew	555.298.4244	Electrical	20	15 watt breakers	$35.00	$700.00	NW Electrical	25.00%
19	Hew Remodel	Ralph & Geri Hew	555.298.4244	Electrical	150	Feet, 3 wire 12 gauge	$1.50	$225.00	NW Electrical	25.00%
20	Hew Remodel	Ralph & Geri Hew	555.298.4244	Electrical	300	Feet. 3 wore 14 gauge	$1.25	$375.00	NW Electrical	15.00%

For another problem, consider what happens when you enter data correctly but inconsistently. The first row has a part named 200-amp panel, whereas the 15th row has a part named Panel, 200-amp. Are these two parts the same item or are they different? It turns out that they are the same item but they were named differently.

A fourth problem concerns partial data. Suppose you know that a supplier offers a 20 percent discount but Carbon River has not yet ordered from the supplier. Where do you record the 20 percent discount?

We can fix this list by breaking it up into separate tables just as we did for the student and art course data. Because this list is more complicated, we will use more tables.

The list in Figure 1-11 has data about four topics: projects, items, price quotations, and suppliers. Accordingly, we create a database with four tables, and relate those four tables using ID values as before. Figure 1-12 shows four such tables and relationships. Observe that the QUOTE table holds a unique quote identifier, a quantity, a price, and then three ID values: one for PROJECT, one for ITEM, and one for SUPPLIER.

Now, if Elizabeth Barnaby changes her phone number, we need make that change only once—in the PROJECT table. Similarly, we need only record a supplier discount once—in the SUPPLIER table.

Processing the Relational Tables

By now, you may have a burning question. It's fine to tear the lists up into pieces in order to eliminate processing problems, but what if the users want to view their data in the format of the original list? With the data separated into different tables, the users will have to jump from one table to another to find the information they want, and this jumping around will become tedious.

This is an important question and one that many people addressed in the 1970s and 1980s. Several approaches were invented for combining, querying, and processing sets of tables. Over time, one of those approaches, a language called **Structured Query Language (SQL)** (pronounced see-quell), emerged as the leading technique. Today, SQL is an international standard. Using SQL, you can reconstruct lists from their underlying tables; you can query for specific data conditions; you can perform computations on data in tables; and you can insert, update, and delete data.

Processing Tables with SQL You will learn how to code SQL statements in Chapter 3. However, to give an idea of the structure of such statements, the following

FIGURE 1-12

Equipment List Tables

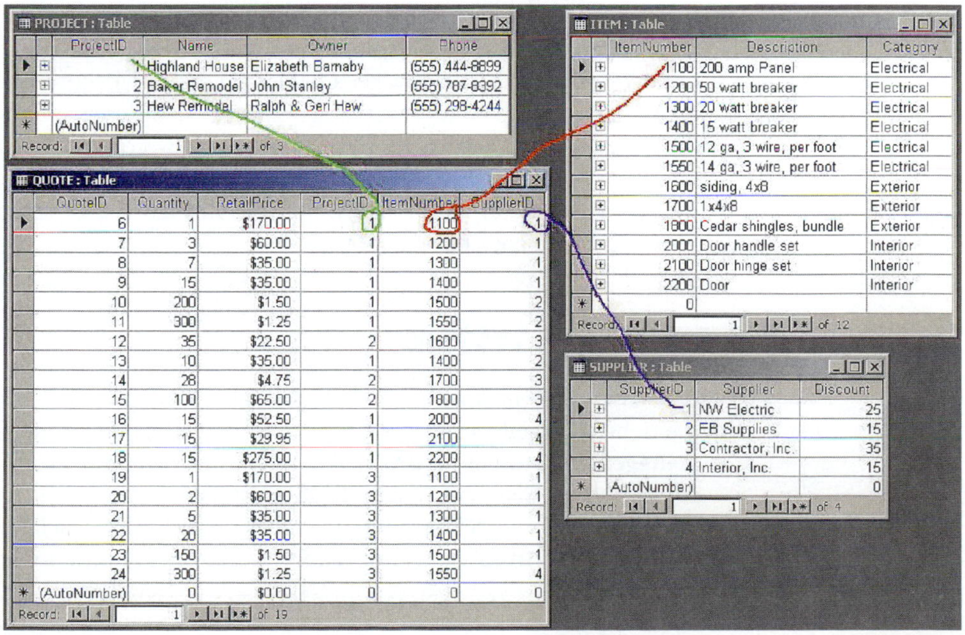

PROJECT : Table

ProjectID	Name	Owner	Phone
1	Highland House	Elizabeth Barnaby	(555) 444-8899
2	Baker Remodel	John Stanley	(555) 787-8392
3	Hew Remodel	Ralph & Geri Hew	(555) 298-4244
(AutoNumber)			

Record: 1 of 3

QUOTE : Table

QuoteID	Quantity	RetailPrice	ProjectID	ItemNumber	SupplierID
6	1	$170.00	1	1100	1
7	3	$60.00	1	1200	1
8	7	$35.00	1	1300	1
9	15	$35.00	1	1400	1
10	200	$1.50	1	1500	2
11	300	$1.25	1	1550	2
12	35	$22.50	2	1600	3
13	10	$35.00	1	1400	2
14	28	$4.75	2	1700	3
15	100	$65.00	2	1800	3
16	15	$52.50	1	2000	4
17	15	$29.95	1	2100	4
18	15	$275.00	1	2200	4
19	1	$170.00	3	1100	1
20	2	$60.00	3	1200	1
21	5	$35.00	3	1300	1
22	20	$35.00	3	1400	1
23	150	$1.50	3	1500	1
24	300	$1.25	3	1550	4
(AutoNumber)	0	$0.00	0	0	0

Record: 1 of 19

ITEM : Table

ItemNumber	Description	Category
1100	200 amp Panel	Electrical
1200	50 watt breaker	Electrical
1300	20 watt breaker	Electrical
1400	15 watt breaker	Electrical
1500	12 ga, 3 wire, per foot	Electrical
1550	14 ga, 3 wire, per foot	Electrical
1600	siding, 4x8	Exterior
1700	1x4x8	Exterior
1800	Cedar shingles, bundle	Exterior
2000	Door handle set	Interior
2100	Door hinge set	Interior
2200	Door	Interior
0		

Record: 1 of 12

SUPPLIER : Table

SupplierID	Supplier	Discount
1	NW Electric	25
2	EB Supplies	15
3	Contractor, Inc.	35
4	Interior, Inc.	15
(AutoNumber)		0

Record: 1 of 4

FIGURE 1-13

Query to Create Art School List

Art School List : Select Query

CustomerName	Phone	CourseDate	AmountPaid	Course	Fee
Ariel Johnson	206.555.1234	10/1/2003	$250.00	Adv Pastels	$500.00
Robin Green	312.555.6689	9/15/2003	$350.00	Beg Oils	$350.00
Charles Jackson	306.555.1488	10/1/2003	$500.00	Adv Pastels	$500.00
Ariel Johnson	206.555.1234	3/15/2003	$350.00	Int Pastels	$350.00
Jeffrey Pearson	212.555.8878	10/1/2003	$500.00	Adv Pastels	$500.00
Miguel Sears	770.555.3289	9/15/2003	$350.00	Beg Oils	$350.00
Leah Kyle	444.555.3833	11/15/2003	$250.00	Adv Pastels	$500.00
Lynda Myers	509.555.3303	10/15/2003	$0.00	Beg Oils	$350.00

Record: 1 of 8

FIGURE 1-14

Query to Compute Amount Due

Amount Due Query : Select Query

CustomerName	Phone	Course	Fee	AmountPaid	Amount Due
Ariel Johnson	206.555.1234	Adv Pastels	$500.00	$250.00	$250.00
Leah Kyle	444.555.3833	Adv Pastels	$500.00	$250.00	$250.00
Lynda Myers	509.555.3303	Beg Oils	$350.00	$0.00	$350.00

Record: 1 of 3

SQL statement will join the three tables in Figure 1-10 to produce the original list. Don't worry about understanding the syntax of this statement now; just realize that it produces the result shown in Figure 1-13.

```
SELECT  CUSTOMER.CustomerName, CUSTOMER.Phone,
        COURSE.CourseDate, ENROLLMENT.AmountPaid,
        COURSE.Course, COURSE.Fee
FROM    CUSTOMER, ENROLLMENT, COURSE
WHERE   CUSTOMER.CustomerNumber = ENROLLMENT.CustomerNumber
        AND COURSE.CourseNumber = ENROLLMENT.CourseNumber;
```

As you will learn in Chapter 3, it is also possible to select rows, to order them, and to make calculations on row data values. Figure 1-14 shows the result of a SQL statement that joins the tables together, computes the difference between the course Fee and the AmountPaid, and stores this result in a new column called AmountDue. It then selects only rows for which AmountDue is greater than zero and presents the results sorted by CustomerName. Check the data in Figure 1-13 to ensure that the results in Figure 1-14 are correct.

WHAT IS A DATABASE SYSTEM?

A database system consists of the four components shown in Figure 1-15. Starting from the right, the **database** is a collection of related tables and other structures. The **database management system (DBMS)** is a computer program used to create, process, and administer the database. The DBMS receives requests encoded in SQL and translates those requests into actions on the database. The DBMS is a large, complicated program that is licensed from a software vendor. Companies almost never write their own DBMS programs.

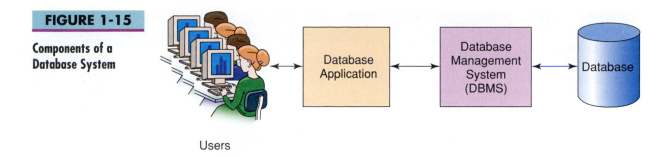

FIGURE 1-15

Components of a
Database System

A database application is a set of one or more computer programs that serves as an intermediary between the user and the DBMS. Application programs read or modify database data by sending SQL statements to the DBMS. Application programs also present data to users in the format of forms and reports. Application programs can be acquired from software vendors, and they are also frequently written in-house. The knowledge you gain from this text will help you to write database applications.

Users are the fourth components of a database system. Users employ the database application to keep track of things. They use forms to read, enter, and query data, and they produce reports. Consider the database, the DBMS, and database application in more detail.

The Database

As shown in Figure 1-15, the right-most component of a database system is the database itself. Before continuing, we need to define more specifically what a database is and describe its components as well.

In the most general case, a database is a self-describing collection of related records. For all relational databases (almost all databases today, and the only type considered in this book), this definition can be modified to say that a database is a self-describing collection of related tables.

The two key terms in this definition are *self-describing* and *related tables*. You already have a good idea of what we mean by related tables. ADVISER and STUDENT are examples of two related tables. They are related by the common column of AdviserName. We will build on this idea of relationships further in the next chapter.

Self-describing means that a description of the structure of the database is contained within the database itself. Because this is so, the contents of a database can always be determined just by looking inside it. It is not necessary to look anywhere else. This situation is akin to that at your campus library. You can tell what is in the library by examining the catalog that resides within the library itself.

All DBMS products provide a set of tools for displaying the structure of their databases. For example, Figure 1-16 shows a diagram produced by Microsoft Access that displays the relationships of the tables in the Art Course database (the tables in Figure 1-10). Other tools describe the structure of the tables and other components.

Data about the structure of a database are called **metadata**. Examples of metadata are the names of tables, the names of columns and the tables to which they belong, properties of tables and columns, and so forth.

Figure 1-17 shows the contents of a database. It has user data and metadata as just described. A database also has indexes and other structures that exist to improve database performance. We will say more about such structures as we proceed. Finally, some databases contain application metadata; these are data that describe application elements such as forms and reports. Microsoft Access, for example, carries application metadata as part of its databases.

FIGURE 1-16

Example Metadata—
Relationship Diagram
for Tables in Figure 1-10

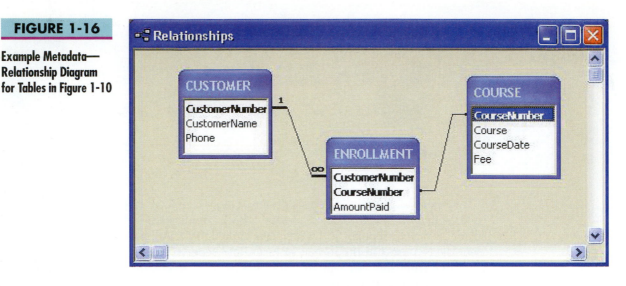

FIGURE 1-17

Database Contents

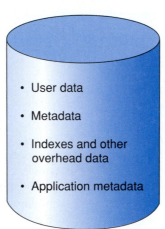

- User data
- Metadata
- Indexes and other overhead data
- Application metadata

The DBMS

The purpose of the DBMS is to create, process, and administer the database. The DBMS is a large, complicated product that is almost always licensed from a software vendor. One such product is Microsoft Access. Other commercial DBMS products are Oracle, from Oracle Corporation; DB2, from IBM Corporation; and SQL Server, from Microsoft Corporation. Dozens of other DBMS products exist, but these four have the lion's share of the market.

DBMS functions are listed in Figure 1-18. The DBMS is used to create the database itself and to create tables and other supporting structures inside that database. As an example of the latter, suppose that we have an EMPLOYEE table with ten thousand

FIGURE 1-18

Functions of a DBMS

- Create database
- Create tables
- Create supporting structures (e.g., indexes, etc.)
- Read database data
- Modify (insert, update, or delete) database data
- Maintain database structures
- Enforce rules
- Control concurrency
- Provide security
- Perform backup and recovery

rows and that this table includes a column, DepartmentName, that records the name of the department in which an employee works. Further, suppose that we frequently need to access employee data by DepartmentName. Because this is a large database, searching through the table to find, for example, all employees in the Accounting Department would take a long time. To improve performance, we can create an index (akin to the index at the back of a book) for DepartmentName to show which employees are in which departments. Such an index is an example of a supporting structure that is created and maintained by the DBMS.

The next two functions of the DBMS are to read and modify database data. To do this, the DBMS receives SQL and other requests and transforms those requests into actions on the database files. Another DBMS function is to maintain all of the database structures. For example, from time to time it might be necessary to change the format of a table or other supporting structure. Developers use the DBMS to make such changes.

With most DBMS products, it is possible to declare rules about data values for the DBMS to enforce. For example, in Figure 1-10, what would happen if a user mistakenly entered a value of 9 for CustomerID in the ENROLLMENT table? No such customer exists, so such a value would cause numerous errors. To prevent this situation, it is possible to tell the DBMS that any value of CustomerID in the ENROLLMENT table must already be a value of CustomerID in the CUSTOMER table. If no such value exists, the insert or update request should be disallowed. Such rules, called **referential integrity constraints**, are enforced by the DBMS.

The last three functions of the DBMS listed in Figure 1-18 have to do with the administration of the database. The DBMS controls concurrency by ensuring that one user's work does not inappropriately interfere with another user's work. This important (and complicated) function will be discussed in Chapter 6. Also, the DBMS contains a security system that is used to ensure that only authorized users perform authorized activities against the database. Users can be prevented from seeing certain data, and their actions can be confined to making only certain data changes on specified data.

Finally, the database, as a centralized repository of data, is a valuable organizational asset. Consider, for example, the value of a book database to a company like Amazon.com. Because the database is so important, steps need to be taken to ensure that no data will be lost in the event of errors, hardware or software problems, or natural catastrophes. The DBMS provides facilities for backing up database data and recovering it from backups when necessary.

Application Programs

Figure 1-19 lists the functions of database applications. First, the application program creates and processes forms. Figure 1-20 shows a typical form for entering and processing customer data for the art course application. Notice that this form hides the structure of the underlying tables from the user. Figure 1-10 shows that data from the ENROLLMENT and the COURSE tables are presented in Course Enrollments. The goal of this form, like that for all data entry forms, is to present the data in a format that is most useful for the users, regardless of the underlying table structure.

Behind the form, the application processes the database in accordance with the users' actions. The application generates a SQL statement to insert, update, or delete data from any of the three tables that underlie this form.

FIGURE 1-19

Functions of Application Programs

- Create and process forms
- Process user queries
- Create and process reports
- Execute application logic
- Control application

FIGURE 1-20

Example Data Entry Form

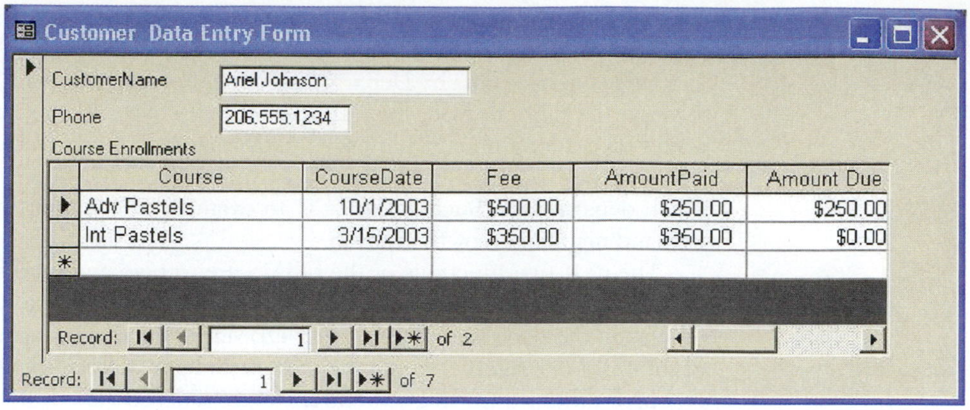

Customer Data Entry Form

| CustomerName | Ariel Johnson |
| Phone | 206.555.1234 |

Course Enrollments

	Course	CourseDate	Fee	AmountPaid	Amount Due
▶	Adv Pastels	10/1/2003	$500.00	$250.00	$250.00
	Int Pastels	3/15/2003	$350.00	$350.00	$0.00
*					

Record: ◀◀ ◀ [1] ▶ ▶▶ ▶* of 2

Record: ◀◀ ◀ [1] ▶ ▶▶ ▶* of 7

The second function of application programs is to process user queries. The application program first generates a query request and sends it to the DBMS. Results are then formatted and returned to the user. The forms in Figure 1-21 illustrate this process. In Figure 1-21(a), the application obtains the name or part of a name of a course. Here, the user has entered the characters *pas*. When the user clicks OK, the application then constructs a SQL query statement to search the database for any course containing these characters. The result of this SQL query is shown in Figure 1-21(b). In this particular case, the application queried for the relevant course, and then joined the ENROLLMENT and CUSTOMER data to the qualifying COURSE rows. Observe that the only rows shown are those with a course name that includes the characters *pas*.

The third function is similar to the second. The application program first queries the DBMS for data (again using SQL), then formats the results of the query as a report. Figure 1-22 shows a report displaying all of the enrollment data in order by course. Notice that the report, like the form in Figure 1-20, is structured according to the users' needs and not according to the underlying table structure.

In addition to generating forms, queries, and reports, the application program takes other action to update the database in accordance with application-specific logic. For example, in an order-entry application, suppose a user requests 10 units of a particular item. Suppose further that when the application program queries the database (via the

FIGURE 1-21

Example Query

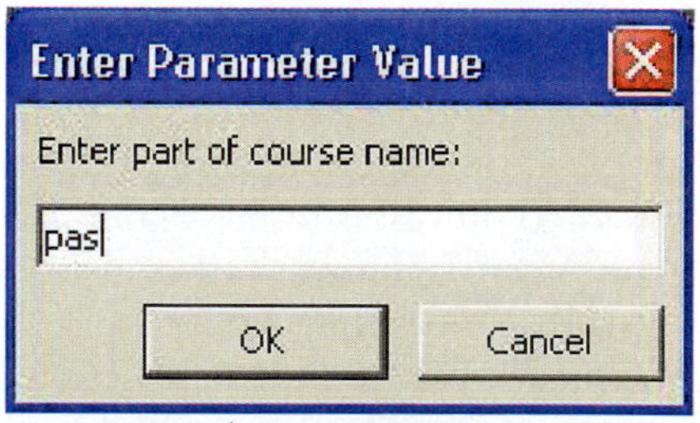

Enter Parameter Value

Enter part of course name:

pas

| OK | Cancel |

(a) Query Parameter Form

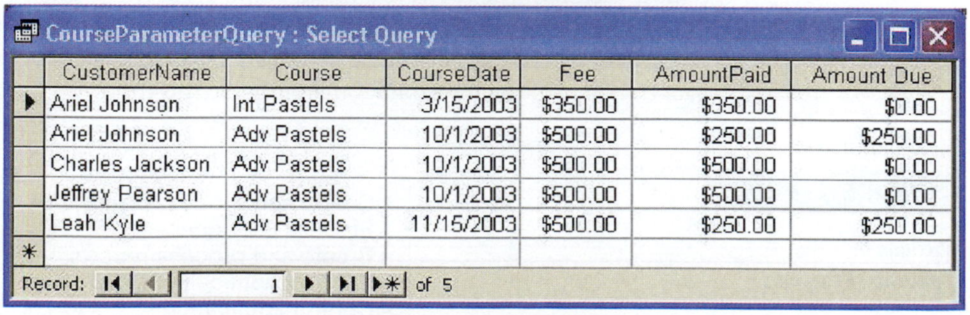

CourseParameterQuery : Select Query

	CustomerName	Course	CourseDate	Fee	AmountPaid	Amount Due
▶	Ariel Johnson	Int Pastels	3/15/2003	$350.00	$350.00	$0.00
	Ariel Johnson	Adv Pastels	10/1/2003	$500.00	$250.00	$250.00
	Charles Jackson	Adv Pastels	10/1/2003	$500.00	$500.00	$0.00
	Jeffrey Pearson	Adv Pastels	10/1/2003	$500.00	$500.00	$0.00
	Leah Kyle	Adv Pastels	11/15/2003	$500.00	$250.00	$250.00
*						

Record: ◀◀ ◀ [1] ▶ ▶▶ ▶* of 5

(b) Query Results

FIGURE 1-22

Example Report

Course Enrollment Report

Course	CourseDate	Fee	CustomerName	AmountPaid	AmountDue	Phone
Adv Pastels	10/1/2003	$500.00				
			Ariel Johnson	$250.00	$250.00	206.555.1234
			Charles Jackson	$500.00	$0.00	306.555.1488
			Jeffrey Pearson	$500.00	$0.00	212.555.8878
			Leah Kyle	$250.00	$250.00	444.555.3833
Beg Oils	10/15/2003	$350.00				
			Lynda Myers	$0.00	$350.00	509.555.3303
			Miguel Sears	$350.00	$0.00	770.555.3289
			Robin Green	$350.00	$0.00	312.555.6689
Int Pastels	3/15/2003	$350.00				
			Ariel Johnson	$350.00	$0.00	206.555.1234

DBMS), it finds that only eight items are in stock. What should happen? It depends on the logic of that particular application. Perhaps no items should be removed from inventory and the user should be notified, or perhaps the eight items should be removed and two more placed on back order. Perhaps some other action should be taken. Whatever the case, it is the job of the application program to execute the appropriate logic.

The last function for application programs listed in Figure 1-19 is to control the application. There are two ways in which this is done. First, the application needs to be written so that only logical options are presented to the user. The application may generate a menu with user choices. If so, the application needs to ensure that only appropriate choices are available. Second, the application needs to control data activities with the DBMS. The application might direct the DBMS, for example, to make a certain set of data changes as a unit. The DBMS might be told either to make all of these changes or none of them. You will learn about such control topics in Chapter 6.

Desktop Versus Organizational Database Systems

Database technology can be used in a wide array of applications. On one end of the spectrum, a researcher might use database technology to track the results of experiments performed in a lab. Such a database might include only a few tables, and each table would have, at most, several hundred rows. The researcher would be the only user of this application.

At the other end of the spectrum, some enormous databases support international organizations. Such databases have hundreds of tables with millions of rows of data and support thousands of concurrent users. These databases are in use 24 hours a day, seven days a week. Just making a backup of such a database is a difficult task.

Figure 1-23 shows the four components of a desktop database application. As you can see from this figure, Microsoft Access (and other personal DBMS products) takes the role of

FIGURE 1-23

Desktop Database System

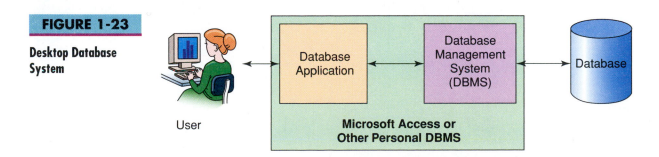

both the database application and the DBMS. Microsoft designed Access this way to make it easier for people to build personal database systems. Using Access, one can switch back and forth from DBMS functions to application functions and never know the difference.

By designing Access this way, Microsoft has hidden many aspects of database processing. For example, behind the scenes, Access uses SQL just as all relational DBMS products do. One must look hard, however, to find it. Figure 1-24 shows the SQL that was used by Access for the query in Figure 1-21. As you examine this figure, you're probably thinking, "I'm just as glad they hid it—it looks complicated and hard." In fact, it looks harder than it is, but we will leave that topic for Chapter 3.

The problem with hiding database technology (and with using lots of wizards to accomplish database design tasks) is that you do not understand what is being done on your behalf. As soon as you need to perform some function that was not anticipated by the Access team, you are lost. Therefore, to be even an average database developer, you have to learn what is behind the scenes.

Furthermore, such products are useful only for desktop database applications. When you want to develop larger database systems, you will have to learn all of the hidden technology. For example, Figure 1-25 shows a database system that has three differ-

FIGURE 1-24

SQL Generated by Access

```
SELECT CUSTOMER.CustomerName, COURSE.Course,
    COURSE.CourseDate, COURSE.Fee,
    ENROLLMENT.AmountPaid, [Fee]–[AmountPaid] AS [Amount Due]

FROM CUSTOMER INNER JOIN
    (COURSE INNER JOIN ENROLLMENT
    ON COURSE.CourseNumber = ENROLLMENT.CourseNumber)
    ON CUSTOMER.CustomerNumber  =
ENROLLMENT.CustomerNumber

WHERE (((COURSE.Course)
    Like "*" & [Enter part of couse name:] & "*"))

ORDER BY CUSTOMER.CustomerName;
```

FIGURE 1-25

Organizational Database System

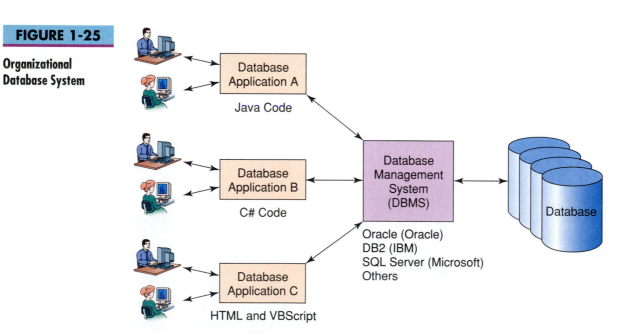

ent applications, and each application has many users. The database itself is spread over many different disks—perhaps even over different computers.

Observe also in Figure 1-25 that the applications are written in three different languages: Java, C#, and a blend of HTML and Visual Basic script. These applications call upon an industrial-strength DBMS product to manage the database. No wizards or simple design tools are available to develop a system like this; instead, the developer writes program code using standard tools such as those in integrated development environments. To write such code, you will need to know SQL and other data access standards.

So, while hiding technology and complexity is good in the beginning, business requirements will soon take you to the brink of your knowledge, and then you will need to know more. To be a part of a team that creates such a database application, you will need to know everything in this book. Over time, you will need to learn a good deal more.

SUMMARY

The importance of database processing increases every day because databases are used in information systems everywhere—and increasingly so. The purpose of this book is to teach you essential database concepts and to help you get started using and learning database technology.

The purpose of a database is to help people keep track of things. Lists can be used for this purpose, but if a list involves more than one topic, problems will occur when data are inserted, updated, or deleted.

Relational databases store data in the form of tables. Almost always, the tables are designed so that each table stores data about a single topic. Lists that involve multiple topics need to be broken up and stored in multiple tables, one for each topic. When this is done, a column needs to be added to show the relationship from a row of one table to a row in a second table.

Structured Query Language (SQL) is an international language for processing relational tables. Using SQL, data in separated tables can be joined together, new tables can be queried, and data can be inserted, updated, and deleted. Using SQL, tables of data can be queried in many ways. Tables can also be joined together to form new tables. SQL can be used to insert, modify, and delete data as well.

The components of a database system are the database, the DBMS, one or more database applications, and users. A database is a self-describing collection of related records. A relational database is a self-describing collection of related tables. A database is self-describing because it contains a description of its contents within itself. Tables are related by storing identifier values. The contents of a database are user data, metadata, supporting structures like indexes, and sometimes application metadata.

A database management system (DBMS) is a large, complicated program used to create, process, and administer the database. DBMS products are almost always licensed from software vendors. Specific functions of the DBMS are summarized in Figure 1-18. The functions of database applications are to create and process forms, to process user queries, and to create and process reports. Application programs also execute specific application logic and control the application. Users provide data and data changes and read data in forms, queries, and reports.

DBMS products for desktop database systems provide functionality for application development and database management. They hide considerable complexity, but at a cost: Requirements unanticipated by the DBMS features cannot be readily implemented. Larger database systems include multiple applications that might be written in multiple languages. These systems may support hundreds or thousands of users.

REVIEW QUESTIONS

1.1 Why is the study of database technology important?

1.2 What is the purpose of this book?

1.3 Describe the purpose of a database.

1.4 Figure 1-26 shows a list of pets and their owners that is used by a veterinary service. Describe three problems that are likely to occur when using this list.

1.5 Name the two topics in the list in Figure 1-26.

1.6 Break the list in Figure 1-26 into two tables, each with data for a single topic. Assume that owners have a unique phone number but that pets have no unique column. Create an ID column for pets like the one created for customers and courses for the art school database in Figure 1-10.

1.7 Show how the tables you created for question 1.6 solve the problems you described in question 1.4.

1.8 What does SQL stand for, and what purpose does it serve?

1.9 Examine Figure 1-27. How many topics does this list have? What are they?

1.10 Break the list in Figure 1-27 into tables, each with a single topic. Create ID columns as you think necessary.

1.11 Show how the tables you created for question 1.10 solve the four problems of lists identified in this chapter.

1.12 Describe in your own words and illustrate with tables how relationships are represented in a relational database.

1.13 Name the four components of a database system.

1.14 Define the term *database*.

1.15 Why do you think it is important for a database to be self-describing?

1.16 List the components of a database.

1.17 What are metadata?

1.18 Describe the use of an index.

1.19 What are application metadata?

1.20 What is the purpose of the DBMS?

1.21 List specific functions of the DBMS.

1.22 Give an example of a referential integrity constraint for the tables you created for question 1.6.

FIGURE 1-26

Pet and Owner List

	A	B	C	D	E	F	G
1	Pet Name	Type	Breed	DOB	Owner	OwnerPhone	OwnerEmail
2	Kino	Dog	Std. Poodle	27-Feb-97	Marsha Downs	555.123.6788	MD@somewhere.com
3	Teddy	Cat	Cashmier	1-Feb-99	Richard James	555.444.0098	RJ@somewhere.com
4	Filo	Dog	Std. Poodle	17-Jul-98	Marsha Downs	555.123.6788	MD@somewhere.com
5	AJ	Dog	Collie Mix	5-May-00	Liz Frier	555.444.5596	LF@somewhere.com
6	Cedro	Cat	Unknown	6-Jun-92	Richard James	555.444.0098	RJ@somewhere.com
7	Woolley	Cat	Unknown	???	Richard James	555.444.0098	RJ@somewhere.com
8	Buster	Dog	Border Collie	11-Dec-95	Miles Trent	555.999.8861	MT@somewhere.com

---

FIGURE 1-27

Second Version of Pet and Owner List

	A	B	C	D	E	F	G	H	I	J
1	Pet Name	Type	Breed	DOB	Owner	OwnerPhone	OwnerEmail	Service	Date	Charge
2	Kino	Dog	Std. Poodle	27-Feb-97	Marsha Downs	555.123.6788	MD@somewhere.com	Ear Infection	17/5/01	$65.00
3	Teddy	Cat	Cashmier	1-Feb-99	Richard James	555.444.0098	RJ@somewhere.com	Nail Clip	5-May-01	$27.50
4	Filo	Dog	Std. Poodle	17-Jul-98	Marsha Downs	555.123.6788	MD@somewhere.com			
5	AJ	Dog	Collie Mix	5-May-00	Liz Frier	555.444.5596	LF@somewhere.com	One year shots	7-May-01	$42.50
6	Cedro	Cat	Unknown	6-Jun-92	Richard James	555.444.0098	RJ@somewhere.com	Nail Clip	5-May-01	$27.50
7	Woolley	Cat	Unknown	???	Richard James	555.444.0098	RJ@somewhere.com	Skin Irritation	5-May-01	$15.00
8	Buster	Dog	Border Collie	11-Dec-95	Miles Trent	555.999.8861	MT@somewhere.com	Laceration Repair	15-Jun-01	$127.00

1.23 Explain the difference between a DBMS and a database.

1.24 List the functions of a database application.

1.25 Explain the differences between a desktop and an organizational database system.

1.26 What is the advantage of hiding complexity from the user of a DBMS? What is the disadvantage?

1.27 Summarize the differences in the database systems in Figures 1-23 and 1-25.

EXERCISES

The following are column headings found in spreadsheets with the indicated names. Use these spreadsheets in answering exercises 1.28 through 1.30.

A. Name of Spreadsheet: EQUIPMENT
Column Headings:
(Number, Description, AcquisitionDate, AcquisitionPrice)

B. Name of Spreadsheet: COMPANY
Columns Headings:
(Name, IndustryCode, Gross Sales, OfficerName, OfficerTitle)

C. Name of Spreadsheet: COMPANY
Columns Headings:
(Name, IndustryCode, Gross Sales, NameOfPresident)

D. Name of Spreadsheet: COMPUTER
Columns Headings:
(SerialNumber, Make, Model, DiskType, DiskCapacity)

E. Name of Spreadsheet: PERSON
Columns Headings:
(Name, DateOfHire, DeptName, DeptManager, ProjectID, NumHours, ProjectManager)

1.28 For each of the spreadsheets provided, indicate the number of themes you think the spreadsheet includes and give an appropriate name for each theme. For some of them, the answer depends on the assumptions you make. In these cases, state your assumptions.

1.29 For the spreadsheets that have more than one theme, break up the columns into sets such that each set has a single theme. Add a column (or columns) to maintain the relationship between the themes.

1.30 For the spreadsheets that have more than one theme, show at least one problem that will occur when inserting, updating, and deleting data.

GARDEN GLORY PROJECT QUESTIONS

Garden Glory is a partnership that provides gardening and yard maintenance services to individuals and organizations. It consists of two partners, two office administrators, and a number of full- and part-time gardeners. Garden Glory will provide one-time garden services, but it specializes in ongoing service and maintenance. Many of its customers have multiple buildings, apartments, and rental houses that require gardening and lawn maintenance services.

A. Create a sample list of owners and properties. Your list will be similar in structure to that in Figure 1-26, but it will concern owners and properties rather than owners and pets. Your list should include, at the minimum, owner name, phone, and billing address, as well as property name, type, and address.

B. Describe problems that are likely to occur if Garden Glory attempts to maintain the list in a spreadsheet.

C. Split the list into tables that each have only one topic. Create IDs as you think appropriate. Use an ID to represent the relationship between a property and an owner.

D. Create a sample list of properties, owners, and services. Your list will be similar to that in Figure 1-27. Your list should include the data items from question A as well as the date, description, and amount charged for each service.

E. Illustrate problems that are likely to occur if Garden Glory attempts to maintain the list from question D in a spreadsheet.

F. Split the list from question D into tables that each have only one topic. Create IDs as you think appropriate. Use an ID to represent relationships.

JAMES RIVER JEWELRY PROJECT QUESTIONS

James River Jewelry is a small jewelry shop that specializes in hard-to-find Asian jewelry. It has a small but loyal clientele, and it wants to further increase customer loyalty by creating a frequent buyer program. In this program, after every 10 purchases customers will receive a credit of 50 percent of the sum of their 10 most recent purchases.

A. Create a sample list of customers and purchases, and a second list of customers and credits. Your lists should include customer data you think would be important to James River along with typical purchase data. Credit data should include the date of the credit, the total amount of the 10 purchases used as the basis of the credit, and the credit amount.

B. Describe problems that are likely to occur if James River attempts to maintain the lists in a spreadsheet.

C. Split the lists into tables that each have only a single topic. Create IDs as you think appropriate. Use an ID to represent the relationship between a purchase and a customer, and another ID to represent the relationship between a credit and a customer.

D. Attempt to combine the two lists you created in question A into a single list. What problems occur as you try to do this? Look closely at Figure 1-27. An essential difference exists between a list of the three themes Customer, Purchase, and Credit and a list of the three themes PetName, Owner, and Service in Figure 1-27. What do you think that difference is?

E. Change the tables from question C so that the Purchase list has not only the ID of Customer but also the ID of Credit. Compare this arrangement to the tables in your answer to question 1.10. What is the essential difference between these two designs?

MID-WESTERN UNIVERSITY CHEMISTRY DEPARTMENT PROJECT QUESTIONS

The chemistry department at Mid-Western University engages in top-level research involving nuclear magnetic resonance (NMR) imaging. The department has three multimillion dollar magnets that support its research activities. The magnets are heavily scheduled for use on a variety of different research grants. In order to justify the expense of these magnets and to bolster the department's future applications for additional magnets, the department maintains a spreadsheet having the following columns: GrantNumber, PI, PIEmailAddress, MagnetID, MagnetLocation, AppointmentDate, AppointmentStartTime, and AppointmentEndTime. *PI* stands for principal investigator; each grant has a single PI. The appointment columns refer to an appointment to use a magnet for a particular grant.

A. Create sample data for this spreadsheet. Use your imagination to develop data values.

B. Describe problems that are likely to occur when inserting, updating, and deleting data in this spreadsheet.

C. Split the spreadsheet into tables having only one topic each. Hint: Your tables will have a structure similar to that in Figure 1-10. Create IDs as you think appropriate and necessary.

D. Explain how the tables in your answer to question C will eliminate the problems you identified in question B.

E. Assume that the department wants to keep track of the start and end dates of the grant as well as the grant number. Further assume that although each grant has only one PI, a PI can have many different grants. Modify your answer to question A in accordance with this additional requirement.

F. Split the spreadsheet in your answer to question E into tables having only one topic each. Create IDs as you think appropriate and necessary. Hint: Your design will be a combination of the designs in Figures 1-8 and 1-10.

The Relational Model

> Learn the conceptual foundation of the relational model
> Understand how relations differ from nonrelational tables
> Learn basic relational terminology
> Learn the meaning and importance of keys, foreign keys, and related terminology
> Understand how foreign keys represent relationships
> Learn the purpose and use of surrogate keys
> Learn the meaning of functional dependencies
> Learn to apply a process for normalizing relations

This chapter explains the relational model, the single most important standard in database processing today. This model, which was developed and published in 1970 by E. F. Codd,[1] then an employee at IBM, was founded on the theory of relational algebra, and the model has since found widespread practical application. Today, it is used for the design and implementation of almost every commercial database worldwide. This chapter describes the conceptual foundation of this model. In Chapter 3, we will present how to use SQL to define and manipulate relations.

---

[1]E. F. Codd, "A Relational Model of Data for Large Shared Databanks," *Communications of the ACM* (June, 1970): 377–387.

▶ RELATIONS

Chapter 1 stated that relational DBMS products store data in the form of tables. However, this is not entirely correct. DBMS products store data in the form of relations, which are a special type of table. Specifically, a **relation** is a two-dimensional table that has the characteristics listed in Figure 2-1. First, each row of the table holds data that pertain to some entity or a portion of some entity. Second, each column of the table contains data that represent an attribute of the entity. Thus, in an EMPLOYEE relation, each row contains data about a particular employee, and each column contains data that represent an attribute of that employee, such as Name, Phone, or EmailAddress.

In addition, to be a relation, the cells of a table must hold a single value; no repeating elements are allowed in a cell. Also, all of the entries in any column must be of the same kind. For example, if the third column in the first row of a table contains EmployeeNumber, then the third column in all other rows must contain EmployeeNumber as well. Further, each column must have a unique name, but the order of the columns in the table is unimportant. Similarly, the order of the rows is unimportant. Finally, no two rows in a table may be identical.

A Sample Relation and Two Nonrelations

Figure 2-2 shows a sample EMPLOYEE table. Consider this table in light of the characteristics listed in Figure 2-1. First, each row is about an EMPLOYEE entity, and each column represents an attribute of employees, so those two conditions are met. Each cell has only one value, and all entries in a column are of the same kind. Column names are unique, and we could change the order of either the columns or the rows and not lose any information. Finally, no two rows are identical. Because this table features all the characteristics listed in Figure 2-1, we can classify it as a relation.

Figures 2-3(a) and 2-3(b) show two tables that are not relations. The EMPLOYEE table in Figure 2-3(a) is not a relation because the Phone column has cells with multiple entries. Tom Caruthers has three values for phone, and Richard Bandalone has two. Multiple entries per cell are not permitted in a relation.

The table in Figure 2-3(b) is not a relation for two reasons. First, the order of the rows is not unimportant. The row under Tom Caruthers contains his fax number. If we rearrange the rows, we may lose track of the correspondence between his name and his fax number. The second reason this table is not a relation is that not all values in the Email column are of the same kind. Some of the values are e-mail addresses, and others are types of phone numbers.

FIGURE 2-1

Characteristics of a Relation

* Rows contain data about an entity
* Columns contain data about attributes of the entity
* Cells of the table hold a single value
* All entries in a column are of the same kind
* Each column has a unique name
* The order of the columns is unimportant
* The order of the rows is unimportant
* No two rows may be identical

FIGURE 2-2

Sample EMPLOYEE Table

EmployeeNumber	FirstName	LastName	Department	Email	Phone
100	Jerry	Johnson	Accounting	JJ@somewhere.com	236-9987
200	Mary	Abernathy	Finance	MA@somewhere.com	444-8898
300	Liz	Smathers	Finance	LS@somewhere.com	777-0098
400	Tom	Caruthers	Accounting	TC@somewhere.com	236-9987
500	Tom	Jackson	Production	TJ@somewhere.com	444-9980
600	Eleanore	Caldera	Legal	EC@somewhere.com	767-0900
700	Richard	Bandalone	Legal	RB@somewhere.com	767-0900

FIGURE 2-3(a)

Table That Is a Nonrelational with Multiple Entries per Cell

EmployeeNumber	FirstName	LastName	Department	Email	Phone
100	Jerry	Johnson	Accounting	JJ@somewhere.com	236-0000
200	Mary	Abernathy	Finance	MA@somewhere.com	444-8898
300	Liz	Smathers	Finance	LS@somewhere.com	777-0098
400	Tom	Caruthers	Accounting	TC@somewhere.com	236-0000, 236-0991, 236-0991
500	Tom	Jackson	Production	TJ@somewhere.com	444-9980
600	Eleanore	Caldera	Legal	EC@somewhere.com	767-0900
700	Richard	Bandalone	Legal	RB@somewhere.com	767-0900, 767-0011

FIGURE 2-3(b)

Table That Is a Nonrelational for Two Reasons

EmployeeNumber	FirstName	LastName	Department	Email	Phone
100	Jerry	Johnson	Accounting	JJ@somewhere.com	236-9987
200	Mary	Abernathy	Finance	MA@somewhere.com	444-8898
300	Liz	Smathers	Finance	LS@somewhere.com	777-0098
400	Tom	Caruthers	Accounting	TC@somewhere.com	236-9987
				Fax:	236-9987
				Home:	555-7171
500	Tom	Jackson	Production	TJ@somewhere.com	444-9980
600	Eleanore	Caldera	Legal	EC@somewhere.com	767-0900
				Fax:	236-9987
				Home:	555-7171
700	Richard	Bandalone	Legal	RB@somewhere.com	767-0900

Although each cell can have only one value, that value can vary in length. Figure 2-4 shows the table in Figure 2-2 with a variable-length Comment attribute. Even though a comment can be lengthy and varies in length from row to row, there is still only one comment per cell. Thus, the table in Figure 2-4 is a relation.

A Note on Terminology

In the database world, people generally use the terms *table* and *relation* interchangeably. Accordingly, from now on this book will do the same. Thus, any time we use the term *table*, we mean a table that meets the characteristics listed in Figure 2-1. Keep in mind, however, that strictly speaking, some tables are not relations.

Sometimes, especially in traditional data processing, people will use the term *file* instead of *table*. When they do so, they will use the term **record** for "row" and the term **field** for "column." To further confound the issue, database theoreticians sometimes use yet another set of terms: They call a table a *relation*, a row a **tuple** (rhymes with *couple*), and a column an **attribute**.

These three sets of terminology are summarized in Figure 2-5. To make things even more confusing, people often mix up these sets of terms. It is not unusual to hear someone refer to a relation that has rows and fields. As long as you know what is intended, this mixing is not important.

Before moving on, there is one other source of confusion to discuss. According to Figure 2-1, a table that has duplicate rows is not a relation. However, in practice this condition is often ignored. Particularly when manipulating relations with a DBMS, we

FIGURE 2-4

Relation with Variable Length Column Values

EmployeeNumber	FirstName	LastName	Department	Email	Phone	Comment
100	Jerry	Johnson	Accounting	JJ@somewhere.com	236-9987	Joined the Accounting Department in March after completing his MBA at night. Will sit for CPA exam this fall.
200	Mary	Abernathy	Finance	MA@somewhere.com	444-8898	
300	Liz	Smathers	Finance	LS@somewhere.com	777-0098	
400	Tom	Caruthers	Accounting	TC@somewhere.com	236-9987	
500	Tom	Jackson	Production	TJ@somewhere.com	444-9980	
600	Eleanore	Caldera	Legal	EC@somewhere.com	767-0900	
700	Richard	Bandalone	Legal	RB@somewhere.com	767-0900	Is a full time consultant to legal on a retainer basis.

Table	Row	Column
File	Record	Field
Relation	Tuple	Attribute

may end up with a table that has duplicate rows. To make that table a relation, we should eliminate the duplicates. On a large table, however, checking for duplication can be time-consuming. Therefore, the default behavior for DBMS products is not to check for duplicate rows. Hence, in practice, tables might exist with duplicate rows that are still called relations. You will see examples of this situation in the next chapter.

▶ TYPES OF KEYS

A **key** is one or more columns of a relation that is used to identify a row. A key can be **unique** or **nonunique**. For example, for the relation in Figure 2-2, EmployeeNumber is a unique key because a value of EmployeeNumber identifies a unique row. Thus, a query to display all employees having an EmployeeNumber of 200 will produce a single row. On the other hand, Department is a nonunique key. It is a key because it is used to identify a row, but it is nonunique because a value of Department potentially identifies more than one row. Thus, a query to display all rows having a Department value of Accounting will produce several rows.

From the data in Figure 2-2, it appears that EmployeeNumber, LastName, and Email are all unique identifiers. However, to decide whether or not this is true, database developers must do more than examine sample data. Rather, the developers must ask the users or other subject-matter experts whether a certain column is unique. The column LastName is an example where this is important. It might turn out that the sample data just happen to have unique values for LastName. The users, however, might say that LastName is not always unique.

Composite Keys

Suppose the users say that, in general, LastName is not unique, but that the combination of LastName and Department is unique. Thus, for some reason, the users know that two people with the same last name will never work in the same department. Two Johnsons, for example, will never work in accounting. If that is the case, then we can say that the combination (LastName, Department) is a unique key. A key that contains two or more attributes is called a **composite key**.

Alternatively, the users may know that the combination (LastName, Department) is not unique, but that the combination (FirstName, LastName, Department) is unique. The latter combination, then, is a composite key with three attributes.

Primary and Candidate Keys

Now, suppose the users tell us that EmployeeNumber is a unique key, that Email is a unique key, and that the combination (FirstName, LastName, Department) is a unique key. When designing a database, we choose one of the unique identifiers to be the primary key. The other unique keys are referred to as **candidate keys** because they are candidates to be the primary key.

The primary key is important not only because it can be used to identify unique rows, but also because it can be used to represent rows in relationships. Although we did not say it, in Figure 1-10 in Chapter 1, CustomerID was the primary key of CUSTOMER. As such, we used CustomerID to represent the CUSTOMER/ENROLLMENT relationship by placing CustomerID in the ENROLLMENT table.

Additionally, many DBMS products use values of the primary key to organize storage for the relation. They also build indexes and other special structures for fast retrieval of rows using primary key values.

Although we are jumping ahead a bit, examine Figure 2-6, which shows a Microsoft Access form that was used to define the structure of the CUSTOMER table in Figure 1-10. The top part of this form has a row for each column of the table being defined. Notice the key symbol next to CustomerID; this symbol means that the developer has defined CustomerID as the primary key for this table.

Foreign Keys and Referential Integrity

As described earlier, to represent a relationship, we place the primary key of one relation into a second relation. When we do this, the attribute in the second relation is referred to as a *foreign key*. For example, to represent the relationship between advisers and students in Figure 1-10, we place CustomerID, the primary key of CUSTOMER, into the ENROLLMENT relation. In this case, CustomerID in ENROLLMENT is referred to as a foreign key. This term is used because CustomerID is the primary key of a relation that is foreign to the table in which it resides.

Consider the following two relations.

EMPLOYEE (EmployeeNumber, FirstName, LastName, Department, Email, Phone)

and

DEPARTMENT (DeptName, BudgetCode, OfficeNumber)

In this notation, the name of the relation is shown first, outside the parentheses, and is followed by the name of each of the columns of the relation within the parentheses.

Suppose EmployeeNumber and DeptName are the primary keys of EMPLOYEE and DEPARTMENT, respectively. In this book, we will indicate primary keys by underlining them. Thus, we write these two relation descriptions as follows.

EMPLOYEE (EmployeeNumber, FirstName, LastName, Department, Email, Phone)

and

DEPARTMENT (DeptName, BudgetCode, OfficeNumber)

FIGURE 2-6

Defining the CUSTOMER Table Using Microsoft Access

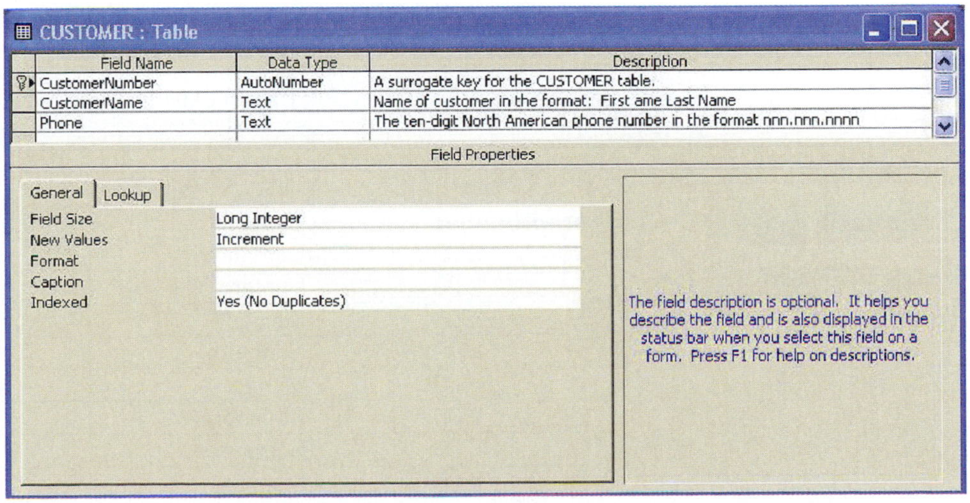

Now suppose that Department (in EMPLOYEE) contains the names of the departments in which employees work, and that DeptName (in DEPARTMENT) also contains these names. Then, Department (in EMPLOYEE) is said to be a foreign key to DEPARTMENT. In this book, we will denote foreign keys by displaying them in italics. Thus, we would write these two relation descriptions as follows.

EMPLOYEE (<u>EmployeeNumber</u>, FirstName, LastName, *Department*, Email, Phone)

and

DEPARTMENT (<u>DeptName</u>, BudgetCode, OfficeNumber)

It is not necessary for the primary key and the foreign key to have the same name. The only requirement is that they have the same set of values. Department must contain values that match values in DeptName.

In most cases, it is important to ensure that every value of a foreign key matches a value of the primary key. In the previous example, the value of Department in every row of EMPLOYEE should match a value of DeptName in DEPARTMENT. If this is the case (and it usually is), then we declare the following rule.

Department in EMPLOYEE must exist in DeptName in DEPARTMENT

Such a rule is called a **referential integrity constraint**. Whenever you see a foreign key, you should look for an associated referential integrity constraint.

Consider the EQUIPMENT relation in Figure 2-7(a). The structure of this relation is:

EQUIPMENT (<u>SerialNumber</u>, Type, AcquisitionCost)

Suppose this equipment can be assigned to the employees shown in Figure 2-2. If the primary key of EMPLOYEE is EmployeeNumber, then we add this attribute as a foreign key to EQUIPMENT, as shown in Figure 2-7(b). These sample data show how this equipment might be allocated to the first three employees in Figure 2-2. (How the equipment assignments were made is unimportant to this discussion.)

The structure of this relation is now:

EQUIPMENT (<u>SerialNumber</u>, Type, AcquisitionCost, *EmployeeNumber*)

The referential integrity constraint is as follows.

EmployeeNumber in EQUIPMENT must exist in EmployeeNumber in EMPLOYEE

FIGURE 2-7(a)

Example EQUIPMENT Relation

SerialNumber	Type	AcquisitionCost
1000	Computer	$2,600.00
1200	Printer	$275.00
1300	Monitor	$350.00
1400	Computer	$1,700.00
1500	Monitor	$400.00
1600	Scanner	$350.00
1700	Computer	$3,100.00
1800	Monitor	$350.00

FIGURE 2-7(b)

EQUIPMENT with Employee Number as Foreign Key

SerialNumber	Type	AcquisitionCost	EmployeeNumber
1000	Computer	$2,600.00	100
1200	Printer	$275.00	100
1300	Monitor	$350.00	100
1400	Computer	$1,700.00	300
1500	Monitor	$400.00	300
1600	Scanner	$350.00	100
1700	Computer	$3,100.00	200
1800	Monitor	$350.00	200

Recall, however, that EMPLOYEE has two candidate keys: Email and the composite key (FirstName, LastName, Department). Consider the alternative designs that result if we use one of these candidate keys as the primary key.

If Email is chosen as the primary key instead of EmployeeNumber, then we need to make Email the foreign key of EMPLOYEE, as shown in Figure 2-7(c). In this case, the structure of EQUIPMENT is:

EQUIPMENT (<u>SerialNumber</u>, Type, AcquisitionCost, *Email*)

The referential integrity constraint is:

Email in EQUIPMENT must exist in Email in EMPLOYEE

Alternatively, we could make the composite key (FirstName, LastName, Department) the primary key of EMPLOYEE. If so, then the foreign key in EQUIPMENT would need to be the composite key (FirstName, LastName, Department), as shown in Figure 2-7(d). The structure of EQUIPMENT in this case is:

EQUIPMENT (<u>SerialNumber</u>, Type, AcquisitionCost, *FirstName, LastName, Department*)

The referential integrity constraint is:

(FirstName, LastName, Department) in EQUIPMENT must exist in (FirstName, LastName, Department) in EMPLOYEE

FIGURE 2-7(c)

EQUIPMENT with Email as Foreign Key

SerialNumber	Type	AcquisitionCost	Email
1000	Computer	$2,600.00	JJ@somewhere.com
1200	Printer	$275.00	JJ@somewhere.com
1300	Monitor	$350.00	JJ@somewhere.com
1400	Computer	$1,700.00	LS@somewhere.com
1500	Monitor	$400.00	LS@somewhere.com
1600	Scanner	$350.00	JJ@somewhere.com
1700	Computer	$3,100.00	MA@somewhere.com
1800	Monitor	$350.00	MA@somewhere.com

FIGURE 2-7(d)

EQUIPMENT with (FirstName, LastName, Department) as Foreign Key

SerialNumber	Type	AcquisitionCost	FirstName	LastName	Department
1000	Computer	$2,600.00	Jerry	Johnson	Accounting
1200	Printer	$275.00	Jerry	Johnson	Accounting
1300	Monitor	$350.00	Jerry	Johnson	Accounting
1400	Computer	$1,700.00	Liz	Smathers	Finance
1500	Monitor	$400.00	Liz	Smathers	Finance
1600	Scanner	$350.00	Jerry	Johnson	Accounting
1700	Computer	$3,100.00	Mary	Abernathy	Finance
1800	Monitor	$350.00	Mary	Abernathy	Finance

Examine the alternative designs in Figures 2-7(b) through (d) and observe how they differ. Which of these designs is best? Most likely the design in Figure 2-7(b) is best because it involves the least amount of foreign key data. However, they all work.

Surrogate Keys

Suppose you work for a company that sells and installs landscaping plants. Your job is to keep track of plant sales and service hours. Assume you have the following tables of data.

PROPERTY (<u>Street</u>, <u>City</u>, <u>State</u>, <u>Zip</u>)

PLANT (<u>ItemNumber</u>, VarietyName, Price)

SERVICE (<u>InvoiceNumber</u>, Date, TotalHours)

Sample data for these three relations are shown in Figure 2-8.

You know that a plant is sold for a particular property, so you decide to create a relationship from PROPERTY to PLANT by placing the primary key of PROPERTY in PLANT. Similarly, you know that a service is rendered for a particular property, so you create a relationship from PROPERTY to SERVICE by placing the primary key of PROPERTY in SERVICE. The resulting relations are as follows.

PROPERTY (<u>Street</u>, <u>City</u>, <u>State</u>, <u>Zip</u>)

PLANT (<u>ItemNumber</u>, VarietyName, Price, *Street, City, State, Zip*)

SERVICE (<u>InvoiceNumber</u>, Date, TotalHours, *Street, City, State, Zip*)

FIGURE 2-8	
Sample Data for PROPERTY, PLANT, and SERVICE Relations	

Street	City	State	Zip
123 East Elm	Riverside	CA	90800-4987
82334 - 188th Street	Oakland	CA	91200-9810
477 North Greenbriar Circle	Riverside	CA	90822-3328
One South Highrent Estates Parkway	Rolling Hills	CA	93455-0080

(a)

ItemNumber	VarietyName	Price
1000	Carpet Rose, White	$9.95
1100	Carpet Rose, Yellow	$11.50
1200	Lilac, 5 gal, purple	$57.55
1300	Lilac, 2 gal, purple	$27.50
1400	Hybrid Tea, Rose	$22.45

(b)

InvoiceNumber	Date	TotalHours
500	5/5/2002	17
550	5/6/2002	6
600	5/9/2002	12
650	5/11/2002	8

(c)

The referential integrity constraints are:

(Street, City, State, Zip) in PLANT must exist in (Street, City, State, Zip) in
PROPERTY
(Street, City, State, Zip) in SERVICE must exist in (Street, City, State, Zip) in
PROPERTY

This design has two problems. First, a considerable amount of data is duplicated. The length of the composite key (Street, City, State, Zip) could be 100 characters or more. If so, every row of PLANT and SERVICE will be 100-plus bytes longer just because of the foreign key. Second, to establish a relationship between a plant or service and a particular property, the users will have to enter values for Street, City, State, and Zip. This will mean considerable keying on their part, an operation that is prone to error. Moreover, when users make an error in entering a foreign key value, they are, in essence, assigning the plant or service to the wrong property. Such a mistake will likely be unpopular with customers.

An alternative design is to create a **surrogate key**. Such a key is a unique, numeric value that is appended to the relation to serve as the primary key. Surrogate key values have no meaning to the users and are normally hidden from them on forms, queries, and reports. Surrogate keys have already been used in Figure 1-10, where we added the surrogate keys CustomerID to the CUSTOMER table and CourseID to the COURSE table.

For the PROPERTY/PLANT/SERVICE example, we will define PropertyID as a surrogate key for PROPERTY. The design of the three tables is now:

PROPERTY (PropertyID, Street, City, State, Zip)

PLANT (ItemNumber, VarietyName, Price, *PropertyID*)

SERVICE (InvoiceNumber, Date, TotalHours, *PropertyID*)

The referential integrity constraints are:

PropertyID in PLANT must exist in PropertyID in PROPERTY
PropertyID in SERVICE must exist in PropertyID in PROPERTY

This design has much less duplicated data and will be far easier to use. Only one value needs to be entered to assign a plant or service to a property.

Most DBMS products have a facility for automatically generating key values. Figure 2-6 shows how surrogate keys are defined with Microsoft Access. The Data Type is set to AutoNumber. With this specification, Access will assign a value of 1 to CustomerNumber for the first row of CUSTOMER, a value of 2 to CustomerNumber for the second row, and so forth.

Enterprise class DBMS products, such as SQL Server, offer more capability. For example, with SQL Server, the developer can specify the starting value of the surrogate key as well as the amount to increment the key for each new row. Figure 2-9 shows how this is done for the definition of a surrogate key for the PROPERTY table. The bottom half of this figure shows the attributes for the PropertyID column. Identity has been set to Yes to indicate to SQL Server that a surrogate key column exists. In SQL Server, the starting value of the surrogate key is called the Identity Seed. Here it is set to 100. Further, the amount to add to the key values is called the Identity Increment. In this example, it is set to 10. These settings mean that when the user creates the first row of the PROPERTY table, SQL Server will give the value 100 to PropertyID. When the second row of PROPERTY is created, SQL Server will give the value 110 to PropertyID, and so forth.

Figure 2-10 shows the data in Figure 2-8 with example relationships using the surrogate key design.

FIGURE 2-9

Defining a Surrogate Key Using SQL Server

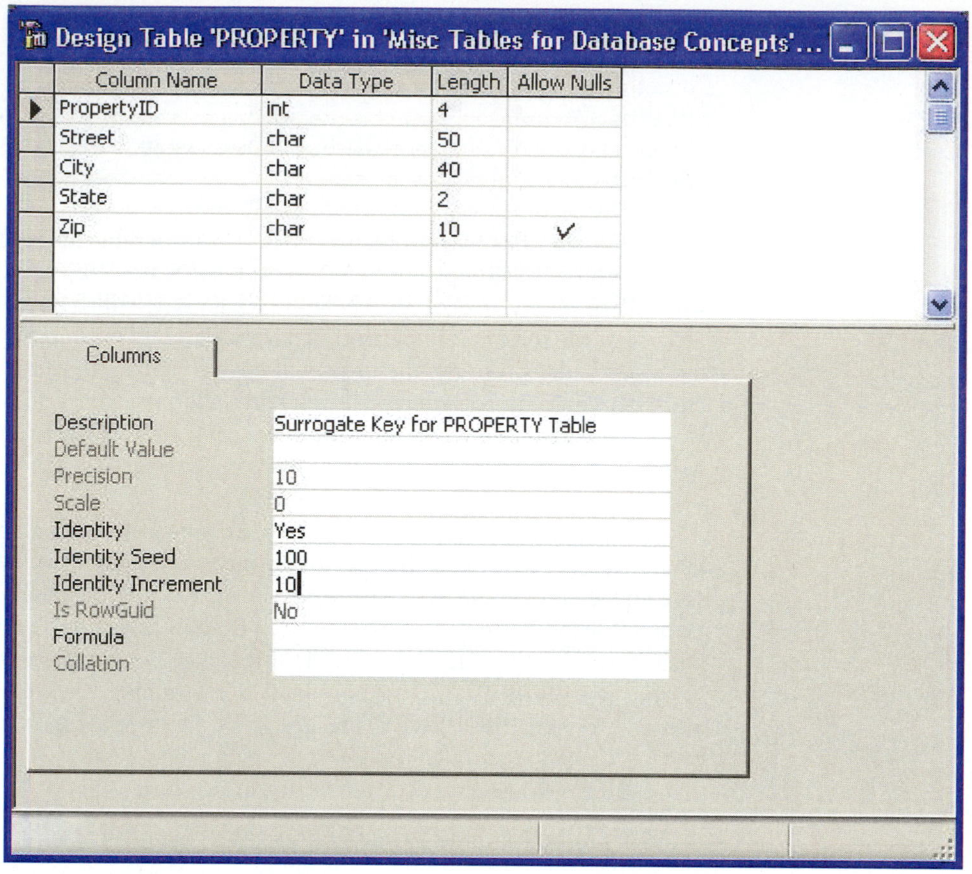

Design Table 'PROPERTY' in 'Misc Tables for Database Concepts'...

Column Name	Data Type	Length	Allow Nulls
PropertyID	int	4	
Street	char	50	
City	char	40	
State	char	2	
Zip	char	10	✓

Columns

Description	Surrogate Key for PROPERTY Table
Default Value	
Precision	10
Scale	0
Identity	Yes
Identity Seed	100
Identity Increment	10
Is RowGuid	No
Formula	
Collation	

FIGURE 2-10

PROPERTY, Plant, and Service Relations Using Surrogate Key Design

PropertyID	Street	City	State	Zip
100	123 East Elm	Riverside	CA	90800-4987
110	82334 - 188th Street	Oakland	CA	91200-9810
120	477 North Greenbriar Circle	Riverside	CA	90822-3328
130	One South Highrent Estates Parkway	Rolling Hills	CA	93455-0080

(a)

ItemNumber	VarietyName	Price	PropertyID
1000	Carpet Rose, White	$9.95	120
1100	Carpet Rose, Yellow	$11.50	130
1200	Lilac, 5 gal, purple	$57.55	120
1300	Lilac, 2 gal, purple	$27.50	130
1400	Hybrid Tea, Rose	$22.45	100

(b)

InvoiceNumber	Date	TotalHours	PropertyID
500	5/5/2002	17	100
550	5/6/2002	6	130
600	5/9/2002	12	120
650	5/11/2002	8	100

(c)

► FUNCTIONAL DEPENDENCIES AND NORMALIZATION

This section introduces some of the concepts used for relational database design; these concepts will be used in the next several chapters and then expanded in scope in Chapter 5. This book presents only the essentials. To learn more, you should consult other, more comprehensive references.[2]

Functional Dependencies

To get started, let's make a short excursion into the world of algebra. Suppose you are buying boxes of cookies and someone tells you that each box costs $5. Knowing this fact, you can compute the cost of several boxes with the formula:

CookieCost = NumberOfBoxes × $5

A more general way to express the relationship between CookieCost and NumberOfBoxes is to say that CookieCost depends upon NumberOfBoxes. Such a statement tells the character of the relationship of CookieCost and NumberOfBoxes, even though it doesn't give the formula. More formally, we can say that CookieCost is **functionally dependent** on NumberOfBoxes. Such a statement can be written as follows.

NumberOfBoxes → CookieCost

This expression also can be read as NumberOfBoxes determines CookieCost. The variable on the left, NumberOfBoxes, is called the **determinant**.

Using another example, we can compute the extended price of a part order by multiplying the quantity of the item times its unit price, or:

ExtendedPrice = Quantity * UnitPrice

In this case, we would say that ExtendedPrice is functionally dependent on Quantity and UnitPrice, or:

(Quantity, UnitPrice) → ExtendedPrice

The composite (Quantity, UnitPrice) is the determinant of ExtendedPrice.

Now, let's expand these ideas. Suppose you know that a sack contains either red, blue, or yellow objects. Further suppose you know that the red objects weigh 5 pounds, the blue objects weigh 3 pounds, and the yellow objects weigh 7 pounds. If a friend looks into the sack, sees an object, and tells you the color of the object, you can tell the weight of the object. We can formalize this is the same way we did in the previous example.

ObjectColor → Weight

Thus, we can say that Weight is functionally dependent on ObjectColor and that ObjectColor determines Weight. The relationship here does not involve an equation, but this functional dependency is still true. Given a value for ObjectColor, you can determine the object's weight.

---

[2]See David Kroenke, *Database Processing*, 9th edition (Upper Saddle River, NJ: Prentice Hall, 2004), and C. J. Date, *An Introduction to Database Systems*, 5th edition (Boston, MA: Addison-Wesley, 1999).

In addition, if we know that the red objects are balls, the blue objects are cubes, and the yellow objects are cubes, we also can say:

ObjectColor → Shape

Thus, ObjectColor determines Shape. We can put these two together to state:

ObjectColor → (Weight, Shape)

Thus, ObjectColor determines Weight and Shape.

Another way to represent these facts is to put them into a table as follows.

Object Color	Weight	Shape
Red	5	Ball
Blue	3	Cube
Yellow	7	Cube

This table meets all of the conditions listed in Figure 2-1, so we can refer to it as a relation. It has a primary key of ObjectColor. We can express this relation as:

OBJECT (ObjectColor, Weight, Shape)

Now, you may be thinking that we have just performed some trick or slight of hand to arrive at a relation, but one can make the argument that the only reason for having relations is to store instances of functional dependencies. Consider a relation such as:

PLANT (ItemNumber, VarietyName, Price, *PropertyID*)

Here, we are simply storing facts that express the following functional dependency.

ItemNumber → (VarietyName, Price, PropertyID)

Primary and Candidate Keys Revisited

With the concept of functional dependency, we can now define primary and candidate keys more formally. Specifically, a primary key of a relation can be defined as "one or more attributes that functionally determine all of the other attributes of the relation." The same definition holds for candidate keys, as well.

Recall the relation in Figure 2-2.

EMPLOYEE (EmployeeNumber, FirstName, LastName, Department, Email, Phone)

This relation has three candidate keys: EmployeeNumber, Email, and the composite (FirstName, LastName, Department). Because this is so, we can state the following.

EmployeeNumber → (FirstName, LastName, Department, Email, Phone)

Or, equivalently, given a value for EmployeeNumber, we can determine FirstName, LastName, Department, Email, and Phone. Similarly, we can say:

Email → (EmployeeNumber, FirstName, LastName, Department, Phone)

Or, given a value for Email, we can determine EmployeeNumber, FirstName, LastName, Department, and Phone. Finally, we also can say:

(FirstName, LastName, Department) → (EmployeeNumber, Email, Phone)

Or given values of FirstName, LastName, and Department, we can determine the EmployeeNumber, Email, and Phone.

These concepts can be used to help in the design of relations, as we will describe next.

Normalization

Normalization is a topic that consumes one or more chapters of more theoretically oriented database books. Here, we will reduce this topic to a few ideas that capture the essence of the process, and we will expand this discussion in Chapter 5. After that, if you are interested in the topic, you should consult the references mentioned earlier for more information.

The problem that normalization addresses is the following: A table can meet all of the characteristics listed in Figure 2-1 and still have the update problems we identified for lists at the start of Chapter 1. Specifically, consider the following ADVISER-LIST relation:

ADVISER-LIST (AdviserID, AdviserName, Department, Phone, Office, StudentNum, StudentName)

What is the primary key of this relation? Given the definition of foreign key, it has to be an attribute that determines all of the other attributes. The only attribute that has this characteristic is StudentNum. Given a value of StudentNum, we can determine the values of all of the other attributes. Or:

StudentNum → (AdviserID, AdviserName, Department, Phone, Office, StudentName)

We can then write this relation as follows.

ADVISER-LIST (AdviserID, AdviserName, Department, Phone, Office, StudentNum, StudentName)

However, this table has update problems. Specifically, an adviser's data are repeated many times in the table, once for each advisee. This means that changes to adviser data might need to be made multiple times. If, for example, an adviser changes offices, that change will need to be completed in all the rows for the person's advisees. If an adviser has 20 advisees, that change will need to be entered 20 times.

Another problem, also mentioned in Chapter 1, can occur when we delete a student from this list. If we delete a student who happens to be the only advisee for an adviser, we will delete not only the student's data, but also the adviser's data. Thus, we will unintentionally lose facts about two entities while attempting to delete one.

If you look closely at this relation, you will see a functional dependency that involves the adviser's data. Specifically:

AdviserID → (AdviserName, Department, Phone, Office)

Now, we can state the problem with this relation more accurately—in terms of functional dependencies. Specifically, this relation is poorly formed because it has a functional dependency that does not involve the primary key. Stated differently, AdviserID is a determinant of a functional dependency, but it is not a candidate key.

Relational Design Principles

From this discussion, we can formulate the following design principles.

> To be a well-formed relation, every determinant must be a candidate key.
> Any relation that is not well formed should be broken into two or more relations that are well formed.

These two principles are the heart of normalization—the process of examining relations and modifying them to make them well formed. This process is called normalization because you can categorize the problems to which relations are susceptible into different types called normal forms.

Any relation that has the characteristics listed in Figure 2-1 is called a relation in first normal form. Other normal forms exist, such as second, third, Boyce-Codd, fourth, fifth, and domain/key normal form. We will describe these further in Chapter 5.

If you follow the aforementioned design principles, you will avoid almost all of the problems associated with unnormalized tables. Some rare problems arise that these principles do not address (see questions 2.38 and 2.39 in the Exercises section), but if you follow these principles, you will be safe most of the time.

Normalization Process

We can apply the principles just described to formulate the following process for normalizing relations.

1. Identify all candidate keys of the relation.
2. Identify all functional dependencies in the relation.
3. Examine the determinants of the functional dependencies. If any determinant is not a candidate key, the relation has normalization problems. In this case:
   a. Place the columns of the functional dependency in a new relation of their own.
   b. Make the determinant of the functional dependency the primary key of the new relation.
   c. Leave a copy of the determinant as a foreign key in the original relation.
   d. Create a referential integrity constraint between the original relation and the new relation.
4. Repeat step 3 as many times as necessary until every determinant of every relation is a candidate key.

To understand this process, consider the following relation.

PRESCRIPTION (PrescriptionNumber, Date, Drug, Dosage, CustomerName, CustomerPhone, CustomerEmail)

Sample data are shown in Figure 2-11.

Step 1 According to the normalization process, we first identify all candidate keys. PrescriptionNumber determines Date, Drug, and Dosage. If we assume that a prescription is for only one person, then it also determines CustomerName CustomerPhone, and CustomerEmail. By law, prescriptions must be for only one person, so PrescriptionNumber is a candidate key.

Does this relation have other candidate keys? Neither Date, Drug, nor Dosage determines prescription because many prescriptions can be written on a given date, many prescriptions can be written for a given drug, and many prescriptions can be written for a given dosage.

What about customer columns? If a customer had only one prescription, then we could say that some identifying customer column—say, CustomerEmail—would deter-

FIGURE 2-11

Sample Prescription Data

PrescriptionNumber	Date	Drug	Dosage	CustomerName	CustomerPhone	CustomerEmail
P10001	5/17/2003	Lipitor	10mg	A.B. Smith	555.123.2233	SmithAB@somewhere.com
P10003	5/17/2003	Amoxicillan	35mg	Jeff Rhodes	555.125.5588	RhodesJ@somewhere.com
P10004	5/17/2003	Lipitor	20mg	Sarah Smith	555.123.2233	SmithS@somewhere.com
P10007	5/19/2003	Nexium	20mg	Michael Frye	555.145.6666	MF@somewhere.com
P10010	5/19/2003	Nexium	20mg	Jeff Rhodes	555.125.5588	RhodesJ@somewhere.com

mine the prescription data. However, people can have more than one prescription, so this assumption is invalid.

Given this analysis, then the only candidate key of PRESCRIPTION is PrescriptionNumber.

Step 2   According to the second step in the normalization process, we now identify all functional dependencies. PrescriptionNumber determines all of the other attributes as just described. If a drug had only one dosage, then we could say that Drug → Dosage, but this is not true; some drugs have several dosages. Therefore, Drug is not a determinant. Dosage is not a determinant because the same dosage can be given for many different drugs.

In examining the customer columns, a functional dependency is found—in particular, CustomerEmail → (CustomerName, CustomerPhone). (Again, to know if this is true for a particular application, we need to look beyond the sample data in Figure 2-11 and to ask the users. For example, it is possible that some customers share the same e-mail address; it is also possible that some customers have do not have e-mail. For now, assume the users say that CustomerEmail is a determinant of the customer attributes.)

Step 3   Now, according to step 3, we ask whether a determinant exists that is not a candidate key. In this example, CustomerEmail is a determinant and not a candidate key. Therefore, PRESCRIPTION has normalization problems. According to step 3, we then split the functional dependency into a relation of its own.

CUSTOMER (CustomerName, CustomerPhone, <u>CustomerEmail</u>)

We make the determinant of the functional dependency, CustomerEmail, the primary key of the new relation.

We leave a copy of CustomerEmail in the original relation as a foreign key. Thus, PRESCRIPTION is now:

PRESCRIPTION (<u>PrescriptionNumber</u>, Date, Drug, Dosage, *CustomerEmail*)

Finally, we create the referential integrity constraint.

CustomerEmail in PRESCRIPTION must exist in CustomerEmail in CUSTOMER.

At this point, neither of these relations has a determinant that is not a candidate key, and we can say the two relations are now normalized.

Normalization Examples

We will now illustrate the use of this process with four examples.

Normalization Example 1   The relation in Figure 2-12(a) shows a table of student residence data named STU-DORM. The first step in normalizing it is to identify all candidate keys. Because StudentNum determines each of the other columns, it is a candidate key. StudentName cannot be a candidate key because two students have the name Smith. None of the other columns can be an identifier either, so StudentNum is the only candidate key.

Next, in step 2, we look for the functional dependencies in the relation. Besides those for StudentNum, a functional dependency appears to exist between DormName and DormCost. Again, we would need to check this out with the users. In this case, assume that the functional dependency DormName → DormCost is true, and assume that our interview with the users indicates that no other functional dependencies exist.

According to step 3, we now ask if any determinants exist that are not candidate keys. In this example, DormName is a determinant, but it is not a candidate key. Therefore, this relation has normalization problems.

StudentNum	StudentName	DormName	DormCost
100	Smith	Stephens	$3,500.00
200	Johnson	Alexander	$3,800.00
300	Abernathy	Horan	$4,000.00
400	Smith	Alexander	$3,800.00
500	Wilcox	Stephens	$3,500.00
600	Webber	Horan	$4,000.00
700	Simon	Stephens	$3,500.00

To fix those problems, we place the columns of the functional dependency (DormName, DormCost) into a relation of their own and call that relation DORM. We make the determinant of the functional dependency the primary key. Thus, DormName is the primary key of DORM. We leave the determinant DormName as a foreign key in STU-DORM. Finally, we find the appropriate referential integrity constraint. The result is:

STU-DORM (<u>StudentNum</u>, StudentName, *DormName*)
DORM (<u>DormName</u>, DormCost)

With constraint:

DormName in STU-DORM must exist in DormName in DORM

The same data for these relations appear as shown in Figure 2-12(b).

Normalization Example 2 Now consider the EMPLOYEE table in Figure 2-13(a). First, we identify candidate keys. From the data, it appears that EmployeeNumber and Email each identify all of the other attributes. Hence, they are candidate keys (again, with the proviso that we cannot depend on sample data to show all cases; we must verify this assumption with the users.)

Step 2 is to identify functional dependencies. From the data, it appears that the only functional dependency is that Department determines DeptPhone. Assuming this is true, then according to step 3, we have a determinant, Department, that is not the same as either of the candidate keys. Thus, EMPLOYEE has normalization problems.

To fix those problems, we place the columns in the functional dependency in a table of their own and make the determinant the primary key of the new table. We leave the determinant as a foreign key in the original table. The result is the two tables:

EMPLOYEE (<u>EmployeeNumber</u>, LastName, Email, *Department*)

and

DEPARTMENT (<u>Department</u>, DeptPhone)

With referential integrity constraint:

Department in EMPLOYEE must exist in Department in DEPARTMENT

The result for the sample data is shown in Figure 2-13(b).

StudentNum	StudentName	DormName
100	Smith	Stephens
200	Johnson	Alexander
300	Abernathy	Horan
400	Smith	Alexander
500	Wilcox	Stephens
600	Webber	Horan
700	Simon	Stephens

DormName	DormCost
Stephens	$3,500.00
Alexander	$3,800.00
Horan	$4,000.00

FIGURE 2-13(a)

Employee Department Data as One Table

EmployeeNumber	LastName	Email	Department	DeptPhone
100	Johnson	JJ@somewhere.com	Accounting	236-9987
200	Abernathy	MA@somewhere.com	Finance	444-8898
300	Smathers	LS@somewhere.com	Finance	444-8898
400	Caruthers	TC@somewhere.com	Accounting	236-9987
500	Jackson	TJ@somewhere.com	Production	444-9980
600	Caldera	EC@somewhere.com	Legal	767-0900
700	Bandalone	RB@somewhere.com	Legal	767-0900

FIGURE 2-13(b)

Employee Department Data as Two Tables

EmployeeNumber	LastName	Email	Department
100	Johnson	JJ@somewhere.com	Accounting
200	Abernathy	MA@somewhere.com	Finance
300	Smathers	LS@somewhere.com	Finance
400	Caruthers	TC@somewhere.com	Accounting
500	Jackson	TJ@somewhere.com	Production
600	Caldera	EC@somewhere.com	Legal
700	Bandalone	RB@somewhere.com	Legal

Department	DeptPhone
Accounting	236-9987
Finance	444-8898
Production	444-9980

Normalization Example 3 Now consider the MEETING table in Figure 2-14(a). We begin by looking for candidate keys. No column by itself can be a candidate key. Attorney determines different sets of data, so it cannot be a determinant. The same is true for ClientNumber, ClientName, and MeetingDate. In the sample data, the only column that does not determine different sets of data is Duration, but this uniqueness is accidental. It is easy to imagine that two more meetings would have the same duration.

The next step is to look for combinations of columns that can be candidate keys. (Attorney, ClientNumber) is one combination, but the values (Boxer, 1000) determine two different sets of data. They cannot be a candidate key. The combination (Attorney, ClientName) fails for the same reason. The only combinations that can be candidate keys of this relation are (Attorney, ClientNumber, MeetingDate) and (Attorney, ClientName, MeetingDate).

Consider those possibilities further. The name of the relation is MEETING and we're asking whether (Attorney, ClientNumber, MeetingDate) or (Attorney, ClientName, MeetingDate) can be a candidate key. Do these combinations make sense as an identifier of a meeting? They do unless more than one meeting of the same attorney and client occurs on the same day. In that case, we need to add a new column, MeetingTime, to the relation and make this new column part of the candidate key. In this example, we will assume this is not the case and that (Attorney, ClientNumber, MeetingDate) and (Attorney, ClientName, MeetingDate) are the candidate keys.

The next step is to identify functional dependencies. Here, two exist:

ClientNumber → ClientName and ClientName → ClientNumber. Each of these determinants is part of one of the candidate keys. For example, ClientNumber is part of (Attorney, ClientNumber, MeetingDate). However, being part of a candidate key is not enough. The determinant must be the same as the entire candidate key. Thus, the MEETING table has normalization problems.

When you are not certain whether or not normalization problems exist, consider the three update operations discussed in Chapter 1. Do problems exist with any of them? For example, in Figure 2-14(a), if you change ClientName in the first row to ABC, Limited,

FIGURE 2-14(a)

Meeting Data as One Table

Attorney	ClientNumber	ClientName	MeetingDate	Duration
Boxer	1000	ABC, Inc	5/5/2002	2.00
Boxer	2000	ZZZ Partners	5/5/2002	5.50
James	1000	ABC, Inc	5/7/2002	3.00
Boxer	1000	ABC, Inc	5/9/2002	4.00
Wu	3000	Malcomb Zoe	5/11/2002	7.00

do inconsistencies arise in the data? The answer is yes, because ClientNumber 1000 would have two different names in the table. This and any of the other problems that were identified in Chapter 1 when inserting, updating, or deleting data are a sure sign that the table has normalization problems.

To fix the normalization problems, we create a new table CLIENT with columns ClientNumber and ClientName. Both of these columns are determinants; thus, either can be the primary key of the new table. However, whichever one is selected as the primary key also should be made the foreign key in MEETING. Thus, two correct designs are possible.

MEETING (<u>Attorney</u>, *<u>ClientNumber</u>*, <u>MeetingDate</u>, Duration)

CLIENT (<u>ClientNumber</u>, ClientName)

ClientNumber in MEETING must exist in ClientNumber in CLIENT

or

MEETING (<u>Attorney</u>, *<u>ClientName</u>*, <u>MeetingDate</u>, Duration)

CLIENT (ClientNumber, <u>ClientName</u>)

ClientName in MEETING must exist in ClientName in CLIENT

Data for the first design are shown in Figure 2-14(b).

Notice in these designs that the attributes ClientNumber and ClientName are foreign keys and also are part of the primary key of MEETING.

One final comment about this design needs to be made: When two attributes each determine one another, they are synonyms. They both must appear in a relation to establish their equivalent values. Given that equivalency, the two columns are interchangeable; one can take the place of the other in any other relation. All things being equal, however, the administration of the database will be simpler if one of the two is used consistently as a foreign key. This policy is just a convenience, however, and not a logical requirement for the design.

Normalization Example 4   For our last example, consider a relation that involves student data. Specifically, consider the following relation.

GRADE (ClassName, Section, Term, Grade, StudentNumber, StudentName, Professor, Department, ProfessorEmail)

Given the confused set of columns in this table, it appears that it will have normalization problems. We can use the normalization process to find what they are and to remove them.

First, what are the candidate keys of this relation? No column by itself is a candidate key. One way to approach this is to realize that a grade is a combination of a class and a student. In this table, which columns identify classes and students? A particular class is identified by (ClassName, Section, Term), and a student is identified by StudentNumber. Possibly, then, a candidate key for this relation is:

(ClassName, Section, Term, StudentNumber)

This statement is equivalent to saying:

(ClassName, Section, Term, StudentNumber) → (Grade, StudentName, Professor, Department, ProfessorEmail)

FIGURE 2-14(b)

Meeting Data as Two Tables

Attorney	ClientNumber	MeetingDate	Duration
Boxer	1000	5/5/2002	2.00
Boxer	2000	5/5/2002	5.50
James	1000	5/7/2002	3.00
Boxer	1000	5/9/2002	4.00
Wu	3000	5/11/2002	7.00

ClientNumber	ClientName
1000	ABC, Inc
2000	ZZZ Partners
3000	Malcomb Zoe

This is a true statement as long as only one professor teaches a class section. For now, we will make that assumption and consider the alternate case later. If only one professor teaches a section, then (ClassName, Section, Term, StudentNumber) is the one and only candidate key.

What are the additional functional dependencies? One involves student data and another involves professor data; specifically, StudentNumber → StudentName and Professor → ProfessorEmail. We also need to ask if Professor determines Department. It will if a professor teaches in only one department. In that case, we can say Professor → (Department, ProfessorEmail). Otherwise, Department must remain in the GRADE relation. Assume professors teach in just one department. Then we have:

StudentNumber → StudentName

and

Professor → (Department, ProfessorEmail)

If you examine the GRADE relation a bit further, however, you can find one other functional dependency. If only one professor teaches a class section, then (ClassName, Section, Term) → Professor.

According to step 3 of the normalization process, GRADE has normalization problems because the determinants StudentNumber, Professor, and (ClassName, Section, Term) are not candidate keys. According to step 3 of the normalization process, we form a table for each of these functional dependencies. As a result, we will have a STUDENT table, PROFESSOR table, and a CLASS_PROFESSOR table. After forming these tables, we then take the appropriate columns out of GRADE. Call the new version of the grade table GRADE1. We now have the following design.

STUDENT (StudentNumber, StudentName)

PROFESSOR (Professor, Department, ProfessorEmail)

CLASS_PROFESSOR (ClassName, Section, Term, *Professor*)

GRADE1 (*ClassName*, *Section*, *Term*, Grade, *StudentNumber*)

with the referential integrity constraints:

StudentNumber in GRADE1 must exist in StudentNumber in STUDENT

Professor in CLASS_PROFESSOR must exist in Professor in PROFESSOR

(ClassName, Section, Term) in GRADE1 must exist in (ClassName, Section, Term) of CLASS_PROFESSOR.

Next, consider what happens if more than one professor teaches a section of a class. In that case, the only change is to make Professor part of the primary key of CLASS_PROFESSOR. Thus, the new relation is:

CLASS_PROFESSOR1 (ClassName, Section, Term, *Professor*)

Class sections that have more than one professor will have multiple rows in this table—one row for each of the professors.

(In the interest of full disclosure, if professors can teach more than one class, then GRADE has what is called a *multi-valued dependency*. We have not discussed such dependencies in this book. If you want to learn about them, see one of the more advanced texts mentioned on page 35 and also Exercise 2.39.)

This example shows how normalization problems can become more complicated than simple examples might indicate. For large commercial applications that potentially involve hundreds of tables, such problems can sometimes consume days or weeks of design time.

FIGURE 2-15

Example ITEM Data

ItemNum	ItemName	Color	Quantity
100	Small T-Shirt	Red	15
150	Small T-Shirt	Blue	5
200	Small T-Shirt	Green	7
300	Med T-Shirt	Red	8
400	Spring Hat		5

▶ THE PROBLEM OF NULL VALUES

We will conclude this introduction to the relational model by discussing a subtle but important topic: null values. Consider the following relation that is used to track finished goods for an apparel manufacturer.

ITEM (ItemNum, ItemName, Color, Quantity)

Sample data for this table are shown in Figure 2-15.

Examine the last row of data; notice that Spring Hat has no value for Color. Such a missing value is called a **null value**. The problem with null values is that they are ambiguous; we do not know how to interpret them because three possible meanings can be construed. First, it might mean that no value of color is appropriate; Spring Hats do not come in different colors. Second, it might mean that the value is known to be blank; that is, Spring Hats have a color, but the color has not yet been decided. Maybe the color is established by placing ribbons around the hats, but this is not done until an order arrives. Or third, the null value might mean that the hats' color is simply unknown; the hats do have a color, but no one has checked yet to see what it is.

Null values can be eliminated by requiring an attribute value. If the attribute is a text value, users can be allowed to enter values such as "not appropriate," "undecided," or "unknown" when necessary. If the attribute is not text, then some other coding system can be developed.

For now, be aware that null values can occur and that they always carry an ambiguity with them. The next chapter will show another, possibly more serious problem of null values.

SUMMARY

The relational model is the most important standard in database processing today. It was first published by E. F. Codd in 1970. Today, it is used for the design and implementation of almost every commercial database.

A relation is a two-dimensional table that has the characteristics listed in Figure 2-1. In this book and in the database world in general, the term *table* is used synonymously with the term *relation*. Three sets of terminology are used for relational structures. The terms *table, row,* and *column* are used most commonly, but *file, record,* and *field* are sometimes used in traditional data processing. Theorists also use the terms *relation, tuple,* and *attribute* for the same three constructs. Sometimes these terms are mixed and matched. Strictly speaking, a relation may not have duplicate rows; however, sometimes this condition is relaxed because eliminating duplicates can be a time-consuming process.

A key is one or more columns of a relation that is used to identify a row. A unique key identifies a single row; a nonunique key identifies several. A composite key is a key that has two or more attributes. A relation has one primary key, which must be a unique key. A relation also may have additional unique keys called candidate keys. A primary key is used to represent the table in relationships, and many DBMS products use values of the primary key to organize table storage. In addition, an index normally is constructed to provide fast access via primary key values.

A foreign key is an attribute that is placed in a relation to represent a relationship. A foreign key is the primary key of a table that is different from (foreign to) the table in which it is placed. Primary and foreign keys may have different names, but they must use the same sets of values. A referential integrity constraint specifies that the values of a foreign key be present in the primary key.

A surrogate key is a unique, numeric value that is appended to a relation to serve as the primary key. Surrogate key values have no meaning to the user and normally are hidden on forms, queries, and reports.

A functional dependency occurs when the value of one attribute (or set of attributes) determines the value of a second attribute (or set of attributes). The attribute on the left side of a functional dependency is called the determinant. One way to view the purpose of a relation is to say that the relation exists to store instances of functional dependencies. Another way to define a primary (and candidate) key is to say that such a key is an attribute that functionally determines all of the other attributes in a relation.

Normalization is the process of evaluating a relation and, when necessary, breaking the relation into two more relations that are better designed. According to normalization theory, a relation is poorly structured if it has a functional dependency that does not involve the primary key. Specifically, in a well-formed relation, every determinant is a candidate key.

A process for normalizing relations is shown on page 38. According to this process, relations that have normalization problems are divided into two or more relations that do not have such problems. Foreign keys are established between the old and new relations, and referential integrity constraints are created.

A null value occurs when no value has been given to an attribute. The problem with a null value is that its meaning is ambiguous. It can mean that no value is appropriate, that a value is appropriate but has not yet been chosen, or that a value is appropriate and has been chosen but is unknown to the user. Null values can be eliminated by requiring attribute values. Another problem with null values will be shown in the next chapter.

REVIEW QUESTIONS

2.1 Why is the relational model important?

2.2 List the characteristics a table must have to be considered a relation.

2.3 Give an example of a relation (other than one in this chapter).

2.4 Give an example of a table that is not a relation (other than one in this chapter).

2.5 Under what circumstances can an attribute of a relation be of variable length?

2.6 Explain the use of the terms *file, record,* and *field.*

2.7 Explain the use of the terms *relation, tuple,* and *attribute.*

2.8 Under what circumstances can a relation have duplicate rows?

2.9 Define the term *unique key* and give an example.

2.10 Define the term *nonunique key* and give an example.

2.11 Give an example of a relation with a unique composite key.

2.12 Explain the difference between a primary key and a candidate key.

2.13 Describe four uses of a primary key.

2.14 Explain the term *foreign key* and give an example.

2.15 Explain how primary keys and foreign keys are denoted in this book.

2.16 Define the term *referential integrity constraint* and give an example of one.

2.17 What is a surrogate key, and under what circumstances would you use one?

2.18 How do surrogate keys obtain their values?

2.19 Why are the values of surrogate keys normally hidden from users on forms, queries, and reports?

2.20 In the following equation, name the functional dependency and identify the determinant(s).
Area = Length × Width

2.21 Explain the meaning of the following expression.
A → (B, C)

Given this expression, tell if it is also true that:
A → B
and
A → C

2.22 Explain the meaning of the following expression:
(D, E) → F

Given this expression, tell if it is also true that:
D → F
and
E → F

2.23 Explain the differences in your answers to questions 2.21 and 2.22.

2.24 Define the term *primary key* in terms of functional dependencies.

2.25 If we assume that a relation has no duplicate data, how do we know there is always at least one primary key?

2.26 How does your answer to question 2.25 change if we allow a relation to have duplicate data?

2.27 Using your own words, describe the nature and purpose of the normalization process.

2.28 Examine the data in Figure 1-26 (see page 20) and state assumptions about functional dependencies in this table. What is the danger of making such conclusions on the basis of sample data?

2.29 Using the assumptions you stated in your answer to question 2.28, what are the determinants of this relation? What attribute(s) can be the primary key of this relation?

2.30 Explain a problem when changing data in the relation in question 2.28 and a second problem when deleting data in this relation.

2.31 Examine the data in Figure 1-27 (see page 20) and state assumptions about functional dependencies in this table.

2.32 Using the assumptions you stated in your answer to question 2.31, what are the determinants of this relation? What attribute(s) can be the primary key of this relation?

2.33 Explain a problem when changing data in the relation in question 2.31 and a second problem when deleting data in this relation.

2.34 Explain three possible interpretations of a null value.

2.35 Give an example of a null value (other than one in this chapter) and explain each of the three possible interpretations for that value.

EXERCISES

2.36 Apply the normalization process to the relation shown in Figure 1-26 to develop a set of normalized relations. Show the results of each of the steps in the normalization process.

2.37 Apply the normalization process to the relation shown in Figure 1-27 to develop a set of normalized relations. Show the results of each of the steps in the normalization process.

2.38 Consider the following relation.

STUDENT (<u>StudentNum</u>, StudentName, <u>SiblingName</u>, Major)

Assume that the values of SiblingName are the names of all of a given student's brothers and sisters; also assume that students have at most one major.

A. Show an example of this relation for two students, one of whom has three siblings and the other of whom has only two siblings.

B. State the functional dependencies in this relation.

C. Explain why this relation does not meet the relational design criteria set out in this chapter.

D. Divide this relation into two relations that do meet the relational design criteria.

2.39 Alter question 2.38 to allow students to have multiple majors. In this case, the relational structure is:

STUDENT (<u>StudentNum</u>, StudentName, <u>SiblingName</u>, <u>Major</u>)

A. Show an example of this relation for two students, one of whom has three siblings and the other of whom has one sibling. Assume each student has a single major.

B. Show the data changes necessary to add a second major only for the first student.

C. Show the data changes necessary to add a second major for the second student.

D. Explain the differences in your answer to questions B and C. Comment on the desirability of this situation.

E. Divide this relation into two relations that do not have the problems described in your answer to question D.

2.40 The text states that one can argue that "the only reason for having relations is to store instances of functional dependencies." Explain what this means in your own words.

GARDEN GLORY PROJECT QUESTIONS

Figure 2-16 shows data that Garden Glory collects about properties and services.

A. Using these data, state assumptions about functional dependencies among the columns of data. Justify your assumptions on the basis of these sample data and also on the basis of what you know about service businesses.

B. Given your assumptions, comment on the appropriateness of the following designs.
   1. PROPERTY (<u>PropertyName</u>, Type, Street, City, Zip, ServiceDate, Description, Amount)
   2. PROPERTY (PropertyName, Type, Street, City, Zip, <u>ServiceDate</u>, Description, Amount)

FIGURE 2-16

Sample Data for
Garden Glory

Property Name	Type	Street	City	Zip	ServiceDate	Description	Amount
Eastlake Building	Office	123 Eastlake	Seattle	98119	5/5/02	Lawn Mow	$42.50
Elm St Apts	Apartment	4 East Elm	Lynnwood	98223	5/7/02	Lawn Mow	$123.50
Jefferson Hill	Office	42 West 7th St	Bellevue	98040	5/7/02	Garden Service	$53.00
Eastlake Building	Office	123 Eastlake	Seattle	98119	5/12/02	Lawn Mow	$42.50
Eastlake Building	Office	123 Eastlake	Seattle	98119	5/19/02	Lawn Mow	$42.50
Elm St Apts	Apartment	4 East Elm	Lynnwood	98223	5/14/02	Lawn Mow	$123.50
Eastlake Building	Office	144 Eastlake	Bellevue	98040	5/10/02	Lawn Mow	$63.00

3. PROPERTY (<u>PropertyName</u>, Type, Street, City, Zip, <u>ServiceDate</u>, Description, Amount)

4. PROPERTY (<u>PropertyID</u>, PropertyName, Type, Street, City, Zip, ServiceDate, Description, Amount)

5. PROPERTY (<u>PropertyID</u>, PropertyName, Type, Street, City, Zip, <u>ServiceDate</u>, Description, Amount)

6. PROPERTY (<u>PropertyID</u>, PropertyName, Type, Street, City, Zip, ServiceDate)

   and

   SERVICE (<u>ServiceDate</u>, Description, Amount)

7. PROPERTY (<u>PropertyID</u>, PropertyName, Type, Street, City, Zip, ServiceDate)

   and

   SERVICE (<u>ServiceID</u>, ServiceDate, Description, Amount)

8. PROPERTY (<u>PropertyID</u>, PropertyName, Type, Street, City, Zip, ServiceDate)

   and

   SERVICE (<u>ServiceID</u>, ServiceDate, Description, Amount, PropertyID)

9. PROPERTY (<u>PropertyID</u>, PropertyName, Type, Street, City, Zip)

   and

   SERVICE (<u>ServiceID</u>, ServiceDate, Description, Amount, PropertyID)

C. Suppose Garden Glory decides to add the following table.

   SERVICE-FEE (PropertyID, ServiceID, Description, Amount)

   Add this table to what you consider to be the best design in your answer to question B. Modify the tables from question B as necessary to minimize the amount of duplicate data. Will this design work for the data in Figure 2-16? If not, modify the data so that this design will work. State the assumption implied by this design.

JAMES RIVER JEWELRY PROJECT QUESTIONS

Figure 2-17 shows data that James River collects for its frequent buyer program.

A. Using these data, state assumptions about functional dependencies among the columns of data. Justify your assumptions on the basis of these sample data and also on the basis of what you know about retail sales.

B. Given your assumptions, comment on the appropriateness of the following designs.

1. CUSTOMER (<u>Name</u>, Phone, Email, InvoiceNumber, Date, PreTaxAmount)

2. CUSTOMER (Name, Phone, Email, <u>InvoiceNumber</u>, Date, PreTaxAmount)

FIGURE 2-17

Sample Data for James River

Name	Phone	Email	InvoiceNumber	Date	PreTaxAmount
Elizabeth Stanley	555.236-7789	ES@somewhere.com	1000	5/5/2002	$155.00
Fred Price	555.236-0091	FP@somewhere.com	1010	5/7/2002	$203.00
Linda Becky	555.236-0392	LB@somewhere.com	1020	5/11/2002	$75.00
Pamela Birch	555.236-4493	PB@somewhere.com	1030	5/15/2002	$67.00
Ricardo Romez	555.236-3334	RB@somewhere.com	1040	5/15/2002	$330.00
Elizabeth Stanley	555.236-7789	ES@somewhere.com	1050	5/16/2002	$25.00
Linda Becky	555.236-0392	LB@somewhere.com	1060	5/16/2002	$45.00
Elizabeth Stanley	555.236-7789	ES@somewhere.com	1070	5/18/2002	$445.00
Samantha Jackson	555.236-1095	SJ@somewhere.com	1080	5/19/2002	$72.00

3. CUSTOMER (Name, Phone, <u>Email</u>, InvoiceNumber, Date, PreTaxAmount)

4. CUSTOMER (<u>CustomerID</u>, Name, Phone, Email, InvoiceNumber, Date, PreTax Amount)

5. CUSTOMER (Name, Phone, <u>Email</u>)

   and

   PURCHASE (<u>InvoiceNumber</u>, Date, PreTax Amount)

6. CUSTOMER (Name, Phone, <u>Email</u>)

   and

   PURCHASE (<u>InvoiceNumber</u>, Date, PreTax Amount, Email)

7. CUSTOMER (Name, <u>Email</u>)

   and

   PURCHASE (<u>InvoiceNumber</u>, Phone, Date, PreTax Amount, Email)

C. Modify what you consider to be the best design in question B to include a column called AwardPurchaseAmount. The purpose of this column is to keep a balance of the customers' purchases for award purposes. Assume that returns will be recorded with invoices having a negative PreTaxAmount.

D. Add a new AWARD table to your answer to question C. Assume that the new table will hold data concerning the date and amount of an award that is given after a customer has purchased 10 items. Ensure that your new table has appropriate primary and foreign keys.

MID-WESTERN UNIVERSITY CHEMISTRY DEPARTMENT PROJECT QUESTIONS

Figure 2-18 shows data that the chemistry department collects about appointments for using the NMR magnets. Assume that one principal investigator (PI) can have many grants but that a grant has only one PI.

A. Using these data, state assumptions about functional dependencies among the columns. Justify your assumptions on the basis of these sample data and also on the basis of what you know about scheduling appointments.

B. Given your assumptions, comment on the appropriateness of the following designs.

1. APPOINTMENT (<u>GrantNum</u>, PI, PI_Email, MagnetID, MagnetLocation, Date, Start, End, User, UserJobTitle)

2. APPOINTMENT (GrantNum, <u>PI</u>, PI_Email, MagnetID, MagnetLocation, Date, Start, End, User, UserJobTitle)

FIGURE 2-18

**Sample Data for
Mid-Western University
Chemistry Department**

GrantNum	PI	PI_Email	MagnetID	MagnetLocation	Date	Start	End	User	UserJobTitle
1001	Jones	Jones@ouru.edu	254	SS213	10/11/2003	9:30	12:00	Chris	Postdoc
1014	Adams	Adams@ouru.edu	254	SS213	10/11/2003	13:00	15:00	James	GradStu
1001	Jones	Jones@ouru.edu	254	SS213	10/12/2003	17:00	23:00	Larry	Associate
1017	Adams	Adams@ouru.edu	718	SS255	10/11/2003	9:30	16:00	Jones	PI
1024	Wu	Wu@ouru.edu	254	SS213	10/17/2003	7:00	12:00	Chris	Postdoc
1014	Adams	Adams@ouru.edu	799	SS308	10/11/2003	9:30	12:00	Adams	PI

3. APPOINTMENT (<u>GrantNum</u>, PI, PI_Email, <u>MagnetID</u>, MagnetLocation, Date, Start, End, User, UserJobTitle)

4. APPOINTMENT (GrantNum, PI, PI_Email, <u>MagnetID</u>, MagnetLocation, <u>Date</u>, <u>Start</u>, End, <u>User</u>, UserJobTitle)

5. APPOINTMENT (*GrantNum*, <u>MagnetID</u>, MagnetLocation, <u>Date</u>, <u>Start</u>, End, User, UserJobTitle)

   and

   GRANT (<u>GrantNum</u>, PI, PI_Email)

6. APPOINTMENT (*GrantNum*, <u>MagnetID</u>, MagnetLocation, <u>Date</u>, <u>Start</u>, End, *User*)

   GRANT (<u>GrantNum</u>, PI, PI_Email)

   and

   USER (<u>User</u>, UserJobTitle)

7. Fix the relations in design 6 to remove remaining normalization problems.

8. State all referential integrity constraints for your design 7.

Structured Query Language

> Learn basic SQL statements for creating database structures
> Learn basic SQL SELECT statements and options for processing a single table
> Learn basic SQL SELECT statements for processing multiple tables with subqueries
> Learn basic SQL SELECT statements for processing multiple tables with joins
> Learn SQL statements to add, modify, and delete data

This chapter describes and discusses Structured Query Language (SQL). SQL is not a complete programming language but rather it is a data sublanguage. SQL consists only of constructs for defining and processing a database. To obtain a full programming language, SQL statements must be embedded in scripting languages such as VBScript or in programming languages such as Java or C#. SQL statements also can be submitted interactively using a DBMS-supplied command prompt. You will learn how to use SQL with Microsoft Access in the Appendix. We will use the command-prompt version in this chapter.

SQL was developed by the IBM Corporation in the late 1970s and was endorsed as a national standard by the American National Standards Institute in 1992. The version presented here is based on that standard, sometimes referred to as SQL-92. A later version, SQL3, incorporates some object-oriented concepts. This later version has received little attention from commercial Database Management System (DBMS) vendors and at present is unimportant for practical database processing. We will not consider it here.

SQL is text oriented. It was developed long before graphical user interfaces and requires only a text processor. Today, Microsoft Access, SQL Server, Oracle, and other DBMS products provide graphical tools for performing many of the tasks that are performed using SQL. However, the key phrase in that last sentence is *many of*. You cannot do everything with graphical tools that you can do with SQL; furthermore, to generate SQL statements dynamically in program code, you must use SQL.

Microsoft Access uses SQL but hides it behind the scenes. Although knowledge of SQL is not a requirement for using Access, you will be a stronger and more effective Access developer if you do know SQL.

SQL can be used to define database structures, to query database data, and to update database data. We will discuss each of these in turn. First, however, we will describe a sample database that will be used for illustration.

▶ A SAMPLE DATABASE

In this chapter, we will use a sample database having the following three relations.

PROJECT (ProjectID, Name, Department, MaxHours)

EMPLOYEE (EmployeeNumber, Name, Phone, Department)

ASSIGNMENT (*ProjectID*, *EmployeeNum*, HoursWorked)

Sample data for these relations are shown in Figure 3-1. The primary key of PROJECT is ProjectID and that of EMPLOYEE is EmployeeNumber. The primary key of ASSIGNMENT is the composite (ProjectID, EmployeeNumber). ProjectID is also a foreign key to PROJECT, and EmployeeNum is a foreign key to EMPLOYEE. (Again note that a foreign key need not have the same name as the primary key to which it refers.)

In this database, each row of PROJECT is potentially related to many rows of ASSIGNMENT. Similarly, each row of EMPLOYEE is potentially related to many rows of ASSIGNMENT.

This example has the following referential integrity constraints.

ProjectID in ASSIGNMENT must exist in ProjectID in PROJECT

FIGURE 3-1

Sample Data for
PROJECT, EMPLOYEE,
and ASSIGNMENT
Relations

PROJECT Relation

ProjectID	Name	Department	MaxHours
1000	Q3 Portfolio Analysis	Finance	75.0
1200	Q3 Tax Prep	Accounting	145.0
1400	Q4 Product Plan	Marketing	138.0
1500	Q4 Portfolio Analysis	Finance	110.0

EMPLOYEE Relation

EmployeeNumber	Name	Phone	Department
100	Mary Jacobs	285-8879	Accounting
200	Keni Numoto	287-0098	Marketing
300	Heather Jones	287-9981	Finance
400	Rosalie Jackson	285-1273	Accounting
500	James Nestor		Info Systems
600	Richard Wu	287-0123	Info Systems
700	Kim Sung	287-3222	Marketing

ASSIGNMENT Relation

ProjectID	EmployeeNum	HoursWorked
1000	100	17.50
1000	300	12.50
1000	400	8.00
1000	500	20.25
1200	100	45.75
1200	400	70.50
1200	600	40.50
1400	200	75.00
1400	700	20.25
1400	500	25.25

and

EmployeeNum in ASSIGNMENT must exist in EmployeeNumber in
EMPLOYEE

Finally, assume the following rules, which also are called **business rules**.

> If a PROJECT row is deleted, then all of the ASSIGNMENT rows that are connected to the deleted PROJECT row also will be deleted.
> If an EMPLOYEE row is deleted and that row is connected to any ASSIGNMENT, the EMPLOYEE row deletion will be disallowed.

The business sense of these rules is the following: If a PROJECT row is deleted, then the project has been canceled, and it is unnecessary to maintain records of assignments to that project. On the other hand, if an EMPLOYEE row is deleted (say the employee is transferred), then someone must take over that employee's assignments. Thus, the application needs someone to reassign assignments before deleting the employee row.

These rules are typical business rules. You will learn more about such rules in Chapter 5.

▶ SQL FOR DATA DEFINITION

The SQL CREATE TABLE statement is used to create table structures as shown in Figure 3-2. The essential format of this statement is shown in the following.

CREATE TABLE newtablename (

three-part column description,

three-part column description,

three-part column description, ·

optional table constraints

. . .

);

The parts of the column definition are column name, column data type, and, optionally, a constraint on column values. Column constraints we will consider in this text are Primary Key, Not Null, Null, and Default. Table constraints are described in the next section.

Consider the table definitions in Figure 3-2. The column ProjectID is of type Integer and has the constraint Primary Key. The next column, Name, is of the type character (signified by Char) and is 25 characters in length. The constraint Not Null indicates that a value must be supplied before a new row can be created.

The third column, Department, is of type VarChar(100) and has the property Null. VarChar means variable-length character. Thus, Department contains character data values that vary in length from row to row, and the maximum length of a Department value is 100 characters. However, if a Department value has only four characters, then only four characters will be stored. Null signifies that null values are allowed.

As implied, Char values are of fixed length. The Char(25) definition for Name means that 25 characters will be stored for every value of Name, regardless of the length of the value entered. Names will be padded with blanks to fill the 25 spaces when necessary.

FIGURE 3-2

SQL CREATE TABLE
Statements

```
CREATE TABLE PROJECT (
    ProjectID          Integer             Primary Key,
    Name               Char(25)            Not Null,
    Department         VarChar(100)        Null,
    MaxHours           Numeric(5,2)        Default 100
);

CREATE TABLE EMPLOYEE(
    EmployeeNumber     Integer             Primary Key,
    Name               Char(25)            Not Null,
    Phone              Char(8),
    Department         VarChar(100)
);

CREATE TABLE ASSIGNMENT(
    ProjectID          Integer             Not Null,
    EmployeeNum        Integer             Not Null,
    HoursWorked        Numeric(5,2)        Default 10
);
```

You might wonder, given the advantage of VarChar, why it isn't used all the time. The reason is that extra processing is required for VarChar columns. A few extra bytes are required to store the length of the value, and the DBMS must go to some trouble to arrange variable-length values in memory and on disk. Vendors of DBMS products usually provide guidelines for when to use which type. See the documentation for your DBMS product.

The fourth column of PROJECT has the data type Numeric (5, 2). This means that MaxHours values consist of five decimal numbers with two numbers assumed to the right of the decimal point. (The decimal point is not stored and does not count as one of the five.) Thus, the stored value 12345 would be displayed by the DBMS as 123.45. The constraint Default 100 means that when a new row is created, if no value is provided for MaxHours, the DBMS is to provide the value 100.

According to the SQL standard, every SQL statement should end with a semicolon as shown in Figure 3-2. Although some DBMS products do not require the semicolon, it is good practice to learn to provide it. Also, as a matter of style, we place the ending parenthesis and the semicolon on a line of its own. This style blocks out the table definitions for easy reading.

The four data types shown in Figure 3-2 are the basic SQL data types, but DBMS vendors have added others to their products. Figures 3-3(a) and (b) show some of the data types allowed by Microsoft SQL Server and by Oracle.

Defining Primary Keys with Table Constraints

Figure 3-4 shows a way of defining the primary key of a table using table constraints. First, the columns of the table are defined. The column to be the primary key must be given the column constraint Not Null. After the table columns are defined, a table constraint, identified by the word CONSTRAINT, is used to create the primary key. Every table constraint has a name followed by the definition of the constraint. Here, the name of the constraint is ProjectPK, and it is defined by the keywords PRIMARY KEY (ProjectID). The name is selected by the developer; the only restriction is that the name must be unique in the database. Usually a standard naming convention is used. In this text, we name primary key constraints using the name of the table followed by the letters *PK*.

FIGURE 3-3(a)

Common SQL Server Data Types

Data Type	Description
Binary	Binary, length 0 to 8000 bytes.
Char	Character, length 0 to 8000 bytes.
Datetime	8-byte datetime. Range from January 1, 1753, through December 31, 9999, with an accuracy of three-hundredths of a second.
Image	Variable length binary data. Maximum length 2,147,483,647 bytes.
Integer	4-byte integer. Value range from −2,147,483,648 through 2,147,483,647.
Money	8-byte money. Range from −922,337,203,685,477.5808 through +922,337,203,685,477.5807, with accuracy to a ten-thousandth of a monetary unit.
Numeric	Decimal—can set precision and scale. Range $-10_{38} + 1$ through $10_{38} - 1$.
Smalldatetime	4-byte datetime. Range from January 1, 1990, through June 6, 2079, with an accuracy of one minute.
Smallint	2-byte integer. Range from −32,768 through 32,767.
Smallmoney	4-byte money. Range from −214,748,3648 through +214,748.3647, with accuracy to a ten-thousandth of a monetary unit.
Text	Variable length text, maximum length 2,147,483,647 characters.
Tinyint	1-byte integer. Range from 0 through 255.
Varchar	Variable-lenghth character, length 0 to 8000 bytes.

FIGURE 3-3(b)

Sample Data Types for SQL Server and Oracle

Common Oracle Data Types

Data Type	Description
BLOB	Binary large object. Up to 4 gigabytes in length.
CHAR(n)	Fixed length character field of length n. Maximum 2,000 characters.
DATE	7-byte field containing both date and time.
INTEGER	Whole number of length 38.
NUMBER(n,d)	Numeric field of length n, d places to the right of the decimal.
VARCHAR(n) or VARCHAR2(n)	Variable length character field up to n characters long. Maximum value of n = 4,000.

FIGURE 3-4

Creating Primary Keys with Table Constraints

```
CREATE TABLE PROJECT (
    ProjectID        Integer             Not Null,
    Name             Char(25)            Unique Not Null,
    Department       VarChar(100)        Null,
    MaxHours         Numeric(6,1)        Default 100,
    CONSTRAINT       ProjectPK           PRIMARY KEY (ProjectID)
);

CREATE TABLE EMPLOYEE(
    EmployeeNumber   Integer             Not Null,
    Name             Char(25)            Not Null,
    Phone            Char(8),
    Department       VarChar(100),
    CONSTRAINT       EmployeePK          PRIMARY KEY (EmployeeNumber)
);

CREATE TABLE ASSIGNMENT(
    ProjectID        Integer             Not Null,
    EmployeeNum      Integer             Not Null,
    HoursWorked      Numeric(5,2)        DEFAULT 10,
    CONSTRAINT       AssignmentPK        PRIMARY KEY (ProjectID, EmployeeNum)
);
```

Defining primary keys using table constraints offers two advantages. First, it is required for defining composite keys because the Primary Key column constraint cannot be used on more than one column. It is not possible to declare the key of ASSIGNMENT using the technique in Figure 3-2. Second, using table constraints, the developer is able to name the constraint that defines the primary key. Naming the constraint has advantages for administering the database, as you will see when we discuss the DROP statement.

Defining Foreign Keys with the Table Constraints

We also can use table constraints to define foreign keys and referential integrity constraints. Figure 3-5 shows two table constraints that do this. The first one defines the constraint ProjectFK (again, the name is up to the developer as long as it is unique) that

FIGURE 3-5

Creating Primary and Foreign Keys with Table Constraints

```
CREATE TABLE PROJECT (
    ProjectID           Integer             Not Null,
    Name                Char(25)            Unique Not Null,
    Department          VarChar(100)        Null,
    MaxHours            Numeric(6,1)        Default 100,
    CONSTRAINT          ProjectPK           PRIMARY KEY (ProjectID)
);

CREATE TABLE EMPLOYEE(
    EmployeeNumber      Integer             Not Null,
    Name                Char(25)            Not Null,
    Phone               Char(8),
    Department          VarChar(100),
    CONSTRAINT          EmployeePK          PRIMARY KEY (EmployeeNumber)
);

CREATE TABLE ASSIGNMENT(
    ProjectID           Integer             Not Null,
    EmployeeNum         Integer             Not Null,
    HoursWorked         Numeric(5,2)        DEFAULT 10,
    CONSTRAINT          AssignmentPK        PRIMARY KEY (ProjectID, EmployeeNum),
    CONSTRAINT          ProjectFK           FOREIGN KEY
        (ProjectID) REFERENCES PROJECT (ProjectID)
                     ON DELETE CASCADE,
    CONSTRAINT          EmployeeFK          FOREIGN KEY
        (EmployeeNum) REFERENCES EMPLOYEE (EmployeeNumber)
                     ON DELETE NO ACTION
);
```

specifies that ProjectID references the ProjectID column in PROJECT. The phrase ON DELETE CASCADE means that when a PROJECT row is deleted, all rows in ASSIGNMENT that are connected to the delete row in PROJECT also should be deleted. Thus, when a PROJECT row is deleted, all ASSIGNMENT rows for that PROJECT row will be deleted, as well. This action implements the first business rule on page 53.

The second table constraint defines the foreign key constraint EmployeeFK. This constraint indicates that the EmployeeNum column references the EmployeeNumber column of EMPLOYEE. The phrase ON DELETE NO ACTION indicates to the DBMS that no EMPLOYEE row deletion should be allowed if that row is connected to an ASSIGNMENT row. This declaration implements the second business rule on page 53.

Because ON DELETE NO ACTION is the default, you can omit the ON DELETE expression, and the declaration will default to no action. However, specifying it makes better documentation.

Table constraints can be used for purposes other than creating primary and foreign keys. One of the most important purposes is to define constraints on data values. See the documentation for your DBMS for more information on this topic.

Submitting SQL to the DBMS

After you have developed a text file with SQL statements like those in Figures 3-2, 3-4, and 3-5, you can submit them to the DBMS. The means by which this is done vary from DBMS to DBMS. With SQL Server, you can type them into the Query Analyzer, or you can enter them via **Visual Studio.Net**. Oracle and DB2 use other similar techniques.

Figure 3-6(a) shows the Query Analyzer window after the SQL statements in Figure 3-5 have been entered and processed. The message "The command(s) completed successfully." indicates that the SQL statements were processed correctly. Figure 3-6(b) shows a SQL Server relationship diagram that shows the relationships created by the definition of the foreign key constraints.

DROP Statements

Many data definition SQL statements exist that we have not described. One of the most useful is DROP TABLE. However, it is also one of the most dangerous, because this statement drops the table's structure along with all of the table's data.

If you wanted to drop a table named CUSTOMER and all of its data, you would issue the following statement.

DROP TABLE CUSTOMER;

The DROP TABLE statement will not work if the table contains or could contain values needed to fulfill referential integrity constraints. EMPLOYEE, for example, could contain values of EmployeeID needed by the foreign key constraint EmployeeFK.

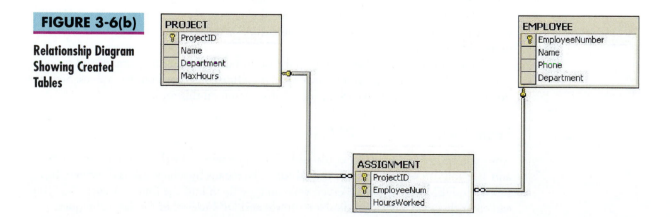

FIGURE 3-6(a)

Processing the CREATE TABLE Statements in Figure 3-5 Using SQL Server

FIGURE 3-6(b)

Relationship Diagram Showing Created Tables

In this case, an attempt to issue the statement DROP TABLE EMPLOYEE will fail, and an error message will be generated.

If you want to drop the EMPLOYEE table, you first need to delete the foreign key constraint EmployeeFK or to drop the ASSIGNMENT table altogether. You can drop the constraint with the statement:

ALTER TABLE ASSIGNMENT DROP CONSTRAINT EmployeeFK;

Or, you can drop the ASSIGNMENT table with:

DROP TABLE ASSIGNMENT;

After either of these, you can then drop the EMPLOYEE table.

▶ SQL FOR RELATIONAL QUERY

After the tables have been defined, you can add data to them, modify data values, and delete data. You also can query data in a multitude of ways. SQL statements for these activities will be easier to learn if we begin with the query statements. After that, we will show SQL for adding, modifying, and deleting data.

For the following, assume that the sample data shown in Figure 3-1 have been entered into the database.

Reading Specified Columns from a Single Table

The following SQL statement will query (read) three of the four columns of the PROJECT table.

SELECT   Name, Department, MaxHours

FROM   PROJECT;

Notice that names of the columns to be queried follow the keyword SELECT, and the name of the relation to use follows the keyword FROM. The result of this statement using the data in the PROJECT table in Figure 3-1 is the following.

Q3 Portfolio Analysis	Finance	75.0
Q3 Tax Prep	Accounting	145.0
Q4 Product Plan	Marketing	138.0
Q4 Portfolio Analysis	Finance	110.0

The result of a SQL SELECT statement is a relation. This is always true for SELECT statements. They start with one or more relations, manipulate them in some way, and then produce a relation. Even if the result of the manipulation is a single number, that number is considered to be a relation with one row and one column.

The order of the column names after the keyword SELECT determines the order of the columns in the resulting table. Thus, if we change the order of columns in the previous SELECT statement to:

SELECT   Name, MaxHours, Department

FROM   PROJECT;

The result will be:

Q3 Portfolio Analysis	75.0	Finance
Q3 Tax Prep	145.0	Accounting
Q4 Product Plan	138.0	Marketing
Q4 Portfolio Analysis	110.0	Finance

The next SQL statement obtains only the Department column from the PROJECT table.

SELECT   Department

FROM   PROJECT;

The result is:

Notice that the first and last rows of this table are duplicates. According to the definition of *relation* given in Chapter 2, such duplicate rows are prohibited. However, as also mentioned in Chapter 2, the process of checking for and eliminating duplicate rows is time-consuming. Therefore, by default, DBMS products do not check for duplication. Thus, in practice duplicate rows can occur.

If the developer wants the DBMS to check for and eliminate duplicate rows, he or she must use the DISTINCT keyword as follows.

SELECT   DISTINCT Department

FROM   PROJECT;

The result of this statement is:

| Finance |
| Accounting |
| Marketing |

The duplicate row has been eliminated as desired.

Reading Specified Rows from a Single Table

In the previous SQL statements, we selected certain columns for all rows of a table. SQL statements also can be used for the reverse; that is, they can be used to select all of the columns for certain rows. For example, the following SQL statement will obtain all of the columns of the PROJECT table for projects sponsored by the finance department.

SELECT   ProjectID, Name, Department, MaxHours

FROM   PROJECT

WHERE   Department = 'Finance';

The result is:

| 1000 | Q3 Portfolio Analysis | Finance | 75.0 |
| 1500 | Q4 Portfolio Analysis | Finance | 110.0 |

A second way to specify all of the columns of a table is to use the special character * after the keyword SELECT. The following SQL statement is equivalent to the previous one.

SELECT   *

FROM   PROJECT

WHERE   Department = 'Finance';

The result is a table of all of the columns of PROJECT for rows having a Department value of Finance.

1000	Q3 Portfolio Analysis	Finance	75.0
1500	Q4 Portfolio Analysis	Finance	110.0

The pattern SELECT/FROM/WHERE is the fundamental pattern of SQL SELECT statements. Many different conditions can be placed in a WHERE clause. For example, the query:

SELECT   *

FROM   PROJECT

WHERE   MaxHours > 100;

selects all columns from PROJECT where the MaxHours column is greater than 100. The result is:

1200	Q3 Tax Prep	Accounting	145.0
1400	Q4 Product Plan	Marketing	138.0
1500	Q4 Portfolio Analysis	Finance	110.0

Notice that when the column data type is Char or VarChar, comparison values must be placed in single quotes. If the column is Integer or Numeric, no quotes are necessary. Thus, we use the notation Department = 'Finance' for a WHERE condition of the VarChar column Department, but we use the notation MaxHours = 100 for the Numeric column MaxHours.

Values placed in quotations are case sensitive. WHERE Department = 'Finance' and WHERE Department = 'FINANCE' are not the same.

More than one condition can be placed in a WHERE clause by using the keyword AND as follows.

SELECT   *

FROM   PROJECT

WHERE   Department = 'Finance' AND MaxHours > 100;

The result of this statement is:

1500	Q4 Portfolio Analysis	Finance	110.0

Reading Specified Columns and Specified Rows from a Single Table

We can combine the techniques just shown to select some columns and some rows from a table. For example, to obtain only the Name and Department values of employees in the accounting department, we use:

SELECT   Name, Department

FROM   EMPLOYEE

WHERE   Department = 'Accounting' ;

The result is:

Mary Jacobs	Accounting
Rosalie Jackson	Accounting

Another use of the WHERE clause is to specify that a column should have one of a set of values by using the IN keyword as follows.

SELECT   Name, Phone, Department

FROM   EMPLOYEE

WHERE   Department IN ['Accounting', 'Finance', 'Marketing'];

The result is:

Mary Jacobs	285-8879	Accounting
Kenji Numoto	287-0098	Marketing
Heather Jones	287-9981	Finance
Rosalie Jackson	285-1273	Accounting
Kim Sung	287-3222	Marketing

In this result, a row is displayed if it has a Department value equal to Accounting, Finance, or Marketing.

To select rows that do not have a Department value with any of these, we would use NOT IN as follows.

SELECT   Name, Phone, Department

FROM   EMPLOYEE

WHERE   Department NOT IN ['Accounting', 'Finance', 'Marketing'];

The result of this query is:

James Nestor		Info Systems
Richard Wu	287-0123	Info Systems

Notice the essential difference between IN and NOT IN. When using IN, the column may equal ANY of the values in the list. When using NOT IN, the column must not be equal to ALL of the values in the list.

Ranges, Wildcards, and Nulls in WHERE Clauses

WHERE clauses also can refer to ranges and partial values. The keyword BETWEEN is used for ranges. For example, the statement:

SELECT   Name, Department

FROM   EMPLOYEE

WHERE   EmployeeNumber BETWEEN 200 AND 500;

will produce the following result.

Kenji Numoto	Marketing
Heather Jones	Finance
Rosalie Jackson	Accounting
James Nestor	Info Systems

This statement is equivalent to:

SELECT   Name, Department

FROM   EMPLOYEE

WHERE   EmployeeNumber = > 200

          AND EmployeeNumber = < 500;

Thus, the end values of BETWEEN (here 200 and 500) are included in the selected range.

The keyword LIKE is used in SQL expressions to select partial values. The underscore symbol (_) represents a single, unspecified character. It can be used to find values that fit a pattern, as in the following.

SELECT   *

FROM   PROJECT

WHERE   Name LIKE 'Q_ Portfolio Analysis';

The underscore means that any character can occur in that spot. The result of this statement is:

1000	Q3 Portfolio Analysis	Finance	75.0
1500	Q4 Portfolio Analysis	Finance	110.0

To find all employees who have a Phone value that begins with 285-, we can use four underscores to represent any last four digits as follows.

SELECT   *

FROM   EMPLOYEE

WHERE   Phone LIKE '285-_ _ _ _';

The result is:

100	Mary Jacobs	285-8879	Accounting
400	Rosalie Jackson	285-1273	Accounting

The percent sign (%) is used to represent a series of one or more unspecified characters. Another way to write the query for employees having a phone number starting with 285- is the following.

SELECT   *

FROM   EMPLOYEE

WHERE   Phone LIKE '285-%';

The result is the same as in the previous example.

If we want to find all the employees who work in departments that end in *ing*, we could use the % character as follows.

SELECT   *

FROM   EMPLOYEE

WHERE   Department LIKE '%ing';

The result is:

100	Mary Jacobs	285-8879	Accounting
200	Kenji Numoto	287-0098	Marketing
400	Rosalie Jackson	285-1273	Accounting
700	Kim Sung	287-3222	Marketing

Unlike the SQL-92 standard, Microsoft Access uses a question mark instead of an underscore and an asterisk instead of a percent sign.

The keyword IS NULL can be used in a WHERE clause to search for null values. The following SQL will find the names and departments of all employees having a null value for Phone.

SELECT   Name, Department

FROM   EMPLOYEE

WHERE   Phone IS NULL;

The result of this query is:

James Nestor	Info Systems

Sorting the Results

The order of rows in the result of a SELECT statement is arbitrary. If this is undesirable, the ORDER BY phrase can be used to sort the rows. For example, the following will display the names and departments of all employees sorted by Department:

SELECT   Name, Department

FROM   EMPLOYEE

ORDER BY   Department;

The result is:

Mary Jacobs	Accounting
Rosalie Jackson	Accounting
Heather Jones	Finance
James Nestor	Info Systems
Richard Wu	Info Systems
Kenji Numoto	Marketing
Kim Sung	Marketing

By default, SQL will sort in ascending order. The keywords ASC and DESC can be used to specify ascending and descending order when necessary. Thus, to sort employees in descending order by Department, use:

SELECT   Name, Department

FROM   EMPLOYEE

ORDER BY   Department DESC;

The result is:

Kenji Numoto	Marketing
Kim Sung	Marketing
Richard Wu	Info Systems
James Nestor	Info Systems
Heather Jones	Finance
Rosalie Jackson	Accounting
Mary Jacobs	Accounting

Two or more columns also can be used for sorting purposes. To sort the employee names and departments first in descending value of Department and then within Department by ascending value of Name, we would specify:

SELECT   Name, Department

FROM   EMPLOYEE

ORDER BY Department DESC, Name ASC;

The result is:

Kenji Numoto	Marketing
Kim Sung	Marketing
James Nestor	Info Systems
Richard Wu	Info Systems
Heather Jones	Finance
Mary Jacobs	Accounting
Rosalie Jackson	Accounting

SQL Built-In Functions

SQL includes five built-in functions: COUNT, SUM, AVG, MAX, and MIN. These functions operate on the results of a SELECT statement. COUNT works regardless of column data type, but SUM, AVG, MAX, and MIN operate only on integer, numeric, and other number-oriented columns.

COUNT and SUM sound similar but are different. COUNT counts the number of rows in the result; SUM totals the set of values of a numeric column. Thus, the SQL statement:

SELECT   COUNT(*)

FROM   PROJECT;

will count the number of rows in the PROJECT table. The result of this statement is the following relation:

4

As stated earlier, the result of a SQL SELECT statement is always a relation. If, as is the case here, the result is a single number, that number is considered to be a relation that has only a single row and a single column.

Consider the following two SELECT statements.

SELECT   COUNT (Department)

FROM   PROJECT;

   and

SELECT   COUNT (DISTINCT Department)

FROM   PROJECT;

The result of the first statement is the relation:

and the result of the second is:

The difference in answers occurs because duplicate rows were eliminated in the count in the second SELECT.

Another example of built-in functions is the following.

SELECT   MIN(MaxHours), MAX(MaxHours), SUM(MaxHours)

FROM   PROJECT

WHERE   ProjectID < 1500;

The result is:

75.00	145.00	358.00

Except as shown with GROUP BY in the example after the next one, column names cannot be mixed with built-in functions. Thus, the following is not allowed.

~~SELECT   MaxHours, SUM(MaxHours)~~

~~FROM   PROJECT~~

~~WHERE   ProjectID < 1500;~~

Also, DBMS products vary in the ways in which built-in functions can be used. In SQL-92 and most other products, built-in functions cannot be used in WHERE clauses. Thus, a where clause such as:

WHERE   MaxHours < AVG(MaxHours)

normally is not allowed.

Built-In Functions and Grouping

To increase the utility of built-in functions, you can apply them to groups of rows. For example, the following statement will count the number of employees in each department.

SELECT   Department, Count(*)

FROM   EMPLOYEE

GROUP BY Department;

The result is:

Accounting	2
Marketing	2
Finance	1
Info Systems	2

The GROUP BY keyword tells the DBMS to sort the table by the named column and then to apply the built-in function to groups of rows having the same value of the named column. When GROUP BY is used, the name of the grouping column and built-in functions may appear in the SELECT phrase. This is the only time that a column and a built-in function can appear together.

We can further restrict the results by applying conditions to the groups that are formed. For example, if we want to consider only groups with more than two members, we could specify:

SELECT   Department, Count(*)

FROM   EMPLOYEE

GROUP BY Department

HAVING   COUNT(*) > 1;

The result of this SQL statement is:

Accounting	2
Marketing	2
Info Systems	2

It is possible to add WHERE clauses when using GROUP BY. However, an ambiguity results when this is done. If the WHERE condition is applied before the groups are formed, we will obtain one result. If, on the other hand, the WHERE condition is applied after the groups are formed, we will get a different result. To resolve this ambiguity, the SQL standard specifies that when WHERE and GROUP BY occur together, the WHERE condition will be applied first. For example, consider the following statement.

SELECT   Department, Count(*)

FROM   EMPLOYEE

WHERE   EmployeeNumber < 600

GROUP BY Department

HAVING   COUNT(*) > 1;

In this expression, first the WHERE clause is applied to select employees with an EmployeeNumber less than 600. Then the groups are formed, and finally the HAVING condition is applied. The result is:

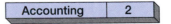

Accounting	2

Querying Multiple Tables with Subqueries

The queries we have considered so far have involved data from a single table. However, at times more than one table must be processed to obtain the desired information. For example, suppose we want to know the names of all employees who have worked more than 40 hours on any single assignment. The names of employees are stored in the EMPLOYEE table, but the hours they have worked are stored in the ASSIGNMENT table.

If we knew that employees 100 and 500 have worked more than 40 hours on an assignment, we could obtain their names with the following expression.

SELECT	Name
FROM	EMPLOYEE
WHERE	EmployeeNumber IN [100, 500];

But according to the problem description, we are not given the employee numbers. We can, however, obtain the appropriate employee numbers with the following.

SELECT	DISTINCT EmployeeNum
FROM	ASSIGNMENT
WHERE	HoursWorked > 40;

The result is:

```
100
400
600
200
```

Now, we can combine these two SQL statements using what is called a **subquery** as follows.

SELECT	Name
FROM	EMPLOYEE
WHERE	EmployeeNumber IN
	(SELECT DISTINCT EmployeeNum
	FROM ASSIGNMENT
	WHERE HoursWorked > 40);

The result of this expression is:

```
Mary Jacobs
Rosalie Jackson
Richard Wu
Kenji Numoto
```

These are indeed the names of the employees who have worked more than 40 hours on any single assignment.

Subqueries can be extended to include three, four, or even more levels. Suppose, for example, we need to know the names of employees who have worked more than 40 hours on an assignment of a project that has been sponsored by the accounting department.

We can obtain the ProjectIDs of projects sponsored by accounting with:

SELECT	ProjectID
FROM	PROJECT
WHERE	Department = 'Accounting';

We can obtain the EmployeeNums of employees working more than 40 hours on those projects with:

```
SELECT      DISTINCT EmployeeNum
FROM        ASSIGNMENT
WHERE       ProjectID IN
            (SELECT   ProjectID
            FROM      PROJECT
            WHERE     Department = 'Accounting');
```

Finally, we can obtain the names of the employees in the above SQL statement with:

```
SELECT      Name
FROM        EMPLOYEE
WHERE       EmployeeNumber IN
            (SELECT   DISTINCT EmployeeNum
            FROM      ASSIGNMENT
            WHERE     ProjectID IN
                (SELECT   ProjectID
                FROM      PROJECT
                WHERE     Department = 'Accounting'));
```

Querying Multiple Tables with Joins

Subqueries are effective for processing multiple tables as long as the results come from a single table. If, however, we need to display data from two or more tables, subqueries will not work. We need to use a **join** operation instead.

The basic idea of a join is to form a new relation by connecting the contents of two or more other relations. Consider the following example.

```
SELECT      Name, HoursWorked
FROM        EMPLOYEE, ASSIGNMENT
WHERE       EmployeeNumber = EmployeeNum;
```

The function of this statement is to create a new table having the two columns Name and HoursWorked. Those columns are to be taken from the EMPLOYEE and ASSIGNMENT tables under the condition that EmployeeNumber (in EMPLOYEE) equals EmployeeNum (in ASSIGNMENT).

You can think of the operation as follows. Start with the first row in EMPLOYEE. Using the value of EmployeeNumber in this first row (100 for the data in Figure 3-1), examine the rows in ASSIGNMENT. When you find a row in ASSIGNMENT where EmployeeNum is also equal to 100, join Name of the first row of EMPLOYEE with HoursWorked from the row you just found in ASSIGNMENT.

For the data in Figure 3-1, the first row of ASSIGNMENT has EmployeeNum equal to 100, so we join Name from the first row of EMPLOYEE with HoursWorked from the first row in ASSIGNMENT to form the first row of the join.

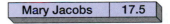
Mary Jacobs | 17.5

Now, still using the EmployeeNumber value of 100, look for a second row in ASSIGNMENT that has EmployeeNum equal to 100. For our data, the fifth row of ASSIGNMENT has such a value. So, join Name from the first row of EMPLOYEE to HoursWorked in the fifth row of ASSIGNMENT to obtain the second row of the join as follows.

Mary Jacobs	17.50
Mary Jacobs	45.75

Continue in this way, looking for matches for the EmployeeNumber value of 100. No more appear in our sample data, so now move to the second row of EMPLOYEE, obtain the new value of EmployeeNumber (200), and begin searching for matches for it in the rows of ASSIGNMENT. In this case, the eighth row has such a match, so we add Name and HoursWorked to our result to obtain:

Mary Jacobs	17.50
Mary Jacobs	45.75
Kenji Numoto	75.00

We continue until all rows of EMPLOYEE have been examined. The final result will be:

Mary Jacobs	17.50
Mary Jacobs	45.75
Kenji Numoto	75.00
Heather Jones	12.50
Rosalie Jackson	8.00
Rosalie Jackson	70.50
James Nestor	20.25
James Nestor	25.25
Richard Wu	40.50
Kim Sung	20.25

A join is just another table, so all of the earlier SQL SELECT commands are available for use. We could, for example, group the rows of the join by employee and sum the hours they worked. The SQL for such a query is the following.

SELECT   Name, SUM(HoursWorked)

FROM   EMPLOYEE, ASSIGNMENT

WHERE   EmployeeNumber = EmployeeNum

GROUP BY   Name;

The result of this query is:

Mary Jacobs	63.25
Kenji Numoto	75.00
Heather Jones	12.50
Rosalie Jackson	78.50
James Nestor	45.50
Richard Wu	40.50
Kim Sung	20.25

Or, we could apply a WHERE clause during the process of creating the join as follows.

SELECT   Name, HoursWorked

FROM   EMPLOYEE, ASSIGNMENT

WHERE   EmployeeNumber = EmployeeNum

        AND   HoursWorked > 40;

The result of this join is:

Mary Jacobs	45.75
Kenji Numoto	75.00
Rosalie Jackson	70.50
Richard Wu	40.50

Now suppose we want to join PROJECT to ASSIGNMENT. We can use the same SQL statement structure as before, except for one complication. Two columns are named ProjectID: one in the PROJECT table and one in the ASSIGNMENT table. We can eliminate the ambiguity in names by appending the name of the table to the column name. Thus, we will refer to the ProjectID in the PROJECT table as PROJECT.ProjectID and the ProjectID in the ASSIGNMENT table as ASSIGNMENT.ProjectID. Using this nomenclature, a join of the PROJECT and ASSIGNMENT tables is as follows.

SELECT   Name, HoursWorked

FROM   PROJECT, ASSIGNMENT

WHERE   PROJECT.ProjectID = ASSIGNMENT.ProjectID;

The result of this expression is:

Q3 Portfolio Analysis	17.50
Q3 Portfolio Analysis	12.50
Q3 Portfolio Analysis	8.00
Q3 Portfolio Analysis	20.25
Q3 Tax Prep	45.75
Q3 Tax Prep	70.50
Q3 Tax Prep	40.50
Q4 Product Plan	75.00
Q4 Product Plan	20.25
Q4 Product Plan	25.25

The results shown here are correct, but a surprising result occurs. What happened to the project named Q4 Portfolio Analysis? It does not appear in the join results because its ProjectID value of 1500 had no match in the ASSIGNMENT table. Nothing is wrong with this result; you just need to be aware that unmatched rows will not appear in the result of a join.

We will consider this problem further, but before we do, suppose we want to know the name of each project, the hours worked on each project, and the names of the employees who worked the hours.

To obtain this result, we will need to join all three tables together as follows.

SELECT   PROJECT.Name, HoursWorked, EMPLOYEE.Name

FROM   PROJECT, ASSIGNMENT, EMPLOYEE

WHERE   PROJECT.ProjectID = ASSIGNMENT.ProjectID

        AND   EMPLOYEE.EmployeeNumber = ASSIGNMENT.EmployeeNum;

The result of this join is:

Q3 Portfolio Analysis	17.50	Mary Jacobs
Q3 Portfolio Analysis	12.50	Heather Jones
Q3 Portfolio Analysis	8.00	Rosalie Jackson
Q3 Portfolio Analysis	20.25	James Nestor
Q3 Tax Prep	45.75	Mary Jacobs
Q3 Tax Prep	70.50	Rosalie Jackson
Q3 Tax Prep	40.50	Richard Wu
Q4 Product Plan	75.00	Kenji Numoto
Q4 Product Plan	20.25	Kim Sung
Q4 Product Plan	25.25	James Nestor

Outer Joins

You saw a moment ago that data can be lost when performing a join. In particular, if a row has a value that does not match the WHERE clause condition, then that row will not be included in the join result. Project Q4 Portfolio Analysis was lost in the previous join because no row in ASSIGNMENT matched its ProjectID value. This kind of loss is not always desirable, so a special type of join called an outer join was created to avoid it.

Outer joins are not part of the SQL-92 specification, but most DBMS products today support them; however, the syntax varies from product to product.

Consider the following example.

SELECT   Name, HoursWorked

FROM   PROJECT LEFT JOIN ASSIGNMENT

WHERE   PROJECT.ProjectID = ASSIGNMENT.ProjectID;

The purpose of this join is to append rows of PROJECT to those of ASSIGNMENT as described previously, except that if any row in the table on the left side of the FROM clause (in this case, PROJECT) has no match, it is included in the results anyway. For the sample data shown in Figure 3-1, the result of this query is:

Q3 Portfolio Analysis	17.50
Q3 Portfolio Analysis	12.50
Q3 Portfolio Analysis	8.00
Q3 Portfolio Analysis	20.25
Q3 Tax Prep	45.75
Q3 Tax Prep	70.50
Q3 Tax Prep	40.50
Q4 Product Plan	75.00
Q4 Product Plan	20.25
Q4 Product Plan	25.25
Q4 Portfolio Analysis	Null

Notice that the last row of this table appends a null value to Q4 Portfolio Analysis.

Right outer joins operate similarly, except that rows in the table on the right-hand side of the FROM clause are included. For example, we could join all three tables together with the following right outer join.

SELECT   PROJECT.Name, HoursWorked, EMPLOYEE.Name

FROM   PROJECT LEFT JOIN ASSIGNMENT RIGHT JOIN EMPLOYEE

WHERE   PROJECT.ProjectID = ASSIGNMENT.ProjectID

            AND EMPLOYEE.EmployeeNumber = ASSIGNMENT.EmployeeNum;

The result of this join is:

Q3 Portfolio Analysis	17.50	Mary Jacobs
Q3 Portfolio Analysis	12.50	Heather Jones
Q3 Portfolio Analysis	8.00	Rosalie Jackson
Q3 Portfolio Analysis	20.25	James Nestor
Q3 Tax Prep	45.75	Mary Jacobs
Q3 Tax Prep	70.50	Rosalie Jackson
Q3 Tax Prep	40.50	Richard Wu
Q4 Product Plan	75.00	Kenji Numoto
Q4 Product Plan	20.25	Kim Sung
Q4 Product Plan	25.25	James Nestor
Q4 Portfolio Analysis	Null	Null

▶ SQL FOR RELATIONAL DATA MODIFICATION

Three data modification operations are possible: insert, modify, and delete. We will consider SQL expressions for each of these in turn.

Inserting Data

Data can be added to a relation using the SQL INSERT command. This command has two forms, depending on whether or not data for all of the columns are supplied. If data for all columns are supplied, the following INSERT can be used.

INSERT INTO PROJECT VALUES (1600, 'Q4 Tax Prep', 'Accounting', 100);

Observe that Integer and Numeric values are not enclosed in quotes, but Char and VarChar values are.

If data for some columns are missing, then the names of the columns for which data are provided must be listed; for example:

INSERT INTO PROJECT (Name, ProjectID) VALUES ('Q4 Tax Prep', 1700);

will add a new row with values for Name and ProjectID and nulls for Department and MaxHours.

Two points should be made regarding the second version of the INSERT command. First, the order of the column names must match the order of the values. In the prior example, the order of the column names is Name, ProjectID, so the order of the values also must be Name, ProjectID. (Note that this is not the order of the columns in the table.) Second, for the insert to work, values for all Not Null columns must be provided.

Notice, too, that if the primary key is a surrogate key, then no value needs to be provided for it; the DBMS will provide the value automatically. Hence, if ProjectID is a surrogate key, we can insert a row as follows.

INSERT INTO PROJECT VALUES ('Q4 Tax Prep', 'Accounting', 100);

The value for ProjectID will be provided by the DBMS. As an aside, if you are using Oracle, inserts with surrogate keys are slightly different. Search the Oracle documentation for the topic Sequences for more information.

Modifying Data

The values of existing data can be modified using the SQL UPDATE command. However, this is a powerful command that needs to be used with care. Consider the following example.

UPDATE   EMPLOYEE

SET   Phone = '287-1435'

WHERE   Name = 'James Nestor';

This command will set the value of the Phone column in the row for James Nestor to 287-1435.

Now consider why this command is dangerous. Suppose that while intending to make this update, you make an error and forget to include the WHERE clause. Thus, you submit the following to the DBMS.

UPDATE   EMPLOYEE

SET   Phone = '287-1435';

After this command has executed, the EMPLOYEE relation will appear as follows.

100	Mary Jacobs	287-1435	Accounting
200	Kenji Numoto	287-1435	Marketing
300	Heather Jones	287-1435	Finance
400	Rosalie Jackson	287-1435	Accounting
500	James Nestor	287-1435	Info Systems
600	Richard Wu	287-1435	Info Systems
700	Kim Sung	287-1435	Marketing

This is clearly not what you intended to do. Had you done this at a new job where there might be, say, 10,000 rows in the EMPLOYEE table, you would experience a sinking feeling in the pit of your stomach and make plans to update your résumé that evening.

The message here is: UPDATE is powerful and easy to use, but also capable of causing disasters.

The update command can modify more than one column value at a time as shown in the following statement.

UPDATE   EMPLOYEE

SET   Phone = '285-0091', Department = 'Production'

WHERE   EmployeeNumber = 200;

This command will change the values of Phone and Department for the indicated employee.

Deleting Data

You can eliminate rows with the SQL DELETE command. However, the same warnings pertain to DELETE as pertain to UPDATE. DELETE is deceptively simple to use and easy to apply in unintended ways. The following, for example, will delete all projects sponsored by the accounting department.

DELETE

FROM   PROJECT

WHERE   Department = 'Accounting';

Given the On Delete Cascade referential integrity constraint, this DELETE operation will not only remove PROJECT rows, it also will remove any related ASSIGNMENT rows. For the data in Figure 3-1, this DELETE operation will remove the fifth, sixth, and seventh rows of the ASSIGNMENT table.

As with UPDATE, if you forget to include the WHERE clause, disaster will ensue. For example, the SQL code

DELETE

FROM   PROJECT;

deletes all of the rows in PROJECT (and because of the On Delete Cascade constraint, all of the ASSIGNMENT rows, as well). This truly would be a disaster.

Observe how the referential integrity constraint differs with the EMPLOYEE table. Here, if we try to process the command:

DELETE

FROM   EMPLOYEE

WHERE   EmployeeNumber = 100;

the DELETE operation will fail because rows in ASSIGNMENT depend on the value of 100 in EMPLOYEE. If you want to delete the row for this employee, you must first reassign or delete his or her rows in ASSIGNMENT.

SUMMARY

Structured Query Language (SQL) is a data sublanguage that has constructs for defining and processing a database. SQL can be embedded into scripting languages like VBScript or programming languages such as Java and C#. SQL statements also can be processed from a command window. SQL was developed by IBM and was endorsed as a national standard by the American National Standards Institute in 1992. A later version, SQL3, has not gained acceptance in industry and is not considered here. Modern DBMS products provide graphical facilities for accomplishing many of the tasks that SQL does. Use of SQL is mandatory for programmatically creating SQL statements.

The CREATE TABLE statement is used for creating relations. Each column is described in three parts: the column name, data type, and optional column constraints. Column constraints considered in this chapter are Primary Key, Null, Not Null, and Default. If no column constraint is specified, the column is Null.

Standard data types are Char, VarChar, Integer, and Numeric. These types have been supplemented by DBMS vendors. Figure 3-3 shows some of the additional data types for SQL Server and Oracle.

If a primary key has only one column, it can be defined using the Primary Key constraint. Another way to define a primary key is to use the table constraint. Such constraints can be used to define single and multicolumn primary keys, and they also can be used to define foreign keys. Foreign key definitions can specify that deletions should cascade. Tables (and their data) can be removed from a database using DROP TABLE. Constraints can be removed using the ALTER TABLE DROP CONSTRAINT command.

The basic format of the SQL SELECT command is SELECT (column names or the symbol *), FROM (table names, separated by commas if there is more than one), WHERE (conditions). SELECT can be used to obtain specific columns, specific rows, or both.

Conditions after the WHERE require quotes around values for Char and VarChar columns, but no quotes for Integer and Numeric columns. Compound conditions can be specified with AND. Sets of values can be used with IN (match any in the set) and NOT IN (not match all in the set). The wildcard symbols _ and % can be used with LIKE to specify a single unknown character or multiple unknown characters, respectively. IS NULL can be used to test for null values.

Results can be sorted using the ORDER BY command. The five SQL built-in functions are COUNT, SUM, MAX, MIN, and AVG. Groups can be created using GROUP BY, and groups can be limited using HAVING. If the keywords WHERE and HAVING both occur in a SQL statement, WHERE is applied before HAVING.

Multiple tables can be queried using either subqueries or joins. If all of the result data come from a single table, then subqueries can be used. If results come from two or more tables, then joins must be used. Rows that do not match the join conditions will not appear in the result. Outer joins can be used to ensure that all rows from a table appear in the result.

Data can be added using the INSERT command, modified using UPDATE, and deleted using DELETE. UPDATE and DELETE can easily cause disasters, so the commands must be used with great care.

REVIEW QUESTIONS

3.1 What does SQL stand for?

3.2 What is a data sublanguage?

3.3 Explain the importance of SQL-92.

3.4 Why is it important to learn SQL?

3.5 Describe in your own words the purpose of the two business rules listed on page 53.

Use the following tables for your answers to questions 3.6 through 3.44.

PET_OWNER (OwnerID, Name, Phone, Email)

PET (PetID, Name, Type, Breed, DOB, *OwnerID*)

(See Figure 1-27 on page 20 for sample data.)

3.6 Code a CREATE TABLE command to create the PET_OWNER table. Justify your choices of column properties.

3.7 Code a CREATE TABLE command to create the PET table. Represent dates using either the SQL Server or Oracle date data types shown in Figure 3-3. Justify your choices of column properties. Why not make every column Not Null?

3.8 Create a referential integrity constraint on OwnerID in PET. Assume that deletions should not cascade.

3.9 Create a referential integrity constraint on OwnerID in PET. Assume that deletions should cascade.

3.10 Code the required SQL statements for the following alternative version of the PET table.

PET1 (Name, Type, Breed, DOB, *OwnerID*)

3.11 Is PET or PET1 a better design? Explain your rationale.

3.12 Code the SQL statements necessary to remove the PET_OWNER table from the database. Assume that the referential integrity constraint is to be removed.

3.13 Code the SQL statements necessary to remove the PET_OWNER table from the database. Assume that the PET table is also to be removed.

3.14 Code a SQL statement to display all columns of all rows of PET. Do not use the * notation.

3.15 Code a SQL statement to display all columns of all rows of PET. Use the * notation.

3.16 Code SQL to display the Breed and Type of all pets.

3.17 Code SQL to display the Breed, Type, and DOB of all pets having the Type Dog.

3.18 Code SQL to display the Breed column of PET.

3.19 Code SQL to display the Breed column of PET. Do not show duplicates.

3.20 Code SQL to display the Breed, Type, and DOB for all pets having the Type Dog and the Breed Std. Poodle.

3.21 Code SQL to display the Name, Breed, and Type for all pets that are not of Type Cat, Dog, or Fish.

3.22 Code SQL to display the PetID, Breed, and Type for all pets having a four-character Name starting with D.

3.23 Code SQL to display the Name and Email of all owners who have an e-mail address ending with somewhere.com. Assume that e-mail account names can be any number of characters.

3.24 Code SQL to display the Name of any owner who has a null value for Phone.

3.25 Code SQL to display the Name and Breed of all pets sorted by Name.

3.26 Code SQL to display the Name and Breed of all pets sorted by Breed in ascending order and by Name in descending order within Breed.

3.27 Code SQL to count the number of pets.

3.28 Code SQL to count the number of distinct breeds.

3.29 For the table:

PET2 (PetID, Name, Type, Breed, Weight, *OwnerID*)

code SQL to display the minimum, maximum, and average Weight of dogs.

3.30 For the PET2 table, code SQL to group the data by Breed and display the average Weight per breed.

3.31 Answer question 3.30, but consider only breeds for which five or more pets are included in the database.

3.32 Answer question 3.31, but do not consider any pet having the breed Spinone Italiano. (Italian pets consider their weight to be personal data!)

3.33 Code SQL to display the Name and Email of any owners of cats. Use a subquery.

3.34 Code SQL to display the Name and Email of any owners of cats with the name Teddy. Use a subquery.

3.35 Suppose the following new table is added to the pet database.

BREED (BreedName, MinWeight, MaxWeight, AverageLifeExpectancy)

Assume that Breed of PET is a foreign key that matches BreedName of BREED. Code SQL to display Name and Email of any owner of a pet that has an AverageLifeExpectancy greater than 15. Use a subquery.

3.36 Answer question 3.33, but use a join.

3.37 Answer question 3.34, but use a join.

3.38 Answer question 3.35, but use joins.

3.39 Answer question 3.33, but use a left outer join. How will your results differ from those in your answer to question 3.36?

3.40 Code SQL to add three new rows to the PET_OWNER table. Assume OwnerID is a surrogate key and the DBMS will provide a value for it. Otherwise, assume you have all of the data.

3.41 Code SQL to add three new rows to the PET_OWNER table. Assume OwnerID is a surrogate key and the DBMS will provide a value for it. Otherwise, you have only Name and Phone; assume Email is Null.

3.42 Code SQL to change the value of Std. Poodle in Breed of PET to Poodle, Std.

3.43 Explain what will happen if you leave the WHERE clause off your answer to question 3.42.

3.44 Code SQL to delete all rows of pets of Type Anteater. What will happen if you forget to code the WHERE clause in this statement?

EXERCISES

3.45 The ALTER TABLE statement can be used to add and delete columns from a table. Using the documentation of your DBMS for reference, code a statement to add the Weight column to the PET table described previously. Assume Weight is Numeric(4,1).

3.46 Under certain circumstances, the ALTER TABLE statement can be used to change the data type of a column. Using the documentation of your DBMS for reference, explain the circumstances under which this can be done. Explain potential problems. Show how to use an ALTER TABLE statement to increase the size of Name of PET that you specified in your answer to question 3.6. Show how to use an ALTER TABLE statement to change the data type of DOB of PET to Char(10).

3.47 The ALTER TABLE statement can be used to create constraints on data values. Using the documentation of your DBMS, write an ALTER TABLE statement that will restrict the values of Type in PET to Dog, Cat, and Bird.

GARDEN GLORY PROJECT QUESTIONS

Assume that Garden Glory designs a database with the following tables.

OWNER (<u>OwnerID</u>, Name, Email, Type)

PROPERTY (<u>PropertyID</u>, Street, City, State, Zip, *OwnerID*)

EMPLOYEE (<u>Initials</u>, Name, CellPhone, ExperienceLevel)

SERVICE (<u>*PropertyID*</u>, <u>*Initials*</u>, Date, HoursWorked)

Type is either Individual or Corporation, and ExperienceLevel is one of Junior, Senior, Master, or SuperMaster. Code SQL statements and answer questions for this database as follows:

A. Code CREATE TABLE statements for each of these tables.

B. Write foreign key constraints for the relationships in each of these tables. Make your own assumptions regarding cascading deletions, and justify those assumptions.

C. Code SQL statements to insert three rows of data into each of these tables. Assume that any primary key with a name ending in ID is a surrogate key whose value will be supplied by the DBMS.

D. Code SQL statements to list all columns of all tables.

E. Code SQL statements to list the Name and CellPhone for all employees having an experience level of Master.

F. Code SQL statements to list the Name and CellPhone for all employees having an experience level of Master and a Name that begins with J.

G. Code SQL statements to list the Name of employees who have worked on a property in New York. Use subquery.

H. Same as question G, but use join.

I. Code SQL statements to list the Name of employees who have worked on a property owned by a Corporation. Use subquery.

J. Same as question I, but use join.

K. Code SQL statements to show the Name and sum of HoursWorked for each employee.

L. Code SQL statements to show the sum of HoursWorked for each ExperienceLevel of EMPLOYEE. Sort the results by ExperienceLevel in descending order.

M. Code SQL statements to show the sum of HoursWorked for each Type of OWNER, but exclude services of employees who have an ExperienceLevel of Junior, and exclude any Type with less than three members.

N. Code SQL statements to modify all EMPLOYEE rows with an ExperienceLevel of Master to SuperMaster.

O. Code SQL statements to switch the values of ExperienceLevel so that all rows currently having the value Junior will have the value Senior, and all rows currently having the value Senior will have the value Junior.

P. Given your assumptions about cascading deletions in your answer to question B, write the fewest number of DELETE statements possible to remove all of the data in your database, but leave the table structures intact.

JAMES RIVER JEWELRY PROJECT QUESTIONS

Assume that James River designs a database with the following tables.

CUSTOMER (CustomerID, Name, Phone, Email)

PURCHASE (InvoiceNumber, Date, PreTaxAmount, *CustomerID*)

PURCHASE_ITEM (*InvoiceNumber*, *ItemNumber*, RetailPrice)

ITEM (ItemNumber, Description, Cost, ArtistName)

Code SQL statements and answer questions for this database as follows:

A. Code CREATE TABLE statements for each of these tables.

B. Write foreign key constraints for the relationships in each of these tables. Make your own assumptions regarding cascading deletions, and justify those assumptions.

C. Code SQL statements to insert three rows of data into each of these tables. Assume that CustomerID of CUSTOMER is a surrogate key column whose values will be supplied by the DBMS.

D. Code SQL statements to list all columns of all tables.

E. Code SQL statements to list the ItemNumber and Description for all items that cost more than $100.

F. Code SQL statements to list the ItemNumber and Description for all items that cost more than $100 and were produced by an artist with a name ending with the letters *son*.

G. Code SQL statements to list the Name of customers who have made at least one purchase with PreTaxAmount greater than $200. Use subquery.

H. Same as question G, but use join.

I. Code SQL statements to list the Name of customers who have purchased an item that costs more than $50. Use subquery.

J. Same as question I, but use join.

K. Code SQL statements to list the Name of customers who have purchased an item that was created by an artist with a name that begins with J. Use subquery.

L. Same as question K, but use join.

M. Code SQL statements to show the Name and sum of PreTaxAmount for each customer.

N. Code SQL statements to show the sum of PreTaxAmount for each ArtistName. Sort the results by ArtistName in descending order.

O. Code SQL statements to show the sum of PreTaxAmount for each ArtistName, but exclude any items that were part of purchases with a PreTaxAmount less than $25.

P. Code SQL statements to modify all ITEM rows with a name of Baker to Rex Baker.

Q. Code SQL statements to switch the values of ArtistName so that all rows currently having the value Baker will have the value Baxter, and all rows currently having the value Baxter will have the value Baker.

R. Given your assumptions about cascading deletions in your answer to question B, write the fewest number of DELETE statements possible to remove all of the data in your database, but leave the table structures intact.

MID-WESTERN UNIVERSITY CHEMISTRY DEPARTMENT PROJECT QUESTIONS

Assume that the chemistry department designs a database with the following relations.

FUNDED_GRANT (<u>GrantNumber</u>, *P_I_Name*, FundingSource)

P_I (<u>Name</u>, Email, OfficeNumber)

MAGNET (<u>ID</u>, Location, Power)

OPERATOR (<u>Name</u>, JobTitle, Email, Phone)

APPOINTMENT (*<u>MagnetID</u>*, *<u>OperatorName</u>*, <u>Date</u>, <u>StartTime</u>, EndTime, *GrantNumber*)

Code SQL statements and answer questions for this database as follows:

A. Code CREATE TABLE statements for each of these tables.

B. Write foreign key constraints for the relationships in each of these tables. Make your own assumptions regarding cascading deletions, and justify those assumptions.

C. Code SQL statements to insert three rows of data into each of these tables. Include one row in P_I with a name equal to 'Baker.'

D. Code SQL statements to list all columns of all tables.

E. Code a SQL statement to list the GrantNumber and P_I_Name for all funded grants with a funding source of 'NIH' (an abbreviation for National Institute of Health).

F. Code a SQL statement to list the GrantNumber and P_I.Name for all funded grants with a funding source of 'NIH' and with a P_I.Name ending in *er.*

G. Code a SQL statement to list the Name and Email of all principal investigators having at least one funded grant with a funding source of 'NIH'. Use subquery.

H. Same as question G, but use join.

I. Code a SQL statement to list the Name of all operators who have an appointment to use a magnet for a funded grant with a funding source other than NIH. Use subquery.

J. Same as question I, but use join.

K. Code a SQL statement to list the Name and Email of all operators who have an appointment to use a magnet for a funded grant with a principal investigator with an Email address that does not end with *edu.* Use subquery.

L. Same as question K, but use join.

M. Code a SQL statement to show the average power of the department's magnets.

N. Code a SQL statement to show the Name and maximum magnet power for appointments by each operator.

O. Code a SQL statement to show the GrantNumber and count of magnet appointments for each funded grant. Sort the results by GrantNumber in descending order.

P. Same as question O, but include only funded grants having more than two appointments.

Q. Code a SQL statement to update all rows with a funding source of NIH to a value of NIH_2003.

R. Code SQL statements to modify all P_I rows with a name of Baker to Rex Baker. Hint: You will have to drop the appropriate referential integrity constraint, make the data changes, and then re-create the constraint. You can do the latter using the command: ALTER TABLE xxx ADD CONSTRAINT yyy, where *xxx* is the name of the table and *yyy* is the referential integrity constraint to add.

PART II

Database Design and Management

So far, you have been introduced to the fundamental concepts and techniques of relational database management. In Chapter 1, you learned that databases consist of related tables, and you learned the major components of a database system. Chapter 2 introduced you to the relational model, and you learned the basic ideas of functional dependencies and normalization. In Chapter 3, you learned how to use basic SQL statements to process a database.

All of this material gives you a background for understanding the nature of database management and the basic tools and techniques. However, you do not yet know how to apply all of this technology to solve a business problem. Imagine, for example, that you walk into a small business—say a bookshop—and are asked to build a database to support a frequent buyer program. How would you proceed? So far, we have assumed that the database design already exists. How would you go about creating the design of the database? Furthermore, once the database exists, what tasks need to be done to manage it over time?

The next three chapters address these important topics. We begin Chapter 4 with an overview of the database design process, and then we describe data modeling—a technique for representing database requirements. In Chapter 5, you will learn how to transform a data model into a relational database design. Finally, in Chapter 6, you will learn about database management. Here, you also will be introduced to many of the problems that occur when a database is concurrently processed by more than one user. Finally, Chapter 7 will conclude the book by surveying important advanced database concepts. After completing these chapters, you will have surveyed all of the basic database technology. This knowledge will give you the necessary background to learn more in the area of your interests or job requirements. For example, you will be able to learn more about SQL, or to learn to use a particular DBMS product such as Oracle or SQL Server, or to learn to publish databases using Internet technology.

Data Modeling and the Entity-Relationship Model

> Learn the basic stages of database development
> Understand the purpose and role of a data model
> Know the principal components of the E-R data model
> Understand how to interpret traditional and UML-style E-R diagrams
> Learn to construct traditional E-R diagrams
> Know how to represent 1:1, 1:N, N:M, and binary relationships with the E-R model
> Know how to represent recursive relationships with the E-R model
> Understand two types of weak entities and know how to use them
> Learn how to create an E-R diagram from source documents

The process of developing a database system consists of three major stages: requirements, design, and implementation. During the requirements stage, system users are interviewed and sample forms, reports, queries, and descriptions of update activities are obtained. These system requirements are used to create a data model, which is a representation of the content, relationships, and constraints of the data needed to support the requirements. Often prototypes, or working demonstrations of selected portions of the future system, are created during the requirements phase. Such prototypes are used to obtain feedback from the system users.

During the design stage, the data model is transformed into a database design. Such a design consists of tables, relationships, and constraints. The design includes the table names and the names of all table columns. The design also includes the data types and properties of the columns, as well as a description of primary and foreign keys. Data constraints consist of limits on data values (e.g., Part Numbers are seven-digit numbers starting with the number three), referential integrity constraints, and business rules. An example of a business rule for a manufacturing company is that every purchased part will have a quotation from at least two suppliers.

The last stage of database development is implementation. During this stage, the database is constructed and filled with data; queries, forms, and reports are created; application programs are written; and all of these are tested. Finally, during this stage users are trained, documentation is written, and the system is installed for use.

In this chapter, we will consider the requirements stage in general and data modeling in particular. You will learn about an important tool, the entity-relationship data model, and you will learn how to apply this tool to represent the data requirements for a small business. Our goal here is to focus only on the database aspects of information systems development. The design and development of other components of an information system are outside the scope of this text; they are the subject matter of a systems development class.

▶ THE REQUIREMENTS STAGE

Sources of user requirements are listed in Figure 4-1. As you will learn in your systems development class, the general practice is to identify the users of the new information system and to interview them. During the interviews, examples of existing forms, reports, and queries are obtained. In addition, the users are asked about the need for changes to existing forms, reports, and queries, and also about the need for new forms, reports, and queries.

Use cases are descriptions of the ways users will employ the features and functions of the new information system. A use case consists of a description of the roles users will play when utilizing the new system, together with descriptions of scenarios of activities. Inputs provided to the system and outputs generated by the system are defined.

FIGURE 4-1

Sources of
Requirements for a
Database Application

User Interviews
Forms
Reports
Queries
Use Cases
Business Rules

Sometimes dozens of such use cases are necessary. Use cases provide sources of requirements and also can be used to validate the data model, design, and implementation.

In addition to these requirements, the development team needs to document characteristics of data items. For each data item in a form, report, or query, the team needs to determine its data type, properties, and limits on values.

Finally, during the process of establishing requirements, system developers need to document business rules that constrain actions on database activity. Generally, such rules arise from business policy and practice. For example, the following business rules could pertain to an academic database.

> Students must declare a major before enrolling in any class.
> Graduate classes can be taken by juniors or seniors with a grade point average of 3.70 or greater.
> No adviser may have more than 25 advisees.
> Students may declare one or two majors, but no more.

THE ENTITY-RELATIONSHIP DATA MODEL

The system requirements described in the prior section, although necessary and important as a first step, are not sufficient for designing a database. In addition, the requirements must be transformed into a data model. When writing application programs, program logic must first be documented in flowcharts or object diagrams; this is also the case with a database—data requirements must first be documented in a data model.

A number of different techniques can be used to create data models. By far the most popular is the **entity-relationship (E-R) model**[1], so this book will focus on it. The E-R model comes in several flavors, or variations. Here we will consider two of them. We begin with the traditional E-R model, which was the first E-R version to achieve prominence. The symbols of the traditional E-R model are understood by all database professionals.

A second version of the E-R model is one that was incorporated into the **Unified Modeling Language (UML)**[2]. UML uses different symbols and notation from the traditional E-R model, and we will introduce that notation so you will be able to interpret E-R models in UML diagrams.

The important elements of the E-R model are entities, attributes, identifiers, and relationships. We will consider each of these in turn.

Entities

An **entity** is something that users want to track. Examples of entities are CUSTOMER John Doe, PURCHASE 12345, PRODUCT A4200, SALES-ORDER 1000, SALESPERSON John Smith, and SHIPMENT 123400. Notice that in this list an entity is a specific thing or an instance of something.

---

[1]P. P. Chen, "The Entity-Relationship Model—Towards a Unified View of Data," *ACM Transactions on Database Systems* (January 1976): 9–36.
[2]Martin Fowler and Kendall Scott, *UML Distilled,* 2nd edition (Boston, MA: Addison-Wesley, 2000).

All of the instances of an entity of a given type are grouped into entity classes. Thus, the PRODUCT entity class is the collection of all PRODUCT entities. In this text, entity classes are printed in capital letters. It is important to understand the differences between an entity class and an entity instance. An entity class is a collection of entities and is described by the structure or format of the entities in that class. An instance of an entity class is the representation of a particular entity, such as CUSTOMER 12345; it is described by the values of attributes of the entity.

An entity class usually includes many instances of an entity. For example, the class ITEM has many instances—one for each item stored in the database. An entity class and two of its instances are shown in Figure 4-2.

When developing a data model, the developers analyze the forms, reports, queries, and other system requirements. Entities are usually the subject of one or more forms or reports, or are a major section in one or more forms or reports. For example, a form entitled PRODUCT Data Entry Form indicates the likelihood of an entity class called PRODUCT. Similarly, a report entitled CUSTOMER PURCHASE Summary indicates that most likely the business has CUSTOMER and PURCHASE entities.

Attributes

Entities have **attributes** that describe the entity's characteristics. Examples of attributes include EmployeeName, DateOfHire, and JobSkillCode. In this text, attributes are printed in uppercase and lowercase letters. The E-R model assumes that all instances of a given entity class have the same attributes.

Attributes have a data type and properties that are determined from the requirements. Typical data types are character, numeric, date, currency, and the like. Properties specify whether the attribute is required, whether it has a default value, whether its value has limits, and any other constraint.

Identifiers

Entity instances have **identifiers**, which are attributes that name, or identify, entity instances. For example, EMPLOYEE instances could be identified by SocialSecurityNumber, by EmployeeNumber, or by EmployeeName. EMPLOYEE instances are not likely to be identified by attributes such as Salary or DateOfHire because these attributes normally are not used in a naming role. Similarly, CUSTOMER instances could be identified by

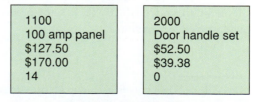

Two Entity Instances

CustomerNumber or CustomerName, and SALES-ORDER instances could be identified by OrderNumber.

The identifier of an entity instance consists of one or more of the entity's attributes. Identifiers that consist of two or more attributes are called **composite identifiers**. Examples are (AreaCode, LocalNumber), (ProjectName, TaskName), and (FirstName, LastName, PhoneExtension).

An identifier may be either unique or nonunique. If it is unique, its value will identify one, and only one, entity instance. If it is nonunique, the value will identify a set of instances. EmployeeNumber is normally a unique identifier, but EmployeeName is most likely a nonunique identifier (more than one John Smith might be employed by the company, for example).

As you can tell from these definitions, identifiers are similar to keys in the relational model, but with two important differences. First, an identifier is a logical concept; it is one or more attributes that users think of as a name of the entity. Such identifiers might or might not be represented as keys in the database design. Second, primary and candidate keys must be unique, whereas identifiers might or might not be unique.

Relationships

Entities can be associated with one another in **relationships**. The E-R model contains relationship classes and relationship instances. Relationship classes are associations among entity classes, and relationship instances are associations among entity instances. According to the original specification of the E-R model, relationships can have attributes; however, in modern practice, only entities have attributes.

A relationship class can involve many entity classes. The number of entity classes in the relationship is known as the degree of the relationship. In Figure 4-3(a), the SUPPLIER-QUOTATION relationship is of degree 2 because it involves two entity classes, SUPPLIER and QUOTATION. The PARENT relationship in Figure 4-3(b) is of degree 3, because it involves three entity classes: MOTHER, FATHER, and CHILD. Relationships of degree 2, which are called **binary relationships**, are the most common.

Three Types of Binary Relationships Figure 4-4 shows the three types of binary relationships. In a 1:1 (read "one-to-one") relationship, a single entity instance of one type is related to a single entity instance of another type. In Figure 4-4(a), the LOCKER-ASSIGNMENT relationship associates a single EMPLOYEE with a single LOCKER. According to this diagram, no employee has more than one locker assigned, and no locker is assigned to more than one employee.

Figure 4-4(b) shows the second type of binary relationship, 1:N (read "one to N" or "one to many"). In this relationship, which is called the ITEM-QUOTE relationship, a single instance of ITEM relates to many instances of QUOTATION. According to this sketch, an item has many quotations, but a quotation has only one item.

Think of the diamond as representing the relationship. The position of the 1 indicates that the relationship has one ITEM; the position of the N indicates that it also has

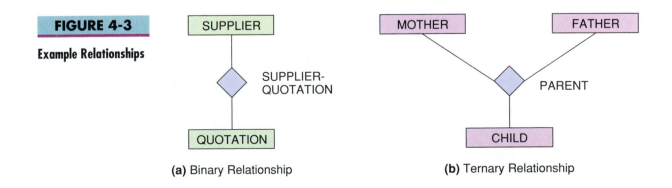

FIGURE 4-3

Example Relationships

(a) Binary Relationship

(b) Ternary Relationship

FIGURE 4-4

Four Types of Binary Relationships

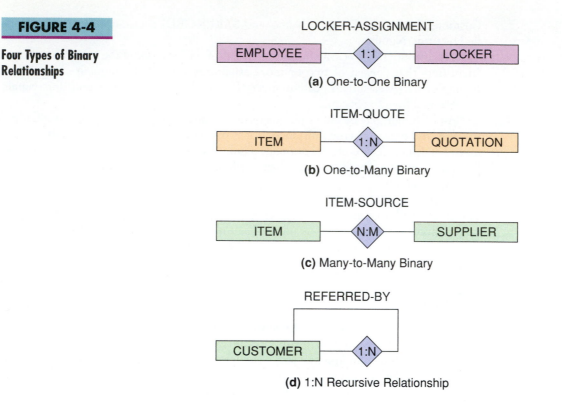

LOCKER-ASSIGNMENT

(a) One-to-One Binary

ITEM-QUOTE

(b) One-to-Many Binary

ITEM-SOURCE

(c) Many-to-Many Binary

REFERRED-BY

(d) 1:N Recursive Relationship

many QUOTATION entities. Thus, each instance of the relationship consists of one ITEM and many QUOTATIONS. If the 1 and the N were reversed and the relationship were written N:1, each instance of the relationship would have many ITEMs and one QUOTATION. However, this is not the case.

Figure 4-4(c) shows the third type of binary relationship, N:M (read "N to M" or "many to many"). This relationship is named ITEM-SOURCE, and it relates instances of ITEM to instances of SUPPLIER. An item can be supplied by many suppliers, and a supplier can supply many items.

The numbers inside the relationship diamond show the maximum number of entities that can occur on one side of the relationship. Such constraints are called the relationship's **maximum cardinality**. The relationship in Figure 4-4(b), for example, is said to have a maximum cardinality of 1:N. However, the cardinalities are not restricted to the values shown here. It is possible, for example, for the maximum cardinality to be other than 1 and N. The relationship between BASKETBALL-TEAM and PLAYER, for example, could be 1:5, indicating that a basketball team has at most five players.

Recursive Relationships   It is possible for an entity to have a relationship to itself. Figure 4-4(d) shows a CUSTOMER entity in which one customer can refer many other customers. As with binary relationships, recursive relationships can be 1:1, 1:N (shown in Figure 4-4[d]), and N:M. We will discuss each of these three types further in Chapter 5.

Entity-Relationship Diagrams

The sketches in Figure 4-4 are called entity-relationship diagrams. Such diagrams are standardized, but only loosely. According to this standard, entity classes are shown by rectangles, relationships are shown by diamonds, and the maximum cardinality of the relationship is shown inside the diamond. The name of the entity is shown inside the rectangle, and the name of the relationship is shown near the diamond. In some cases, the attributes of the entity are listed in the entity rectangle. You will see examples of this later in this chapter.

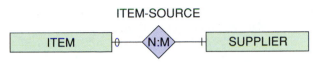

ITEM-SOURCE

FIGURE 4-5

Relationship with Minimum Cardinalities

As stated, the maximum cardinality indicates the maximum number of entities that can be involved in a relationship. The diagrams do not indicate the minimum. For example, Figure 4-4(b) shows that a quotation is related, at maximum, to one item, but it does not show whether a quotation must be related to an item.

Minimum cardinality can be shown in several different ways. One way, illustrated in Figure 4-5, is to place a hash mark across the relationship line to indicate that an entity must exist in the relationship, and to place an oval across the relationship line to indicate that an entity might or might not be in the relationship. Accordingly, Figure 4-5 shows that an ITEM must have a relationship with at least one SUPPLIER, but that a SUPPLIER is not required to have a relationship with an ITEM. The complete relationship restrictions are that an ITEM has a minimum cardinality of one and a maximum cardinality of many SUPPLIER entities. A SUPPLIER has a minimum cardinality of zero and a maximum cardinality of many ITEM entities.

Weak and ID-Dependent Entities

The E-R model defines a special type of entity called a **weak entity**. Such entities are those that cannot exist in a database unless another type of entity also exists in the database. An entity that is not weak is called a strong entity.

To understand weak entities, consider a human resource database with EMPLOYEE and DEPENDENT entity classes. Suppose the business has a rule that an EMPLOYEE instance can exist without having a relationship to any DEPENDENT entity, but a DEPENDENT entity cannot exist without having a relationship to a particular EMPLOYEE entity. In such a case, DEPENDENT is a weak entity. This means that DEPENDENT data can be stored in the database only if the DEPENDENT data have a relationship with an EMPLOYEE entity.

As shown in Figure 4-6(a), weak entities are signified by rounding the corners of the entity rectangle. In addition, the relationship on which the entity depends for its existence is shown in a diamond with rounded corners. Alternatively, in some E-R diagrams (not shown here) weak entities are depicted by using a double line for the boundary of the weak entity rectangle and double diamonds for the relationship on which the entity depends.

The E-R model includes a special type of weak entity called an **ID-dependent entity**. Such an entity is one in which the identifier of one entity includes the identifier of another entity. Consider the entities BUILDING and APARTMENT. Suppose the identifier of BUILDING is BuildingName, and the identifier of APARTMENT is the composite identifier (BuildingName, ApartmentNumber). Because the identifier of APARTMENT contains the identifier of BUILDING (BuildingName), APARTMENT is ID-dependent on BUILDING. Contrast Figure 4-6(b) with Figure 4-6(a). Another way to think of this is that logically and physically, an APARTMENT simply cannot exist unless a BUILDING exists.

FIGURE 4-6

Weak Entities

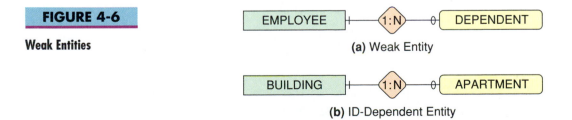

(a) Weak Entity

(b) ID-Dependent Entity

ID-dependent entities are common. Another example is the entity VERSION in the relationship between PRODUCT and VERSION, where PRODUCT is a software product and VERSION is a release of that software product. The identifier of PRODUCT is ProductName, and the identifier of VERSION is (ProductName, ReleaseNumber). A third example is EDITION in the relationship between TEXTBOOK and EDITION. The identifier of TEXTBOOK is Title, and the identifier of EDITION is (Title, EditionNumber).

Unfortunately, an ambiguity is hidden in the definition of *weak entity*, and this ambiguity is interpreted differently by different database designers (as well as different textbook authors). The ambiguity is this: In a strict sense, if a weak entity is defined as any entity whose presence in the database depends on another entity, then any entity that participates in a relationship having a minimum cardinality of one to a second entity is a weak entity. Thus, in an academic database, if a STUDENT must have an ADVISER, then STUDENT is a weak entity, because a STUDENT entity cannot be stored without an ADVISER.

This interpretation seems too broad to some people. A STUDENT is not physically dependent on an ADVISER (unlike an APARTMENT to a BUILDING), and a STUDENT is not logically dependent on an ADVISER (despite how it might appear to either the student or the adviser); therefore, STUDENT should be considered a strong entity.

To avoid such situations, some people interpret the definition of *weak entity* more narrowly. To be a weak entity, an entity must logically depend on another entity. According to this definition, DEPENDENT and APARTMENT are weak entities, but STUDENT is not. A DEPENDENT cannot be a dependent unless it has someone to depend on, and an APARTMENT cannot exist without a BUILDING in which to be located. However, a STUDENT can logically exist without an ADVISER, even if a business rule requires it.

To illustrate this interpretation, consider several examples. Suppose a data model includes the relationship between an ORDER and a SALESPERSON, as shown in Figure 4-7(a). Although we might say that an ORDER must have a SALESPERSON, it does not necessarily require one for its existence. (The ORDER could be a cash sale in which the salesperson is not recorded.) Hence, the minimum cardinality of one arises from a business rule, not from logical necessity. Thus, ORDER requires a SALESPERSON but is not existence-dependent on it, and ORDER is thus a strong entity.

Now consider the relationship of PATIENT and PRESCRIPTION in Figure 4-7(b). Here, a PRESCRIPTION cannot logically exist without a PATIENT. Hence, not only is the minimum cardinality one, but also the PRESCRIPTION is existence-dependent on PATIENT. PRESCRIPTION is thus a weak entity.

Finally, consider ASSIGNMENT in Figure 4-7(c), where the identifier of ASSIGNMENT contains the identifier of PROJECT. Here, not only does ASSIGNMENT

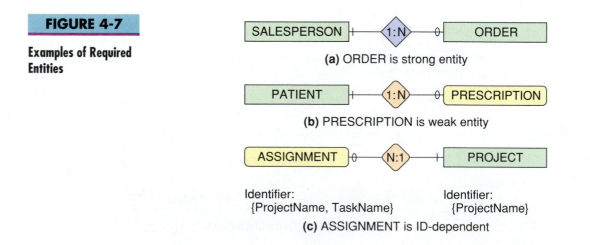

FIGURE 4-7

Examples of Required Entities

(a) ORDER is strong entity

(b) PRESCRIPTION is weak entity

Identifier:
{ProjectName, TaskName}

Identifier:
{ProjectName}

(c) ASSIGNMENT is ID-dependent

have a minimum cardinality of one, and not only is ASSIGNMENT existence-dependent on PROJECT, but ASSIGNMENT is also ID-dependent on PROJECT, because its identifier includes the key of another entity. Thus, ASSIGNMENT is a weak entity.

This text defines *weak entities* as those that logically depend on another entity. Hence, not all entities that have a minimum cardinality of one in relationship to another entity are weak. Only those that are logically dependent are weak. This definition implies that all ID-dependent entities are weak. In addition, every weak entity has a minimum cardinality of one on the entity on which it depends, but every entity that has a minimum cardinality of one is not necessarily weak.

▶ THE E-R MODEL IN UML

The Unified Modeling Language (UML) is a set of diagrams and structures for modeling and designing object-oriented programs (OOP) and applications. UML is not a methodology for developing OOP programs but rather is a set of tools that support the development of such programs. UML has received prominence via the Object Management Group, an organization that has been developing OOP models, technologies, and standards since the 1980s. UML also has begun to receive widespread use among OOP practitioners. UML is the basis of the object-oriented design tools from Rational Systems, recently purchased by IBM.

Because UML concerns program and application development, it is a subject for a course on systems development and is of limited concern to us. However, you may encounter UML-style E-R diagrams, so you should be familiar with their style. Realize that when it comes to database design, they are treated just the same as traditional E-R diagrams.

UML Entities and Relationships

Figure 4-8 shows the UML representation of the designs in Figure 4-4. Each entity is represented by an entity class, which is shown as a rectangle with three segments. The top segment shows the name of the entity and other data that pertain to OOP and is not important for our purposes. The second segment lists the names of the attributes in the entity, and the third documents constraints and lists methods (program procedures) that belong to the entity. Here, we will show constraints but will not be concerned with the OOP methods.

Relationships are shown with a line between the two entities. Cardinalities are represented in the format x..y, where *x* is the minimum required and *y* is the maximum allowed. Thus, 0..1 means that no entity is required and at most one is allowed. An asterisk represents an unlimited number. Thus, 1..* means that one is required and an unlimited number is allowed. Examine Figures 4-8(a) through (c) for examples of 1:1, 1:N, and N:M maximum-cardinality relationships.

Figure 4-8 illustrates a subtle but important point. With E-R diagrams, whether traditional or UML style, foreign keys are never shown. The relationship is represented only by the diamond or line between the entities. The placement of foreign keys is considered a database design task that is done only when the tables are designed, and not before. You will see one reason for this in Chapter 5, when we show the relational representation of N:M relationships.

UML Representation of Weak Entities

Figure 4-9 shows the UML representation of weak entities. A filled-in diamond is placed on the line going to the weak entity's parents (the entity on which the weak entity depends). In Figure 4-9(a), PRESCRIPTION is the weak entity and PATIENT is the parent entity. Every weak entity has a parent, and thus the cardinality on the parent side of the weak relationship is always 1..1. Because this is so, the cardinality on the parent entity is shown simply as 1. Figure 4-9(a) shows a weak entity that is not ID-dependent. This is denoted by the expression <nonidentifying> on the PATIENT-PRESCRIPTION

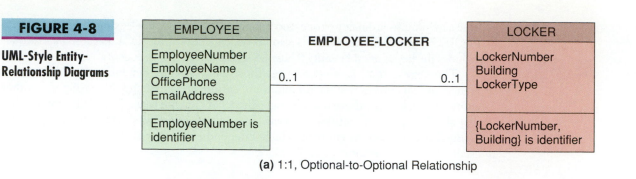

FIGURE 4-8

UML-Style Entity-Relationship Diagrams

(a) 1:1, Optional-to-Optional Relationship

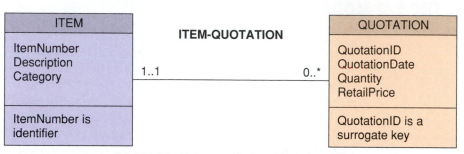

(b) 1:N, Mandatory-to-Optional Relationship

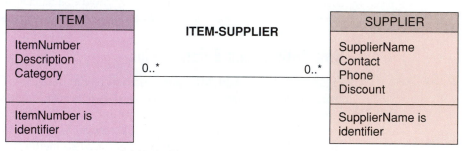

(c) N:M, Optional-to-Optional Relationship

relationship. Figure 4-9(b) shows a weak entity that is ID-dependent. That is denoted with the label <identifying>.

With this background, you should be able to interpret UML-style E-R diagrams. However, for the rest of this text we will use the more traditional, and common, notation.

▶ DEVELOPING AN EXAMPLE E-R DIAGRAM

The best way to gain proficiency with data modeling is to do it. In this section, we will examine a set of documents used by a small business and create a data model from those documents. After you have read this section, you should practice creating data models with one or more of the projects at the end of the chapter.

Heather Sweeney Designs

Heather Sweeney is an interior designer who specializes in home kitchen design. She offers a variety of seminars at home shows, kitchen and appliance stores, and other public locations. The seminars are free; she offers them as a way of building her customer base. She earns revenue by selling books and videos that instruct people on kitchen design. She also offers custom-design consulting services.

After someone attends a seminar, Heather wants to leave no stone unturned in attempting to sell that person one of her products or services. Accordingly, she would like

FIGURE 4-9

UML Representation of
Weak Entities

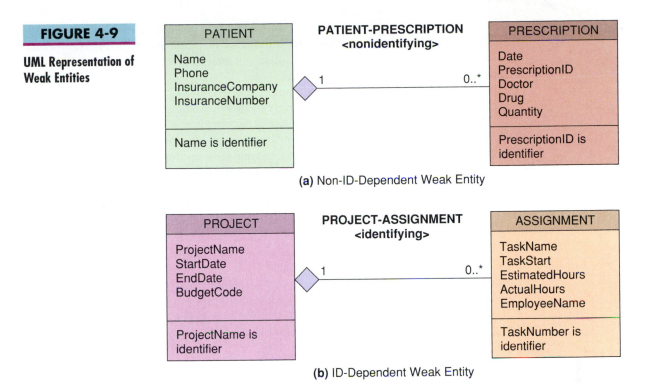

(a) Non-ID-Dependent Weak Entity

(b) ID-Dependent Weak Entity

to develop a database to keep track of customers, the seminars they have attended, the contacts she has made with them, and the purchases they have made. She wants to use this database to continue to contact her customers and offer them products and services.

The Seminar Customer List

Figure 4-10 shows the seminar customer list that Heather or her assistant fills out at seminars. It includes basic data about the seminar as well as the name, phone, and e-mail address of all the attendees at the seminar. If we examine this list in terms of a data model, two potential entities are found: SEMINAR and CUSTOMER.

FIGURE 4-10

Seminar Customer List
Example

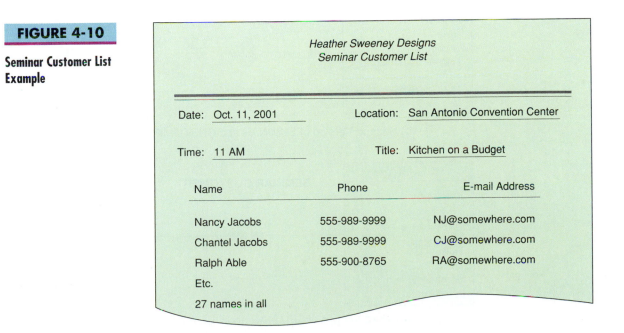

From the form in Figure 4-10, we can conclude that a SEMINAR relates to many CUSTOMERs, and we can make the initial E-R diagram shown in Figure 4-11(a). However, from this single document a number of facts cannot be determined. The missing facts are denoted with question marks.

Having missing facts is typical during the data-modeling process. We examine documents and conduct user interviews, then create a data model with the data that we have. We also note where data are missing and supply that data later as we learn more. Thus, there is no need to stop data modeling when something is unknown; we just note that it is unknown and keep going with the goal of supplying missing information at some later point.

Suppose we talk with Heather and determine that customers can attend as many seminars as they would like, but that she would like to be able to record customers even if they have not been to a seminar. ("Honey, I'll take a customer wherever I can find one!" was her actual response.) Also, she never offers a seminar to fewer than 10 attendees. Given this information, we can fill out more of the E-R diagram as shown in Figure 4-11(b).

Before continuing, consider the minimum cardinality of the relationship from SEMINAR to CUSTOMER in Figure 4-11(b). The notation says that a seminar must have at least 10 customers, which is what we were told. However, this means that we cannot add a new SEMINAR to the database unless it already has 10 customers. This is incorrect. When Heather first schedules a seminar, it probably has no customers at all, but she still would like to record it in the database. Therefore, even though she has a

FIGURE 4-11

Initial E-R Diagram for Heather Sweeney Designs

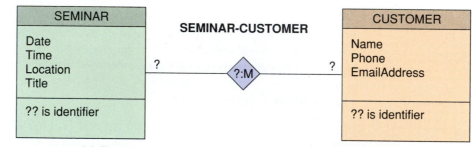

(a) First Version of SEMINAR and CUSTOMER E-R Diagram

(b) Second Version of SEMINAR and CUSTOMER E-R Diagram

(c) Third Version of SEMINAR and CUSTOMER E-R Diagram

business policy of requiring at least 10 customers at a seminar, we cannot place this limit as a constraint in the data model.

In Figure 4-11(b), neither of the entities has an identifier. For SEMINAR, the composites (Date, Time, Location) and (Date, Time, Title) are probably unique and could be the identifier. However, identifiers will become table keys during database design, and these will be large character keys. A surrogate key is probably a better idea here, so we will add one. Also, looking at our data and thinking about the nature of e-mail addresses, we can reasonably suppose that EmailAddress can be the identifier of CUSTOMER. All of these decisions are shown for the E-R diagram in Figure 4-11(c).

The Customer Form Letter

Figure 4-12 shows a form letter that Sweeney Designs uses. Eventually, Heather would like to send messages like this via e-mail, as well. Accordingly, we will represent this form letter with an entity called CONTACT, which could be a letter, an e-mail, or some other form of

FIGURE 4-12

Customer Form Letter

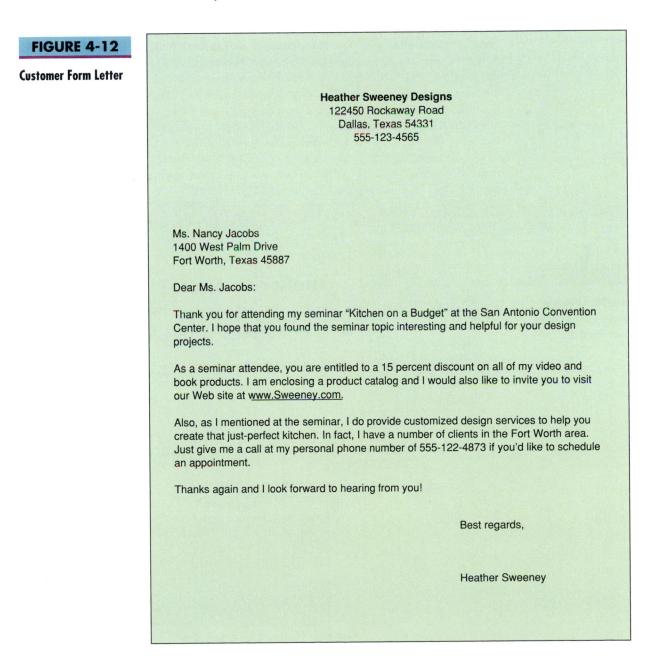

Heather Sweeney Designs
122450 Rockaway Road
Dallas, Texas 54331
555-123-4565

Ms. Nancy Jacobs
1400 West Palm Drive
Fort Worth, Texas 45887

Dear Ms. Jacobs:

Thank you for attending my seminar "Kitchen on a Budget" at the San Antonio Convention Center. I hope that you found the seminar topic interesting and helpful for your design projects.

As a seminar attendee, you are entitled to a 15 percent discount on all of my video and book products. I am enclosing a product catalog and I would also like to invite you to visit our Web site at www.Sweeney.com.

Also, as I mentioned at the seminar, I do provide customized design services to help you create that just-perfect kitchen. In fact, I have a number of clients in the Fort Worth area. Just give me a call at my personal phone number of 555-122-4873 if you'd like to schedule an appointment.

Thanks again and I look forward to hearing from you!

Best regards,

Heather Sweeney

customer contact. She uses several different form letters (and, in the future, e-mails); Heather refers to each one by a number. Thus, she has form letter 1, form letter 2, and so forth. For now, we will represent the attributes of CONTACT as ContactNumber and Type, where Type can be either Form Letter or, in the future Email or some other type.

Reading the form letter, we see that it refers to a seminar and a customer. Therefore, we will add it to the E-R diagram with relationships to both of these entities as shown in Figure 4-13(a). A seminar can result in many contacts and a customer may receive many contacts, so the maximum cardinality of these relationships is N. However, neither a customer nor a seminar need generate a contact, so the minimum cardinality of these relationships is zero.

Working from CONTACT back to SEMINAR and CUSTOMER, we can determine that the contact is for a single CUSTOMER and refers to a single SEMINAR, so the maximum cardinality in that direction is one. Also, some of the form letters refer to seminars and some do not, so the minimum cardinality back to SEMINAR is zero. However, a contact must have a customer, so the minimum cardinality of that relationship is one. These cardinalities are shown in Figure 4-13(a).

Now, however, consider the identifier of CONTACT, which is shown as unknown in Figure 4-13(a). What could be the identifier? None of the attributes by themselves suffice because many contacts will have the same values for ContactNumber, ContactType, or Date. Reflect on this for a minute, and you will begin to realize that some attribute of CUSTOMER has to be part of CONTACT. That realization is a signal that something is wrong. In a data model, the same attribute should not logically need to be part of two different entities.

Could it be that CONTACT is a weak entity? Can a CONTACT logically exist without a SEMINAR? Yes, because not all CONTACTs refer to a SEMINAR. Can a CONTACT logically exist without a CUSTOMER? The answer to that question has to be no. Whom would we be contacting without a CUSTOMER? Aha! That's it: CONTACT is a weak entity, depending on CUSTOMER; in fact, it is an ID-dependent entity because the identifier of CONTACT includes the identifier of CUSTOMER.

Figure 4-13(b) shows the data model with CONTACT as a weak entity on CUSTOMER. After further interviews with Heather, it was determined that she never

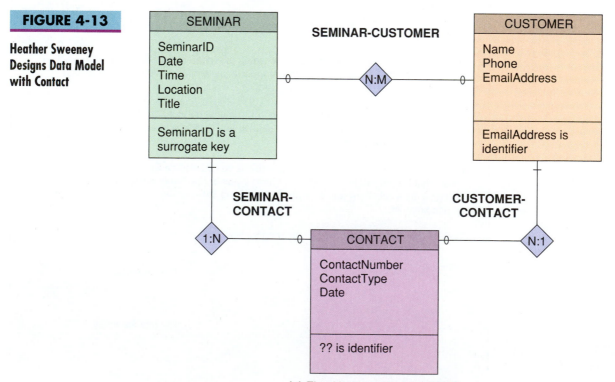

FIGURE 4-13

Heather Sweeney Designs Data Model with Contact

(a) First Version with CONTACT

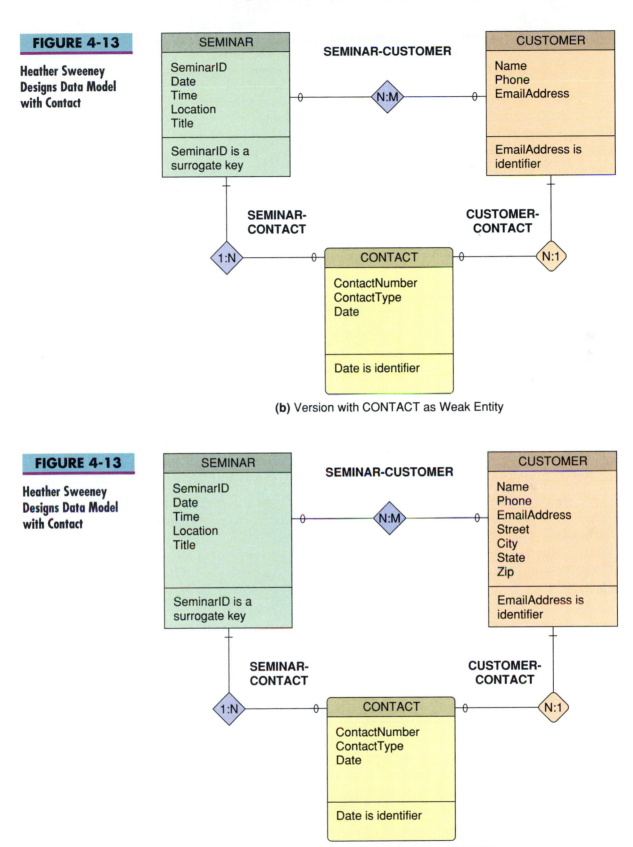

FIGURE 4-13

Heather Sweeney Designs Data Model with Contact

(b) Version with CONTACT as Weak Entity

FIGURE 4-13

Heather Sweeney Designs Data Model with Contact

(c) Version with Amended CUSTOMER

contacts a customer more than once on the same day, so Date can be the identifier of CONTACT (as ID-dependent within CUSTOMER).

This E-R diagram has one other problem. The contact letter has the customer's address, but the CUSTOMER entity has no address attributes. Consequently, they need to be added as shown in Figure 4-13(c). This adjustment is typical; as more forms and reports are obtained, new attributes and other changes will need to be made to the data model.

The Sales Invoice

The sales invoice that Heather uses to sell books and videos is shown in Figure 4-14. The sales invoice itself will need to be an entity, and because the sales invoice has customer data, it will have a relationship back to CUSTOMER. (Note that we do not duplicate the customer

---

FIGURE 4-14

Sales Invoice

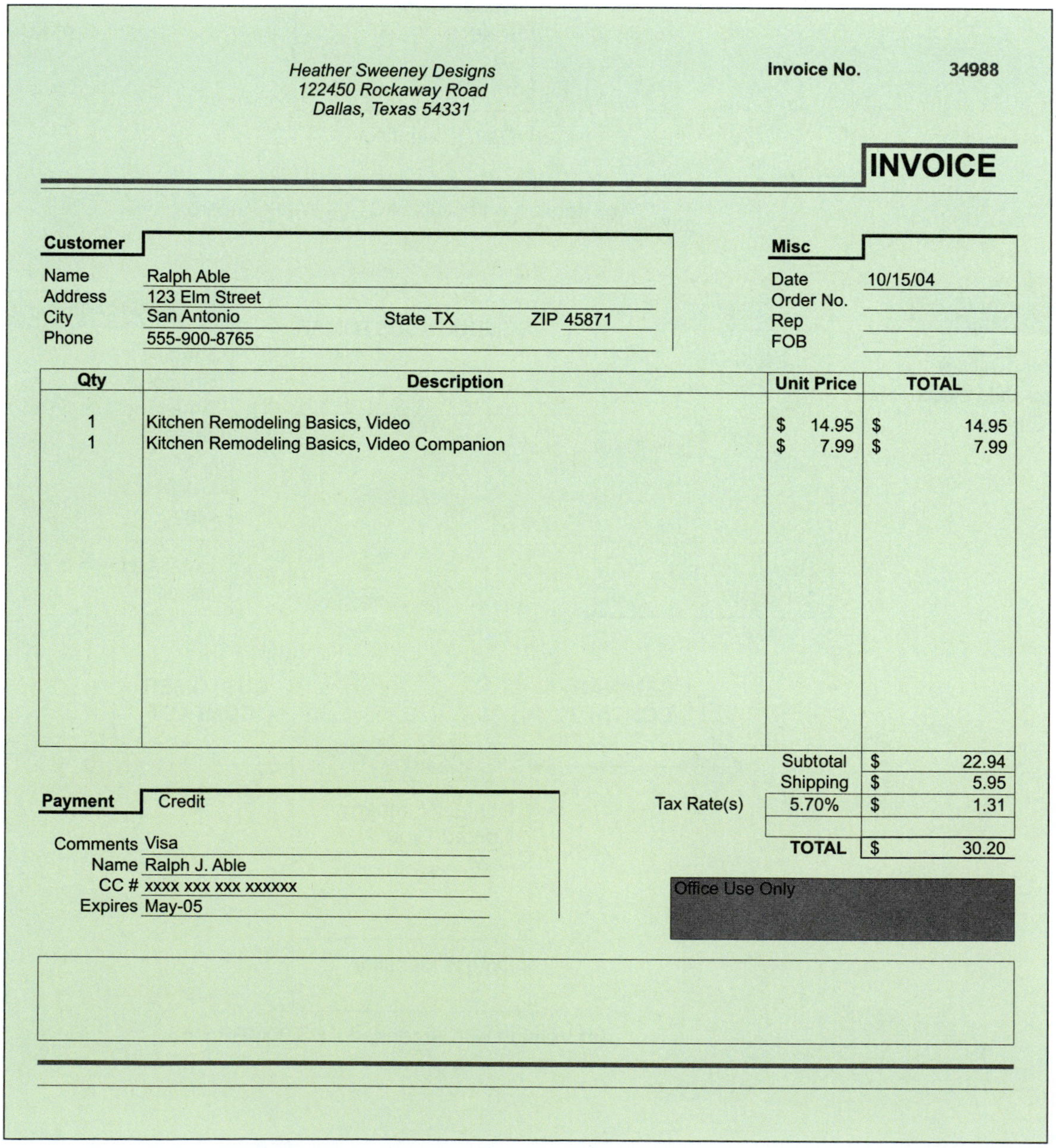

Heather Sweeney Designs *122450 Rockaway Road* *Dallas, Texas 54331*	**Invoice No.** 34988

INVOICE

Customer		**Misc**	
Name	Ralph Able	Date	10/15/04
Address	123 Elm Street	Order No.	
City	San Antonio State TX ZIP 45871	Rep	
Phone	555-900-8765	FOB	

Qty	Description	Unit Price	TOTAL
1	Kitchen Remodeling Basics, Video	$ 14.95	$ 14.95
1	Kitchen Remodeling Basics, Video Companion	$ 7.99	$ 7.99

Subtotal	$ 22.94
Shipping	$ 5.95
Tax Rate(s) 5.70%	$ 1.31
TOTAL	$ 30.20

Payment   Credit

Comments Visa
    Name Ralph J. Able
    CC # xxxx xxx xxx xxxxxx
    Expires May-05

Office Use Only

data, because we can obtain data items via the relationship; if data items are missing, we add them to CUSTOMER.) Because Heather runs her computer with lax security, she decided that she did not want to record credit card numbers in her computer database. Instead, she records only the PaymentType value in the database and files the credit card receipts in a (locked) physical file with a notation that relates them back to an invoice number.

Figure 4-15(a) shows a first cut at the data model with INVOICE. This diagram is missing data about the line items on the order. Because there are multiple line items, the line item data cannot be stored in INVOICE. Instead, a weak entity, LINE-ITEM, must be defined. The need for a weak entity is typical for documents that contain a group of repeating data; if the repeating group is not logically independent, then it must be made into a weak entity. Figure 4-15(b) shows the adjusted design.

As shown, LINE-ITEM has no identifier. Because it belongs to an identifying relationship from INVOICE, it needs an attribute that can be used to identify a particular LINE-ITEM within an INVOICE. We could use Description, but that would imply that the same item may not appear on a given invoice more than once, and this might be too constraining. Another option is to add a LineNumber attribute that identifies the line on which an item appears. We will add a LineItem attribute to our design.

We need to make one more correction to this data model. Heather sells standard products—her books and videos have standardized names and prices. She does not want the person who fills out an order to be able to use nonstandard names or prices. Accordingly, we need to add a PRODUCT entity and relate it to LINE-ITEM as shown in Figure 4-15(c).

Observe that UnitPrice is an attribute of both PRODUCT and LINE-ITEM. This was done so that Heather can update UnitPrice without impacting the recorded orders. At the

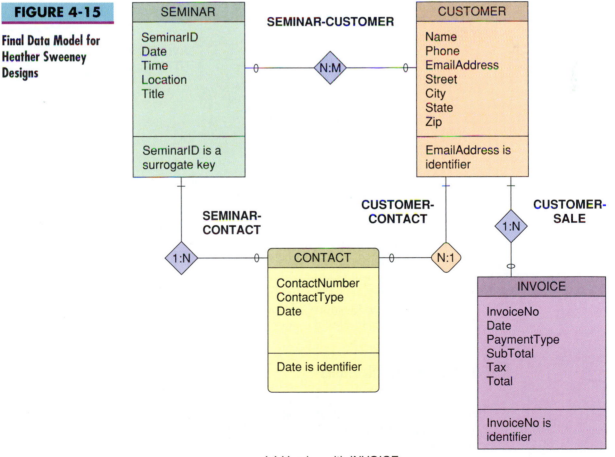

FIGURE 4-15

Final Data Model for Heather Sweeney Designs

(a) Version with INVOICE

FIGURE 4-15

Final Data Model for Heather Sweeney Designs

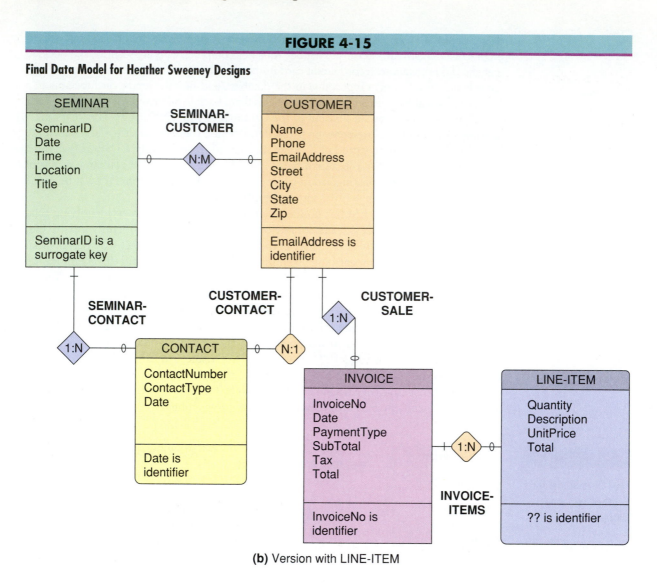

(b) Version with LINE-ITEM

time a sale is made, UnitPrice in LINE-ITEM is set equal to UnitPrice in PRODUCT. The LINE-ITEM UnitPrice never changes. However, as time passes and Heather changes prices for her products, she can update UnitPrice in PRODUCT. If UnitPrice were not copied into LINE-ITEM, when the PRODUCT price changes, the price in already-stored LINE-ITEMs would change as well, and Heather does not want this to occur. This means that although two attributes are named UnitPrice, they are different attributes used for different purposes.

Also note in Figure 4-15(c) that based on interviews with Heather, we have added ProductNumber and QuantityOnHand to PRODUCT. These attributes do not appear in any of the documents, but they are known by Heather and are important to her.

Attribute Specifications

The data model in Figure 4-15(c) shows entities, attributes, and entity relationships, but it does not document details about attributes. To do that, the development team needs to create a table like that shown in Figure 4-16. Here, the data format and properties of the attributes of each entity are documented. These attributes and properties are used to create the tables in the database design, as you will see in the next chapter.

FIGURE 4-15

Final Data Model for Heather Sweeney Designs

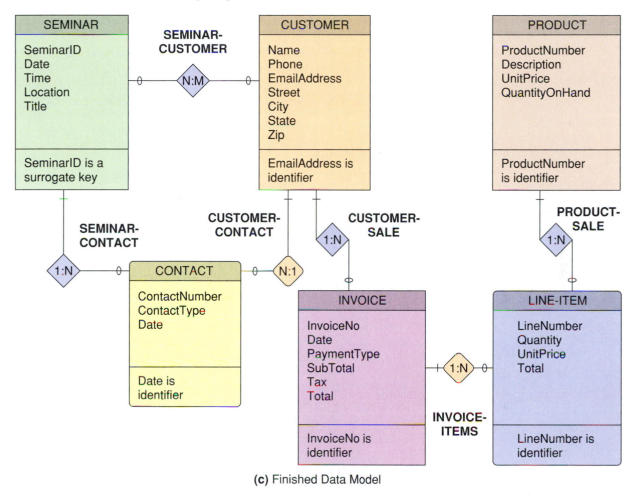

(c) Finished Data Model

FIGURE 4-16

Attribute Specifications

Entity Name	Attribute Name	Data Format (Length)	Required?	Default Value	Input Mask	Remarkable Constraints
SEMINAR	SeminarID	AutoNumber	Yes	DBMS supplied		Surrogate
SEMINAR	Date	Date	Yes	None	mm/dd/yyyy	09/01/2003
SEMINAR	Time	Text(4)	No	None	hh(AM/PM)	
SEMINAR	Location	Text(7)	Yes	None	None	
SEMINAR	Title	Text(35)	Yes	'Intro'	None	
CUSTOMER	Name	Text(35)	Yes	None	None	
CUSTOMER	Phone	Text(10)	No	None	(nnn)nnn-nnnn	
CUSTOMER	Email Address	Text(50)	No	None		
CUSTOMER	• • •					

Business Rules

While creating the data model, the development team needs to be on the lookout for business rules that constrain data values and the processing of the database. We encountered such a business rule with regard to CONTACT, when Heather stated that no more than one form letter or e-mail per day is to be sent to a customer.

In more complicated data models, many such business rules would exist. These rules are generally too specific or too complicated to be enforced by the DBMS. Rather, application programs or other forms of procedural logic need to be developed to enforce such rules. You will learn more about this when we discuss stored procedures and triggers in the next chapter.

Validating the Data Model

After the data model has been completed, it needs to be validated. The most common way to do this is to show it to the users and obtain their feedback. However, a large, complicated data model is off-putting to many users, so often the data model needs to be broken into sections and validated piece by piece or expressed in some other terms that are more understandable.

As mentioned earlier in this chapter, prototypes are sometimes constructed for users to review. This is because prototypes are easier for users to understand and evaluate than data models. Prototypes can be developed that show the consequences of data model design decisions without requiring the users to learn E-R modeling. For example, showing a form with room for only one customer is a way of indicating that the maximum cardinality of a relationship is one. If the users respond to such a form with the question "But where do I put the second customer?" you know that the maximum cardinality is greater than one.

It is relatively easy to create mock-ups of forms and reports using Microsoft Access wizards. Such mock-ups are often developed even in situations where Access is not going to be used as the operational DBMS. The mock-ups are used to demonstrate the consequences of data modeling decisions.

Finally, the data model needs to be evaluated against all use cases. For each use case, the development team needs to verify that all of the data and relationships necessary to support the use case are present and accurately represented in the data model.

Data model validation is exceedingly important. It is far easier and cheaper to correct errors at this stage than it is to correct them after the database has been designed and implemented. Changing a cardinality in a data model is a simple adjustment to a document; changing the cardinality later might require the construction of new tables, new relationships, new queries, new forms, new reports, and so forth. So, every minute spent validating a data model will pay great dividends down the line.

SUMMARY

The process of developing a database system consists of three stages: requirements, design, and implementation. During the requirements stage, users are interviewed, systems requirements are documented, and a data model is constructed. Often prototypes of selected portions of the future system are created. During the design phase, the data model is transformed into a relational database design. During the implementation stage, the database is constructed and filled with data, and queries, forms, reports, and application programs are created.

In addition to a data model, the development team also must determine data-item data types, properties, and limits on data values. Business rules that constrain database activity also need be documented.

The entity-relationship model is the most popular tool used to develop a data model. With the E-R model, entities—which are identifiable things of importance to the users—are defined. All of the entities of a given type form an entity class. A particular entity is called an instance. Attributes describe the characteristics of entities, and one or more attributes identify an entity. Identifiers can be unique or nonunique.

Relationships are associations among entities. The E-R model explicitly defines relationships. Each relationship has a name, and there are relationship classes as well as relationship instances. According to the original specification of the E-R model, relationships may have attributes; however, this is not common in contemporary data models.

The degree of a relationship is the number of entities participating in the relationship. Most relationships are binary. The three types of binary relationships are 1:1, 1:N, and N:M. A recursive relationship occurs when an entity has a relationship to itself.

In traditional E-R diagrams such as the traditional E-R model, entities are shown in rectangles, and relationships are shown in diamonds. The maximum cardinality of a relationship is shown inside the diamond. The minimum cardinality is indicated by a hash mark or an oval.

A weak entity is one whose existence depends on another entity; an entity that is not weak is called a strong entity. Weak entities are shown in rectangles with rounded corners, and the relationship on which the entity depends is indicated by a diamond with rounded corners. In this text, we further define a weak entity as an entity that logically depends on another entity. An entity can have a minimum cardinality of one in a relationship with another entity and not necessarily be a weak entity.

Unified Modeling Language (UML), an object-oriented program (OOP) design tool, has defined a new style of E-R diagrams. You should be familiar with diagrams of that style, but you also should realize that when creating a database design, no fundamental difference exists between the traditional style and the UML style.

In addition to E-R diagrams, a data model includes attribute specifications such as those shown in Figure 4-16. Also, while creating a data model, the development team needs to document business rules that constrain database activity.

After E-R models are completed, they must be evaluated. The development team can show the data model, or portions of the data model, directly to the users for evaluation. This requires the users to learn how to interpret an E-R diagram. Sometimes, instead of the data model, prototypes that demonstrate the consequences of the data model are shown to the users. Such prototypes are easier for users to understand.

REVIEW QUESTIONS

4.1   Name the three stages in the process of developing database systems. Summarize the tasks in each.

4.2   What is a data model and what is its purpose?

4.3   What is a prototype and what is its purpose?

4.4   What is a use case and what is its purpose?

4.5   Give an example of a data constraint.

4.6   Give an example of a business rule that would need to be documented in a database development project.

4.7   Define the term *entity* and give an example.

4.8   Explain the difference between an entity class and an entity instance.

4.9   Define the term *attribute* and give examples for the entity you created in question 4.7.

4.10   Which attribute defined in your answer to question 4.9 identifies the entity?

4.11   Explain what a composite identifier is and give an example.

4.12   Define the term *relationship* and give an example.

4.13   Explain the difference between a relationship class and a relationship instance.

4.14 Define the term *degree of relationship*. Give an example, other than the one in this text, of a relationship greater than degree 2.

4.15 List and give an example of the three types of binary relationships. Draw an E-R diagram for each.

4.16 Give an example of a recursive relationship other than the one shown in this chapter.

4.17 Define the terms *maximum cardinality* and *minimum cardinality*.

4.18 Name and sketch the traditional symbols used in E-R diagrams for (a) an entity, (b) a relationship, and (c) a weak entity and its relationship.

4.19 Give an example E-R diagram for the entities DEPARTMENT and EMPLOYEE, which have a 1:N relationship. Assume that a DEPARTMENT does not need to have an EMPLOYEE, but that every EMPLOYEE does have a DEPARTMENT.

4.20 Show example attributes for DEPARTMENT and EMPLOYEE (from question 4.19). Use traditional symbols.

4.21 Define the term *weak entity* and give an example other than one in this text.

4.22 Explain the ambiguity in the definition of the term *weak entity*. Explain how this book interprets this term. Give examples, other than those in this text, of each type of weak entity.

4.23 Define the term *ID-dependent entity* and give an example other than one in this text.

4.24 List important attribute properties that need to be developed as part of a data model.

4.25 Create example properties for five of the attributes from your work for question 4.20.

4.26 Give an example of a business rule for your work for question 4.19.

4.27 Describe why it is important to evaluate a data model.

4.28 Summarize one technique for evaluating a data model, and explain how that technique could be used to evaluate the data model in Figure 4-15.

EXERCISES

4.29 Suppose that Heather Sweeney wants to include records of her consulting services in her database. Extend the data model in Figure 4-15(c) to include CONSULTING-PROJECT and DAILY-PROJECT-HOURS entities. CONSULTING-PROJECT contains data about a particular project for one of her customers, and DAILY-PROJECT-HOURS contains data about the hours spent and a description of the work accomplished on a particular day for a particular project. Use strong and/or weak entities as appropriate. Specify minimum and maximum cardinalities. Use traditional E-R model diagrams.

4.30 Extend your work for question 4.29 to include supplies that Heather uses on a project. Assume that she wants to track the description, price, and amount used of each supply. Supplies are used on multiple days of a project.

4.31 Develop a model of the boxcars on a railway train. Use recursive relationships.

4.32 Develop a model of a genealogical diagram. Model only biological parents; do not model stepparents. Use more than one relationship if necessary.

4.33 Develop a model of a genealogical diagram. Model all parents, including stepparents. Use more than one relationship if necessary.

GARDEN GLORY PROJECT QUESTIONS

Garden Glory wants to expand its database applications beyond the recording of property services. The company still wants to maintain data on owners, properties, employees, and services, but it wants to include other data as well. Specifically, Garden Glory wants to track equipment, how it is used during services, and equipment repairs. In addition, employees need to be trained before using certain equipment, and management wants to be able to determine who has obtained training on which equipment.

With regard to properties, Garden Glory has determined that most of the properties it services are too large and complex to be described in one record. The company wants the database to allow for many subproperty descriptions of a property. Thus, a particular property might have subproperty descriptions of Front Garden, Back Garden, Second-Level Courtyard, and so on. For better accounting to the customers, services are to be related to the subproperties rather than to the overall property.

Develop an E-R data model that will meet Garden Glory's new requirements. Use traditional-style diagrams, and specify entities and relationships only. For brevity, do not specify attributes. Justify the decisions you make regarding minimum and maximum cardinality. Describe how you would go about validating this model.

JAMES RIVER JEWELRY PROJECT QUESTIONS

James River Jewelry wants to expand its database applications beyond the recording of purchases for awards. The company still wants to maintain data on customers, purchases, and awards, but it wants to include other data, as well. Specifically, James River wants to record artists and styles and to keep track of which customers are interested in which artists and styles.

Also, most of the jewelry is sold on consignment, so the company does not pay the artist of a piece of jewelry until it is sold. Typically, the company pays artists 60 percent of the sales price, but the terms are negotiated separately for each item. For some items, the artists earn a larger percentage, and for others they earn less. Artists and James River personnel agree on the initial sales price at the time the item is brought to the shop. When an item has been in the shop for some time, James River may reduce the price; sometimes it renegotiates the sales percentage.

Develop an E-R data model that will meet James River's new requirements. Use traditional-style diagrams, and specify entities and relationships only. For brevity, do not specify attributes. Justify the decisions you make regarding minimum and maximum cardinality. Describe how you would go about validating this model.

MID-WESTERN UNIVERSITY CHEMISTRY DEPARTMENT PROJECT QUESTIONS

The chemistry department wants to expand the data it keeps about its NMR magnets and their use. They still want to track principal investigators, grants, magnets, users, and appointments as described at the end of Chapter 3, but they want to track other data, as well.

Specifically, the department conducts several different training courses for each magnet. They want to keep track of which users have taken which training, and when they took the training. They also want to track who conducted the training. (The courses are taught be the users themselves.)

Create an E-R model for the chemistry department's database. Include entities and relationships for the tables listed at the end of Chapter 3, as well as entities and relationships for the new requirements. Specify attributes that you think are applicable for the new entities.

Database Design

> Learn how to transform E-R data models into relational designs

> Practice applying the normalization process from Chapter 2

> Understand the need for denormalization

> Learn how to represent weak entities with the relational model

> Know how to represent 1:1, 1:N, and N:M binary relationships

> Know how to represent 1:1, 1:N, and N:M recursive relationships

> Learn SQL statements for creating joins over binary and recursive relationships

> Understand the nature and background of normalization theory

This chapter describes a process for converting E-R data models into relational designs. We begin by explaining how entities are expressed as relations. Next, we apply the role of the normalization process that you learned in Chapter 2 and describe normalization in more detail. Then, we show how to represent three types of relationships using foreign keys. We also show how to use these techniques for representing recursive relationships. Finally, we apply all of these techniques to design a database for the data model of Heather Sweeney Designs, developed in Chapter 4.

▶ REPRESENTING ENTITIES WITH THE RELATIONAL MODEL

The representation of entities using the relational model is direct and straightforward. First, define a relation for each entity and give that relation the same name as the entity. Then, create a column in the relation for each attribute in the entity. Make the primary key of the relation the identifier of the entity. Finally, apply the normalization process described in Chapter 2 to remove any normalization problems. To understand this process, consider the following three examples.

Representing the ITEM Entity

Consider the ITEM entity shown in Figure 5-1, which contains the attributes ItemNumber, Description, Cost, ListPrice, and QuantityOnHand. To represent this entity with a relation, we define a relation for the entity and place the attributes in it as columns in the relation. ItemNumber is the identifier of the entity and becomes the primary key of the relation. The result is:

ITEM (<u>Itemnumber</u>, Description, Cost, ListPrice, QuantityOnHand)

As in earlier chapters, the key of the relation is underlined.

The table that results from converting an entity in this way might have normalization problems. Therefore, the next step is to apply the normalization process from Chapter 2. In the case of ITEM, the primary key is ItemNumber, and no other functional dependencies exist; therefore, the ITEM table is normalized.

Representing the CUSTOMER Entity

To understand an entity that gives rise to normalization problems, consider the CUSTOMER entity in Figure 5-2. If we transform the entity as just described, we obtain the following relation.

CUSTOMER (<u>CustomerNumber</u>, CustomerName, Address, City, State, Zip, Contact, PhoneNumber)

CustomerNumber is the key of the relation. According to the normalization process (page 38), we need to check for functional dependencies besides those involving the primary key. At least one exists, namely, Zip → (City, State).

Zip is not a candidate key for this relation; therefore, this relation is not normalized. Furthermore, another functional dependency involving PhoneNumber is possible. Is PhoneNumber the phone number of the company, or is it the phone number of the contact? If PhoneNumber is the phone number of the company, then CustomerNumber → PhoneNumber, and no additional normalization problem exists. However, if the PhoneNumber is that of the contact, then Contact → PhoneNumber and, because Contact is not a candidate key, there are normalization problems involving it, as well.

The answer to this question can be resolved only by asking the users. Assume that we do that, and the users say that indeed it is the phone number of the contact. Thus, Contact → PhoneNumber.

ITEM
ItemNumber Description Cost ListPrice QuantityOnHand
ItemNumber is identifier

FIGURE 5-2

The CUSTOMER Entity

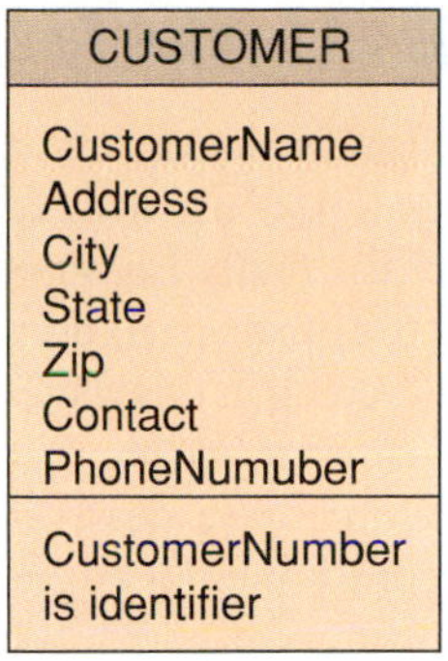

```
          CUSTOMER
  CustomerName
  Address
  City
  State
  Zip
  Contact
  PhoneNumuber
  CustomerNumber
  is identifier
```

Given these facts, then according to step 3 of the normalization process, we pull the attributes of the functional dependencies out of the relation, making a copy of their determinants in the original relation as foreign keys. The result is the three relations:

CUSTOMER (<u>CustomerNumber</u>, CustomerName, Address, *Zip*, *Contact*)

ZIP (<u>Zip</u>, City, State)

CONTACT (<u>Contact</u>, PhoneNumber)

with the referential integrity constraints:

Zip in CUSTOMER must exist in Zip in ZIP
Contact in CUSTOMER must exist in Contact in CONTACT

These three relations are normalized, and we can continue with the design process. However, before proceeding consider another perspective on normalization.

Denormalization

It is possible to take normalization too far. In fact, most practitioners would consider the construction of a separate ZIP table to be going too far. People are accustomed to writing their city, state, and zip as a group, and breaking City and State away from Zip will make the design hard to use. It also will mean that the DBMS has to read two separate tables just to get the customer's address. Hence, even though it results in normalization problems, a better overall design would result by leaving Zip, City, and State in the CUSTOMER relation. This is an example of **denormalization**.

What are the consequences of this decision do denormalize? To answer that question, consider the three basic operations: insert, update, and delete. If we leave Zip, City, and State in CUSTOMER, then we will not be able to insert data for a new zip code until a customer has that zip code. However, we will never want to do that. We only care about zip code data when one of our customers has that zip code. Therefore, leaving the zip data in CUSTOMER does not pose problems when inserting.

What about modifications? If a city changes its zip code, then we might have to change multiple rows in CUSTOMER. How frequently do cities change their zip code though? Because the answer is almost never, updates in the denormalized relation are not a problem. Finally, what about deletes? If only one customer has the zip data (80210, Denver, Colorado), then if we delete that customer, we will lose the fact that 80210 is in Denver. This does not really matter though because when another customer with this zip code is inserted, that customer also will provide the city and state.

Therefore, denormalizing CUSTOMER by leaving the attributes Zip, City, State in the relation will make the design easier to use and not cause modification problems. The denormalized design is better.

The need for denormalization also can arise for reasons such as security and performance. If the cost of the modification problems is low (like for zip code) and if other factors cause denormalized relations to be preferred, then denormalizing is a good idea.

A Relational Design for the SALES-COMMISSION Entity

To summarize the discussion so far, when representing an entity with the relational model, the first step is to construct a relation that has all of the entity's attributes as columns. The identifier of the entity becomes the primary key of the relation. Then the relation is normalized. If the normalized design is too pure, the relation is then denormalized.

By proceeding in this way, we always consider the normalized design. If we make a decision to denormalize, we are doing so from a position of knowledge and not from ignorance.

To reenforce these ideas, consider a third example—that for the SALES-COMMISSION entity in Figure 5-3. First, we create a relation having all of the attributes as columns:

SALES-COMMISSION (SalespersonNumber, SalespersonName, Phone, <u>CheckNumber</u>, CheckDate, CommissionPeriod, TotalCommissionSales, CommissionAmount, BudgetCategory)

As shown, the primary key of the table is CheckNumber, the identifier of the entity.

The attributes of the relation have two additional functional dependencies:

SalespersonNumber → (SalespersonName, Phone, BudgetCategory) and (Salesperson-Number, CommissionPeriod) → (TotalCommissionSales, CommissionAmount).

According to the normalization process, we extract the attributes of these functional dependencies from the original table and make the determinants the keys of the new table. We also leave a copy of the determinants in the original table as foreign keys. The result is the following:

SALES-COMMISSION (*SalespersonNumber*, <u>CheckNumber</u>, CheckDate, *CommissionPeriod*)

SALESPERSON (<u>SalespersonNumber</u>, SalespersonName, Phone)

SALES (<u>SalespersonNumber</u>, <u>CommissionPeriod</u>, TotalCommissionSales, CommissionAmount)

with referential integrity constraints:

SalespersonNumber in SALES-COMMISSION must exist in SalespersonNumber in SALESPERSON

and

(SalespersonNumber, CommissionPeriod) in SALES-COMMISSION must exist in (SalespersonNumber, CommissionPeriod) in SALES

Now consider denormalization. Is there any reason not to create the SALESPERSON or SALES relations? Is the design better if we leave them in the SALES-COMMISSION relation? In this case, there is no reason to denormalize, so we leave the normalized relations alone.

SALES-COMMISSION

SalespersonNumber
SalespersonName
Phone
CheckNumber
CheckDate
CommissionPeriod
TotalCommissionSales
CommissionAmount
BudgetCategory

CheckNumber
is identifier

Normal Forms

E. F. Codd, the father of the relational model, defined three normal forms in an early paper on the relational model. He defined any table that meets the definition of a relation (see Figure 2-1 on page 26) as being in first normal form (written 1NF). He pointed out that such tables can have anomalies, and he defined a second normal form (2NF) that eliminated some of those anomalies. However, the conditions of 2NF did not eliminate all of them, so he defined 3NF. For a short period of time, 3NF relations were considered to be the best, and even today you will hear people brag that their relations are in 3NF.

Not long after Codd published his paper on normal forms, it was pointed out to him that even relations in 3NF could have anomalies. As a result, he and R. Boyce defined Boyce-Codd Normal Form (BCNF), which eliminated the anomalies that had been found with 3NF.

All of these definitions were made in such a way that a relation in a higher normal form is defined to be in all lower normal forms. Thus, a relation in BCNF is automatically in 3NF, a relation in 3NF is automatically in 2NF, and a relation in 2NF is automatically in 1NF.

There the matter rested until others discovered another kind of dependency called a multi-valued dependency. Such dependencies were discussed in Exercise 2.39 at the end of Chapter 2. To eliminate such dependencies, 4NF was defined. A little later, another kind of anomaly involving tables that can be split apart but not correctly joined back together was identified, and 5NF was defined to eliminate that type of anomaly.

You can see how the knowledge evolved; none of these normal forms were perfect—each one eliminated certain anomalies, and none asserted that it was vulnerable to no anomaly at all. At this stage, in 1981, R. Fagin took a different approach and asked why, rather than just chipping away at anomalies, we don't look for conditions that would have to exist in order for a relation to have no anomalies at all. He did just this and in the process defined domain/key normal form (DK/NF). Fagin proved that a relation in DK/NF can have no anomalies, and he further proved that a relation that has no anomalies is also in DK/NF.

For some reason, DK/NF never caught the fancy of the general database population, but it should have. As you can tell, no one should brag that their relations are in 3NF; instead, we all should brag that our relations are in DK/NF. But for some reason (perhaps because there is fashion in database theory, just as there is fashion in clothes), it just isn't done.

You're probably wondering what the conditions of DK/NF are. Without getting into the details, DK/NF requires that all of the constraints on data values be logical implications of the definition of domains and keys. To the level of detail of this text, and to the level of detail experienced by 99 percent of all database practitioners, this can be restated as follows: Every determinant of a functional dependency must be a candidate key. This is exactly where we started.

You can broaden this statement a bit to include multivalued dependencies and say that every determinant of a functional or multivalued dependency must be a candidate key. The trouble with this statement is that as soon as one constrains a multivalued dependency in this way, it is transformed into a functional dependency. Our original statement is fine. It is like saying that good health comes to overweight people who lose weight until they are of an appropriate weight. As soon as they lose their excess weight, they are no longer overweight. Hence, good health comes to people who have appropriate weight.

So, as Paul Harvey says, now you know the rest of the story. Just ensure that every determinant of a functional dependency is a candidate key, and you can claim that your relations are fully normalized. You do not want to say they are in DK/NF until you learn more about it though, because someone might ask you what that means. However, for most practical purposes, your relations are in DK/NF as well.

---

[1]For more information on DK/NF, see David Kroenke, *Database Processing*, 9th edition (Upper Saddle River, NJ: Prentice Hall, 2004): 133–138.

FIGURE 5-4

Relational
Representation of a
Weak Entity:
(a) Example Weak
Entity, (b) Relation
Representing LINE-
ITEM with Improper
Key, and (c) LINE-
ITEM Relation with
Proper Key

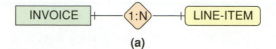

(a)

LINE-ITEM (<u>LineNumber</u>, Qty, ItemNumber, Description, Price, ExtPrice)

(b)

LINE-ITEM (<u>InvoiceNumber</u>, *<u>LineNumber</u>*, Qty, ItemNumber, Description, Price, ExtPrice)

(c)

Representing Weak Entities

This process works for all entity types, but weak entities sometimes require special treatment. Recall that a weak entity logically depends on another entity. If a weak entity is not ID-dependent, it can be represented using the techniques just described. The dependency needs to be recorded in the relational design so that no application will create a weak entity without its proper parent (the entity on which the weak entity depends). Moreover, a business rule needs to be implemented so that when the parent is deleted, the weak entity also is deleted. These rules are part of the relational design.

The situation is slightly different if a weak entity is also ID-dependent. In Figure 5-4(a), LINE-ITEM is an ID-dependent weak entity. It is weak because its logical existence depends on INVOICE, and it is ID-dependent because its identifier contains the identifier of INVOICE.

When creating a relation for an ID-dependent entity, we must ensure that the identifier of the parent and the identifier of the entity itself appear in the relation. For example, consider what would happen if we established a relation for LINE-ITEM without including the key of INVOICE. Such a relation is shown in Figure 5-4(b). What is the key of this relation? Because LINE-ITEM is ID-dependent, it does not have a complete key; in fact, this relation would likely have duplicate rows. (This would happen if two invoices had the same quantity of the same item on the same line.)

Thus, for an ID-dependent weak entity, it is necessary to add the key of the parent entity to the weak entity's relation, and this added attribute becomes part of the weak entity's key. In Figure 5-4(c), we have added InvoiceNumber, the key of INVOICE, to the attributes in LINE-ITEM. The key of LINE-ITEM is the composite (InvoiceNumber, LineNumber).

▶ REPRESENTING RELATIONSHIPS

So far, you have learned how to create a relational design for the entities in an E-R model. However, to convert a data model to a relational design, we also must represent the relationships.

The techniques used to represent E-R relationships depend on the maximum cardinality of the relationships. As you saw in the last chapter, three relationship possibilities exist: one to one, one to many, and many to many. A fourth possibility, many to one, is represented in the same way as one to many, so we need not consider it as separate case.[2] The following sections will consider each of these types of relationships in turn.

Representing One-to-One Relationships

The simplest form of binary relationship is a one-to-one (1:1) relationship, in which an entity of one type is related to at most one entity of another type. An example is shown in Figure 5-5. According to this diagram, an employee is assigned at most one automobile, and an auto is assigned to at most one employee.

---

[2]Another type of relationship exists among subtype entities, but we do not address them in this text. See David Kroenke, *Database Processing*, 9th edition, if you want to learn about subtypes and their representation.

FIGURE 5-5

Example of a 1:1 Relationship

EMPLOYEE —— 1:1 —— AUTO

Representing a 1:1 relationship with the relational model is straightforward. First, each entity is represented with a relation as just described, and then the key of one of the relations is placed in the other as a foreign key. In Figure 5-6(a), the key of AUTO is stored in EMPLOYEE as a foreign key, and in Figure 5-6(b), the key of EMPLOYEE is stored in AUTO as a foreign key.

In general, for a 1:1 relationship, the key of either table can be placed as a foreign key in the other table. To verify that this is so, consider both cases in Figure 5-6. Suppose that for the design in Figure 5-6(a), we have an employee and want the auto assigned to that employee. To get the employee data, we use EmployeeNumber to obtain the employee's row in EMPLOYEE. From this row, we obtain the LicenseNumber of the auto assigned to that employee. We then use this number to look up the auto data in AUTO.

Now consider the other direction. Assume that we have an auto and want to know which employee is assigned to that auto. Using the design in Figure 5-6(a), we access the EMPLOYEE table and look up the row that has the given license number. The data about the employee who has been assigned that auto appear in that row.

We take similar actions to travel in either direction for the alternative design in which the foreign key of EmployeeNumber is placed in AUTO (Figure 5-6(b)). Using this design, to go from EMPLOYEE to AUTO, we go directly to the AUTO relation and look up the row in AUTO that has the given employee's number as its value of EmployeeNumber. To travel from AUTO to EMPLOYEE, we look up the row in AUTO having a given LicenseNumber. From this row, we extract the EmployeeNumber and use it to access the employee data in EMPLOYEE.

In this situation, we are using the term *look up* to mean "to find a row given a value of one of its columns." Another way to view this is in terms of joins. For the relations in Figure 5-6(a), we can form the following join.

```
SELECT       *
FROM         EMPLOYEE, AUTO
WHERE        EMPLOYEE.LicenseNumber = AUTO.LicenseNumber;
```

Because the relationship is 1:1, the result of this join will have a single row for a given employee/auto combination. The row will have all columns from both tables.

FIGURE 5-6

Alternatives for Representing 1:1 Relationships: (a) Placing the Key of AUTO in EMPLOYEE and (b) Placing the Key of EMPLOYEE in AUTO

EMPLOYEE (<u>EmployeeNumber</u>, EmployeeName, Phone, . . . *LicenseNumber*)

AUTO (<u>LicenseNumber</u>, SerialNumber, Color, Make, Model, . . .)

Referential integrity constraint:
    LicenseNumber in EMPLOYEE must exist in LicenseNumber in AUTO
(a)

EMPLOYEE (<u>EmployeeNumber</u>, EmployeeName, Phone, . . .)

AUTO (<u>LicenseNumber</u>, SerialNumber, Color, Make, Model, . . . *EmployeeNumber*)

Referential integrity constraint:
    EmployeeNumber in AUTO must exist in EmployeeNumber in EMPLOYEE
(b)

For the relations in Figure 5-6(b), we can join the two tables on EmployeeNumber as follows.

```
SELECT        *
FROM          EMPLOYEE, AUTO
WHERE         EMPLOYEE.EmployeeNumber = AUTO.EmployeeNumber;
```

Again, one row will be found for each employee/auto combination. In both of these joins, neither unassigned employees nor unassigned autos will appear.

Although the two designs in Figure 5-6 are equivalent in concept, they may differ in performance. For instance, if a query in one direction is more common than a query in the other, we might prefer one design to the other. Also, depending on underlying structures, if an index for EmployeeNumber is in both tables but no index on LicenseNumber is in either table, then the first design is better. In addition, considering the join operation, if one table is much larger than the other, then one of these joins might be faster to perform than the other.

Questionable One-to-One Relationships

Figure 5-7 shows another 1:1 relationship—one in which each EMPLOYEE has a JOB-EVALUATION and each JOB-EVALUATION corresponds to a particular EMPLOYEE. Observe from the hash marks that the relationship is mandatory in both directions. When a relationship is 1:1 and mandatory in both directions, it is likely that the records are describing different aspects of the same entity, especially if, as is the case in Figure 5-7, both entities have the same key. When this occurs, the records generally should be combined into one relation. Learn to regard such 1:1 mandatory relationships with suspicion.

However, the separation of a single entity into two relations can sometimes be justified. One justification concerns performance. For example, suppose the JOB-EVALUATION data are lengthy and are used far less frequently than are the other employee data. In these circumstances, it might be appropriate to store job evaluations in a separate table so that the more common requests for nonevaluation employee data can be processed faster.

Better security is the second justification for separating a single logical entity into two. If the DBMS does not support security at the column level, the JOB-EVALUATION data might need to be separated in order to prevent unauthorized users from accessing them. As an alternative, it might be desirable to place JOB-EVALUATION in a separate table so that the table can be placed on disk media that are accessible only by certain users.

Do not conclude from this discussion that all 1:1 relationships are questionable; only those that appear to describe different aspects of the same entity are suspect. For example, the 1:1 mandatory relationship between EMPLOYEE and AUTO is suitable because each relation describes a logically different thing.

Representing One-to-Many Relationships

The second type of binary relationship, known as one to many (1:N), is a relationship in which an entity of one type can be related to many entities of another type. Figure 5-8 is an E-R diagram of a one-to-many relationship between professors and students. In this relationship, PROFESSOR is related to the many STUDENTs that the professor advises. As stated in Chapter 4, the oval means that the relationship between PROFESSOR

FIGURE 5-7

Suspect 1:1
Relationship

FIGURE 5-8

Examples of One-to-
Many Relationships:
(a) Optional-to-
Mandatory 1:N
Relationship,
(b) Optional-to-
Optional 1:N
Relationship, and
(c) 1:N Relationship
with Weak Entity

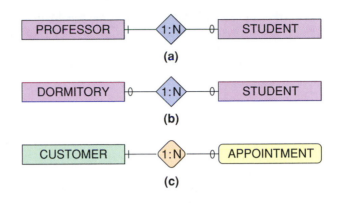

and STUDENT is optional; that is, a professor need not have any advisees. The bar across the line at the other end means that a STUDENT row must correspond to a PROFESSOR row.

The terms *parent* and *child* are sometimes applied to relations in 1:N relationships. The parent relation is on the "one" side of the relationship, and the child relation is on the "many" side. In Figure 5-8(a), PROFESSOR is the parent entity, and STUDENT is the child entity.

Figure 5-8 shows two other 1:N relationships. In Figure 5-8(b), a DORMITORY entity corresponds to many STUDENT entities, but a STUDENT entity corresponds to only one DORMITORY. Furthermore, a dormitory does not have to have any students assigned to it, nor is a student required to live in a dormitory.

In Figure 5-8(c), a CUSTOMER is related to many APPOINTMENT entities, but a particular APPOINTMENT corresponds to only one CUSTOMER. Moreover, a CUSTOMER might or might not have an APPOINTMENT, but every APPOINTMENT must correspond to a CUSTOMER.

Representing 1:N relationships is simple and straightforward. First, each entity is represented by a relation as described, and then the key of the relation representing the parent entity is placed in the relation representing the child entity. Thus, to represent the relationship in Figure 5-8(a), we place the key of PROFESSOR, ProfessorName, in the STUDENT relation as shown in the **data structure diagram** in Figure 5-9. In this diagram, a crow's foot is used to indicate the "many" side of the relationship. The line between PROFESSOR and STUDENT thus means that one PROFESSOR row can be related to many STUDENT rows. The hash mark and oval represent required and optional rows, respectively.

Notice that with ProfessorName stored as a foreign key in STUDENT, we can process the relationship in both directions. Given a StudentNumber, we can look up the appropriate row in STUDENT and get the name of the student's adviser from the row data. To obtain the rest of the PROFESSOR data, we use the professor name obtained from STUDENT to look up the appropriate row in PROFESSOR. To determine all of

FIGURE 5-9

Relational
Representation of
PROFESSOR and
STUDENT Entities in
Figure 5-8(a)

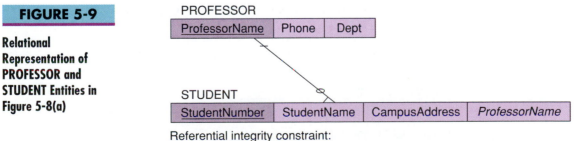

the students advised by a particular faculty member, we look up all rows in STUDENT having the professor's name as a value for ProfessorName. Student data are then taken from those rows.

In terms of joins, we can obtain the professor and student in one table with the following.

SELECT   *

FROM   PROFESSOR, STUDENT

WHERE   PROFESSOR.ProfessorName = STUDENT.ProfessorName;

Contrast this 1:N relationship design strategy with that for 1:1 relationships. In both cases, we store the key of one relation as a foreign key in the second relation. However, in a 1:1 relationship, we can place the key of either relation in the other. In a 1:N relationship though, the key of the parent relation *must* be placed in the child relation.

To understand this better, notice what would happen if we tried to put the key of the child into the parent relation (placing StudentNumber in PROFESSOR). Because attributes in a relation can have only a single value, each PROFESSOR record has room for only one student. Consequently, such a structure cannot be used to represent the many side of the 1:N relationship. Hence, to represent a 1:N relationship, we must place the key of the parent relation in the child relation.

Figure 5-10 shows the representation of the CUSTOMER and APPOINTMENT entities. We represent each entity with a relation. APPOINTMENT is an ID-dependent weak entity, so it has a composite key consisting of the key of the entity on which it depends plus at least one attribute from itself. Here the key is (CustomerNumber, Date, Time). To represent the 1:N relationship, we normally would add the key of the parent to the child. However, in this case the key of the parent (CustomerNumber) is already part of the child, so we do not need to add it.

Representing Many-to-Many Relationships

The third and final type of binary relationship is many to many (M:N), in which an entity of one type corresponds to many entities of the second type, and an entity of the second type corresponds to many entities of the first type.

Figure 5-11(a) presents an E-R diagram of the many-to-many relationship between students and classes. A STUDENT entity can correspond to many CLASS entities, and a CLASS entity can correspond to many STUDENT entities. Notice that both participants in the relationship are optional: A student does not need to be enrolled in a class, and a class does not need to have any students. Figure 5-11(b) gives sample data.

Many-to-many relationships cannot be represented directly by relations in the same way that one-to-one and one-to-many relationships are. To understand why this is so, try using the same strategy as for 1:1 and 1:N relationships—placing the key of one relation

FIGURE 5-10

Relational
Representation of the
Weak Entity in
Figure 5-8(c)

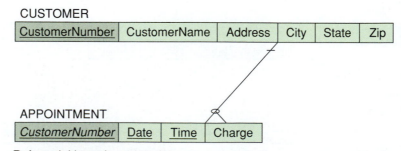

Referential integrity constraint:
    CustomerNumber in APPOINTMENT must exist in CustomerNumber in
    CUSTOMER

FIGURE 5-11

Example of an M:N Relationship: (a) E-R Diagram of STUDENT to CLASS Relationship, and (b) Sample Data for STUDENT to CLASS Relationship

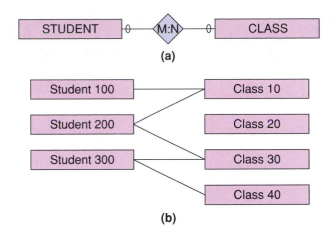

(a)

(b)

as a foreign key in the other relation. First, define a relation for each of the entities; call them STUDENT and CLASS. Now try to put the key of STUDENT (say, StudentNumber) in CLASS. Because multiple values are not allowed in the cells of a relation, we have room for only one StudentNumber, so we have no place to record the StudentNumber of the second and subsequent students.

A similar problem will occur if we try to put the key of CLASS (say, ClassNumber) in STUDENT. We can readily store the identifier of the first class in which a student is enrolled, but we have no place to store the identifier of additional classes.

Figure 5-12 shows another (but incorrect) strategy. In this case, we have stored a row in the CLASS relation for each STUDENT enrolled in one class, so we have two records for Class 10 and two for Class 30. The problem with this scheme is that we duplicate the class data and thus create modification anomalies. Many rows will need to be changed if, say, the schedule for Class 10 is modified. Also, consider the insertion and deletion anomalies: How can we schedule a new class until a student has enrolled? In addition, what will happen if Student 300 drops out of Class 40? This strategy is unworkable.

The solution to this problem is to create a third relation that represents the relationship itself. Relation STU-CLASS has been defined in Figure 5-13(a). An instance of this relation is shown in Figure 5-13(b). Such relations are called **intersection relations** because each row documents the intersection of a particular student with a particular class. Notice in Figure 5-13(b) that the intersection relation has one row for each line between STUDENT and CLASS in Figure 5-11(b).

The data structure diagrams for the STUDENT-CLASS relationship appear in Figure 5-14. The relationship from CLASS to STU-CLASS is 1:N, and the relationship

FIGURE 5-12

Incorrect Representation of an M:N Relationship

SID	Other STUDENT Data
100	. . .
200	. . .
300	. . .

STUDENT

ClassNumber	ClassTime	Other CLASS Data	SID
10	10:00 MWF	. . .	100
10	10:00 MWF	. . .	200
30	3:00 TH	. . .	200
30	3:00 TH	. . .	300
40	8:00 MWF	. . .	300

CLASS

STUDENT (<u>StudentNumber</u>, StudentName)

CLASS (<u>ClassNumber</u>, ClassName)

STU-CLASS (<u>*StudentNumber*</u>, <u>*ClassNumber*</u>)

Referential integrity constraints:
  ClassNumber in STU-CLASS must exist in ClassNumber in CLASS
  StudentNumber in STU-CLASS must exist in StudentNumber in STUDENT

(a)

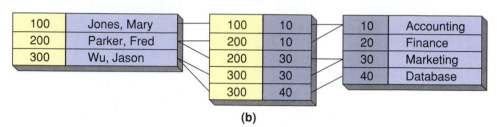

(b)

from STUDENT to STU-CLASS is also 1:N. In essence, we have decomposed the M:N relationship into two 1:N relationships. The key of STU-CLASS is the combination of the keys of both of its parents, (StudentNumber, ClassNumber). The key for an intersection relation is always the combination of parent keys. Also, note that the parent relations are both required. A parent now must exist for each key value in the intersection relation.

We can obtain data about students and classes using the following SQL statement.

```
SELECT      *

FROM        STUDENT, CLASS, STU-CLASS

WHERE       STUDENT.StudentNumber = STU-CLASS.StudentNumber

  AND       STU-CLASS.ClassNumber = CLASS.ClassNumber;
```

The result of this SQL statement is a table with all columns for a student and the classes the student takes. The student data will be repeated in the table for as many classes as the student takes, and the class data will be repeated in the relation for as many students as are taking the class.

Representing Recursive Relationships

A recursive relationship is a relationship among entities of the same class. Recursive relationships are not fundamentally different from other relationships and can be represented using the same techniques. As with nonrecursive relationships, three types of recursive relationships are possible: 1:1, 1:N, and N:M. Figure 5-15 shows an example of each.

Consider first the SPONSOR relationship in Figure 5-15(a). As with a regular 1:1 relationship, one person can sponsor another person, and each person is sponsored by no more than one person. Figure 5-16(a) shows sample data for this relationship.

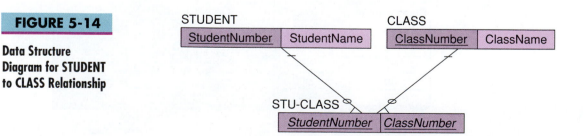

FIGURE 5-15

Examples of Recursive Relationships: (a) 1:1 Recursive Relationship, (b) 1:N Recursive Relationship, and (c) N:M Recursive Relationship

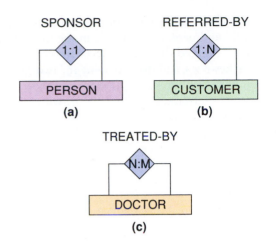

To represent 1:1 recursive relationships, we take an approach nearly identical to that for regular 1:1 relationships; that is, we can place the key of the person being sponsored in the row of the sponsor, or we can place the key of the sponsor in the row of the person being sponsored. Figure 5-16(b) shows the first alternative, and Figure 5-16(c) shows the second. Both work.

FIGURE 5-16

Example of a 1:1 Recursive Relationship: (a) Sample Data for 1:1 Recursive Relationship, (b) First Alternative for Representing a 1:1 Recursive Relationship, and (c) Second Alternative for Representing a 1:1 Recursive Relationship

Person

Jones
Smith
Parks
Myrtle
Pines

(a)

PERSON1 Relation

Person	PersonSponsored
Jones	Smith
Smith	Parks
Parks	null
Myrtle	Pines
Pines	null

Referential integrity constraint:
PersonSponsored in PERSON1
must exist in Person in PERSON1

(b)

PERSON2 Relation

Person	PersonSponsoredBy
Jones	null
Smith	Jones
Parks	Smith
Myrtle	null
Pines	Myrtle

Referential integrity constraint:
PersonSponsoredBy PERSON2
must exist in Person in PERSON2

(c)

This technique is identical to that for nonrecursive 1:1 relationships, except that the child and parent rows reside in the same relation. You can think of the process as follows: Pretend that the relationship is between two different relations. Determine where the key goes, and then combine the two relations into a single one.

We also can use SQL joins to process recursive relationships; to do so, however, we need to introduce additional SQL syntax. In the FROM clause, it is possible to assign a synonym for a table name. For example, the expression FROM CUSTOMER A assigns the synonym A to the table CUSTOMER. Using this syntax, we can create a join on a recursive relationship for the design in Figure 5-16(b) as follows.

```
SELECT      *
FROM        PERSON1 A, PERSON1 B
WHERE       A.Person = B.PersonSponsored;
```

The result will be a table with one row for each person. It will have all of the columns of the person and also of the person they sponsor.

Similarly, to create a join of the recursive relationship shown in Figure 5-16(c), we would use:

```
SELECT      *
FROM        PERSON2 A, PERSON2 B
WHERE       A.Person = B.PersonSponsoredBy;
```

The result will be a table with a row for each person. It will have all of the columns of the person and also of the sponsoring person.

Now consider the 1:N recursive relationship REFERRED-BY in Figure 5-15(b). This is a 1:N relationship, as shown in the sample data in Figure 5-17(a). When these data are placed in a relation, one row represents the referrer, and the other rows represent

<table>
<tr><td>**FIGURE 5-17**</td></tr>
</table>

Example of a 1:N Recursive Relationship: (a) Sample Data for the REFERRED-BY Relationship, and (b) Representing a 1:N Recursive Relationship by Means of a Relation

Customer Number	Referred These Customers
100	200, 400
300	500
400	600, 700

(a)

CUSTOMER Relation

CustomerNumber	CustomerData	ReferredBy
100	. . .	null
200	. . .	100
300	. . .	null
400	. . .	100
500	. . .	300
600	. . .	400
700	. . .	400

Referential integrity constraint:
ReferredBy in CUSTOMER must exist in
CustomerNumber in CUSTOMER

(b)

those who have been referred. The referrer row takes the role of the parent, and the referred rows take the role of the child. As with all 1:N relationships, we place the key of the parent in the child. In Figure 5-17(b), we place the CustomerNumber of the referrer in all the rows for people who have been referred.

We can join the 1:N recursive relationship with:

SELECT   *

FROM   CUSTOMER A, CUSTOMER B

WHERE   A.CustomerNumber = B.ReferredBy;

The result will be a row for each customer that is joined to the data for the customer who referred the person.

Now consider M:N recursive relationships. The TREATED-BY relationship in Figure 5-15(c) represents a situation in which doctors give treatments to each other. Sample data are shown in Figure 5-18(a). As with other M:N relationships, we must create an intersection table that shows pairs of related rows. The name of the doctor in the first column is the one who provided the treatment, and the name of the doctor in the

FIGURE 5-18

Example of an M:N Recursive Relationship: (a) Sample Data for the TREATED-BY Relationship, and (b) Representing an M:N Recursive Relationship by Means of Relations

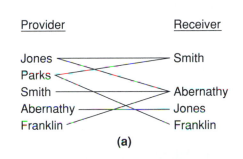

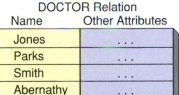

Referential integrity constraints:
    Physician in TREATMENT-INTERSECTION
    must exist in Name in DOCTOR

    Patient in TREATMENT-INTERSECTION
    must exist in Name in DOCTOR

(b)

second column is the one who received the treatment. This structure is shown in Figure 5-18(b). We can join the M:N relationship with:

```
SELECT    *
FROM      DOCTOR A, TREATMENT-INTERSECTION, DOCTOR B
WHERE     A.Name = TREATMENT-INTERSECTION.Physician
AND       TREATMENT-INTERSECTION.Patient = B.Name;
```

The result of this will be a table having rows of doctor (as treatment provider) joined to doctor (as patient). The doctor data will be repeated once for every patient treated and once for every time the doctor was treated.

Recursive relationships are thus represented in the same way as are other relationships; however, the rows of the tables can take two different roles. Some are parent rows, and others are child rows. If a key is supposed to be a parent key and the row has no parent, its value will be null. If a key is supposed to be a child key and the row has no child, its value will be null.

▶ DATABASE DESIGN AT HEATHER SWEENEY DESIGNS

Figure 5-19 shows the final E-R diagram for Heather Sweeney Designs, the example database discussed in Chapter 4. To transform this E-R diagram into a relational design, we follow the process described in the last sections. First, represent each entity with a relation of its own.

SEMINAR (<u>SeminarID</u>, Date, Time, Location, Title)

CUSTOMER (Name, Phone, <u>EmailAddress</u>, Street, City, State, Zip)

PRODUCT (<u>ProductNumber</u>, Description, UnitPrice, QuantityOnHand)

CONTACT (ContactNumber, ContactType, <u>Date</u>)

INVOICE (<u>InvoiceNo</u>, Date, PaymentType, SubTotal, Tax, Total)

LINE-ITEM (<u>LineNumber</u>, Quantity, UnitPrice, Total)

Next, apply the normalization process to each of these tables. Do any of them have a functional dependency that does not involve the primary key? From what we know so far, the only such functional dependency is Zip → (City, State). However, for the reasons explained before, we will choose not to place Zip into its own table.

One possible functional dependency concerns locations, dates, times, or titles. If, for example, Heather offers seminars only at certain times in some locations, or if she only gives certain seminar titles in some locations, then a functional dependency would exist with Location as its determinant. It would be important for the design team to check this out, but for now assume that no such dependency exists.

Weak Entities

The next step is to examine the weak entities. There are two, and they both are ID-dependent. CONTACT is a weak entity, and its identifier depends in part on the identifier of CUSTOMER. Thus, we will place the key of CUSTOMER, which is EmailAddress, into CONTACT. Similarly, LINE-ITEM is a weak entity, and its identifier depends on

---

FIGURE 5-19

Finished Data Model for Heather Sweeney Designs

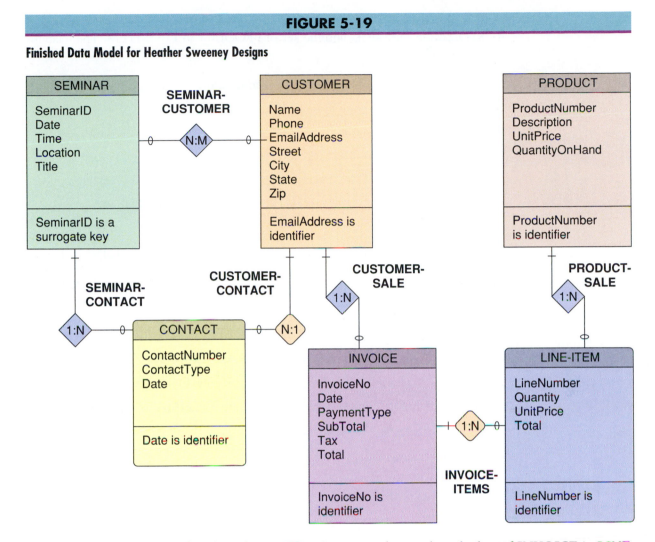

the identifier of INVOICE. Consequently, we place the key of INVOICE in LINE-ITEM. The relations now appear as follows.

SEMINAR (SeminarID, Date, Time, Location, Title)

CUSTOMER (Name, Phone, EmailAddress, Street, City, State, Zip)

PRODUCT (ProductNumber, Description, UnitPrice, QuantityOnHand)

CONTACT (ContactNumber, ContactType, Date, *EmailAddress*)

INVOICE (InvoiceNo, Date, PaymentType, SubTotal, Tax, Total)

LINE-ITEM (LineNumber, Quantity, UnitPrice, Total, *InvoiceNo*)

Note that CONTACT.EmailAddress and LINE-ITEM.InvoiceNo are underlined and italicized because they are part of a primary key and also a foreign key.

Relationships

Now, considering the relationships in this diagram, 1:N relationships exist between SEMINAR and CONTACT, between CUSTOMER and INVOICE, and between PRODUCT and LINE-ITEM. For each of these, we place the key of the parent in the child as a foreign key. Thus, we will place the key of SEMINAR in CONACT, the key of CUSTOMER in INVOICE, and the key of PRODUCT in LINE-ITEM. The relations are now as follows.

SEMINAR (<u>SeminarID</u>, Date, Time, Location, Title)

CUSTOMER (Name, Phone, <u>EmailAddress</u>, Street, City, State, Zip)

PRODUCT (<u>ProductNumber</u>, Description, UnitPrice, QuantityOnHand)

CONTACT (ContactNumber, ContactType, <u>Date</u>, <u>EmailAddress</u>, *SeminarID*)

INVOICE (<u>InvoiceNo</u>, Date, PaymentType, SubTotal, Tax, Total, *EmailAddress*)

LINE-ITEM (<u>LineNumber</u>, Quantity, UnitPrice, Total, <u>InvoiceNo</u>, *ProductNumber*)

Finally, one N:M relationship exists between SEMINAR and CUSTOMER. To represent it, we create an intersection table, which we will name SEMINAR-CUST. As with all intersection tables, its columns are the keys of the two tables involved in the N:M relationship. The final set of tables is:

SEMINAR (<u>SeminarID</u>, Date, Time, Location, Title)

CUSTOMER (Name, Phone, <u>EmailAddress</u>, Street, City, State, Zip)

PRODUCT (<u>ProductNumber</u>, Description, UnitPrice, QuantityOnHand)

CONTACT (ContactNumber, ContactType, <u>Date</u>, <u>EmailAddress</u>, *SeminarID*)

INVOICE (<u>InvoiceNo</u>, Date, PaymentType, SubTotal, Tax, Total, *EmailAddress*)

LINE-ITEM (<u>LineNumber</u>, Quantity, UnitPrice, Total, <u>InvoiceNo</u>, *ProductNumber*)

SEMINAR-CUST (*<u>SeminarID</u>*, *<u>EmailAddress</u>*)

Now, to express the minimum cardinalities of children back to their parents, we need to decide whether or not foreign keys are required. In Figure 5-19, we see that an INVOICE is required to have a CUSTOMER, and that LINE-ITEM is required to have a PRODUCT. Thus, we will make INVOICE.EmailAddress and LINE-ITEM.ProductNumber required. CONTACT.SeminarID will not be required because a contact is not required to refer to a seminar. The final design is shown in the data structure diagram in Figure 5-20. In this figure, nonkey columns are omitted and shown with an ellipsis.

Enforcing Referential Integrity

Figure 5-21 summarizes relationship enforcement for Heather Sweeney Designs. SeminarID is a surrogate key, so no cascading update behavior will be necessary for any of the relationships that it carries. Similarly, InvoiceNo in INVOICE is an unchanging value, so its relationships do not need cascading updates, either. However, updates of EmailAddress and ProductNumber do need to cascade through their relationships.

With regard to cascading deletions, rows in the intersection table require a SEMINAR and a CUSTOMER parent. Therefore, when a user attempts to cancel a seminar or to remove a customer record, the deletion must either cascade or be prohibited. The development team must discuss this issue with Heather and her employees and determine whether they want users to be able to remove seminars that have customers enrolled or to remove customers that have enrolled in a seminar. As shown in Figure 5-21, the team decided that removing such seminar or customer records would be permitted; hence, both of these relationships have cascading deletions.

FIGURE 5-20

Data Structure Diagram for Heather Sweeney Designs

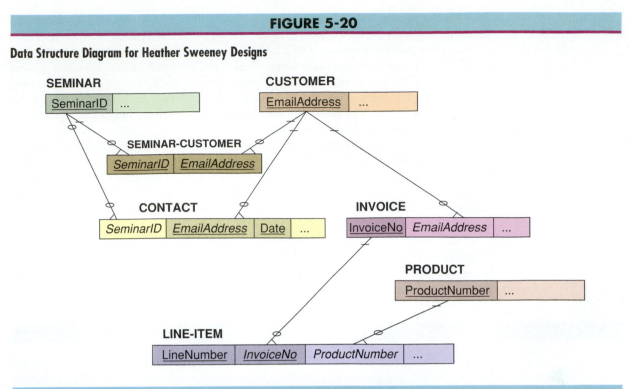

FIGURE 5-21

Summary of Relationship Enforcement for Heather Sweeney Designs

Relationship	Referential Integrity Constraint	Cascading Behavior
SEMINAR to SEMINAR-CUST	SeminarID in SEMINAR-CUST must be in SeminarID in SEMINAR	• Cascade update unnecessary • Cascade delete
CUSTOMER to SEMINAR-CUST	EmailAddress in SEMINAR-CUST must be in EmailAddress in CUSTOMER	• Cascade update of EmailAddress • Cascade delete
SEMINAR to CONTACT	SeminarID in CONTACT must be in SeminarID in SEMINAR	• Cascade update unnecessary • Do not cascade delete
CUSTOMER to CONTACT	EmailAddress in CONTACT must be in EmailAddress in CUSTOMER	• Cascade update of EmailAddress • Cascade delete
CUSTOMER to INVOICE	EmailAddress in INVOICE must be in EmailAddress in CUSTOMER	• Cascade update of EmailAddress • Do not cascade delete
INVOICE to LINE-ITEM	InvoiceNo in LINE-ITEM must be IN InvoiceNo in INVOICE	• Cascade update unnecessary • Cascade delete
PRODUCT to LINE-ITEM	ProductNumber in LINE-ITEM must be in ProductNumber in PRODUCT	• Cascade update of ProductNumer • Do not cascade delete

Other decisions reached by the design team are shown in this figure. The deletion of a seminar will not cascade to contact, so any seminar that has a contact record cannot be deleted. However, the deletion of a CUSTOMER row will trigger a cascading deletion of CONTACT. These decisions make sense. The cancellation of a seminar should not cause the deletion of the record of a customer contact. In fact, because a contact has occurred with a customer about a seminar, it is important for Heather to keep a record of what the seminar was. On the other hand, if a customer record is deleted, all of the contacts for the customer should be deleted, as well.

As shown in Figure 5-21, an attempt to delete a CUSTOMER with one or more ORDERs will fail because the relationship is required. The delete will not cascade, but the deletion of an INVOICE will cause the deletion of related LINE-ITEMs. Finally, an attempt to delete a PRODUCT that is related to one or more LINE-ITEMs will fail; cascading the deletion here would cause LINE-ITEMs to disappear out of ORDERs, a situation that cannot be allowed.

At this point, the design of the database for Heather Sweeney is complete enough to create tables, columns, relationships, and referential integrity constraints using a DBMS. Before going on, the team would need to document any additional business rules to be enforced by application programs, stored procedures, or triggers (defined in the next chapter).

SUMMARY

To transform an E-R data model into a relational database design, a relation is created for each entity. The attributes of the entity become the columns of the relation, and the identifier of the entity becomes the primary key of the relation. The normalization process is then applied to each relation, and additional relations are created if necessary. In some cases, relations are denormalized. If so, the relation will have insertion, update, and deletion problems. Denormalization makes sense if the benefit of not normalizing needs to be weighed against such modification problems.

Weak entities are represented by a relation. ID-dependent entities must include the key columns of the relations upon which they depend, as well as of the identifiers of the entities themselves. Non-ID-dependent entities must have their existence dependence recorded as business rules.

The E-R model has three types of binary relationships: 1:1, 1:N, and N:M. To represent a 1:1 relationship, we place the key of one relation into the other relation. One-to-one relationships sometimes indicate that two relations have been defined on the same entity and so should be combined into one relation. To represent a 1:N relationship, we place the key of the parent in the child. Finally, to represent an M:N relationship, we create an intersection relation that contains the keys of the other two relations.

Recursive relationships are relationships in which the participants in the relationship arise from the same entity class. The three types are 1:1, 1:N, and N:M. The types are represented in the same way as are nonrecursive relationships. For 1:1 and 1:N relationships, we add a foreign key to the relation that represents the entity. For an N:M recursion, we create an intersection table that represents the M:N relationship.

REVIEW QUESTIONS

5.1 Explain how entities are transformed into relations.

5.2 Why is it necessary to apply the normalization process to the relations created according to your answer to question 5.1?

5.3 What is denormalization?

5.4 When is denormalization justified?

5.5 Explain the problems that unnormalized relations have for insert, update, and delete actions.

5.6 Explain how the representation of weak entities differs from the representation of strong entities.

5.7 List the three types of binary relationships and give an example of each. Do not use the examples given in this text.

5.8 Define the term *foreign key* and give an example.

5.9 Show two different ways to represent the 1:1 relationship in your answer to question 5.7. Use data structure diagrams.

5.10 For your answers to question 5.9, describe a method for obtaining data about one of the entities, given the key of the other. Describe a method for obtaining data about the second entity, given the key of the first. Describe methods for both of your alternatives in question 5.9.

5.11 Code SQL statements to create a join having all data about both relations from your work for question 5.9.

5.12 Why are some 1:1 relationships considered suspicious? Under what conditions should relations in a 1:1 relationship be combined into one relation?

5.13 Define the terms *parent* and *child* and give an example of each.

5.14 Show how to represent the 1:N relationship in your answer to question 5.7. Use a data structure diagram.

5.15 For your answer to question 5.14, describe a method for obtaining data for all of the children, given the key of the parent. Describe a method for obtaining data for the parent, given a key of the child.

5.16 For your answer to question 5.14, code a SQL statement that creates a relation having all data from both tables.

5.17 For a 1:N relationship, explain why you must place the key of the parent in the child, rather than placing the key of the child in the parent.

5.18 Give examples of binary 1:N relationships, other than those in this text, for an optional-to-optional relationship, an optional-to-mandatory relationship, a mandatory-to-optional relationship, and a mandatory-to-mandatory relationship. Illustrate your answer using data structure diagrams.

5.19 Show how to represent the N:M relationship in your answer to question 5.7. Use a data structure diagram.

5.20 For your answer to question 5.19, describe a method for obtaining the children for one entity, given the key of the other. Also, describe a method for obtaining the children for the second entity, given the key of the first.

5.21 For your answer to question 5.19, code a SQL statement that creates a relation having all data from all tables.

5.22 Why is it not possible to represent N:M relationships with the same strategy used to represent 1:N relationships?

5.23 Explain the meaning of the term *intersection relation*.

5.24 Define three types of recursive binary relationships and give an example of each.

5.25 Show how to represent the 1:1 recursive relationship in your answer to question 5.24. How does this differ from the representation of 1:1 nonrecursive relationships?

5.26 Code a SQL statement that creates a table with all columns from the parent and child tables in your answer to question 5.25.

5.27 Show how to represent the 1:N recursive relationship in your answer to question 5.24. How does this differ from the representation of 1:N nonrecursive relationships?

5.28 Code a SQL statement that creates a table with all columns from the parent and child tables in your answer to question 5.27.

5.29 Show how to represent the M:N recursive relationship in your answer to question 5.24. How does this differ from the representation of M:N nonrecursive relationships?

5.30 Code a SQL statement that creates a table with all columns from the parent and child tables in your answer to question 5.29. Code a SQL statement using a left outer join that creates a table with all columns from the parent and child tables. Explain the difference between these two SQL statements.

EXERCISES

5.31 Consider the following relation that holds data about employee assignments:

ASSIGN (<u>EmployeeNumber</u>, <u>ProjectNumber</u>, ProjectName, HoursWorked)

Assume that ProjectNumber determines ProjectName, and explain why this relation is not normalized. Demonstrate an insertion anomaly, a modification anomaly, and a deletion anomaly. Apply the normalization process to this relation. State the referential integrity constraint.

5.32 Consider the following relation that holds data about employee assignments:

ASSIGN (<u>EmployeeNumber</u>, ProjectNumber, ProjectName, HoursWorked)

Assume that ProjectNumber determines ProjectName, and explain why this relation is not normalized. Demonstrate an insertion anomaly, a modification anomaly, and a deletion anomaly. Apply the normalization process to this relation. State the referential integrity constraint.

5.33 Explain the difference between the two ASSIGN relations in questions 5.31 and 5.32. Under what circumstances is the relation in question 5.31 more correct? Under what circumstances is the relation in question 5.32 more correct?

5.34 Create a relational design for the data model you developed for question 4.29.

5.35 Create a relational design for the data model you developed for question 4.30.

5.36 Create a relational design for the data model you developed for question 4.31.

5.37 Create a relational design for the data model you developed for question 4.32.

5.38 Create a relational design for the data model you developed for question 4.33.

GARDEN GLORY PROJECT QUESTIONS

Use the data model you constructed for Garden Glory at the end of Chapter 4 and convert that data model to a relational design. (Alternatively, your instructor may provide a data model for you to use.) Document your design as follows.

A. Specify tables, primary keys, and foreign keys.

B. Describe how you have represented weak entities if any exist.

C. Create a data structure diagram similar to that in Figure 5-20.

D. Document relationship enforcement; use Figure 5-21 as a guide.

E. Document any business rules that you think might be important.

F. Describe how you would validate that your design is a good representation of the data model upon which it is based.

JAMES RIVER JEWELRY PROJECT QUESTIONS

Use the data model you constructed for James River at the end of Chapter 4 and convert that data model to a relational design (alternatively, your instructor may provide a data model for you to use). Document your design as follows.

A. Specify tables, primary keys, and foreign keys.

B. Describe how you have represented weak entities if any exist.

C. Create a data structure diagram similar to that in Figure 5-20.

D. Document relationship enforcement; use Figure 5-21 as a guide.

E. Document any business rules that you think may be important.

F. Describe how you would validate that your design is a good representation of the data model upon which it is based.

MID-WESTERN UNIVERSITY CHEMISTRY DEPARTMENT PROJECT QUESTIONS

Use the data model you constructed for the chemistry department at the end of Chapter 4, and convert that data model to a relational design. (Alternatively, your instructor may provide a data model for you to use.) Document your design as follows.

A. Specify tables, primary keys, and foreign keys.

B. Describe how you have represented weak entities if any exist.

C. Create a data structure diagram similar to that in Figure 5-20.

D. Document relationship enforcement; use Figure 5-21 as a guide.

E. Document any business rules that you think might be important.

F. Describe how you would validate that your design is a good representation of the data model upon which it is based.

Database Administration

> Understand the need for and importance of database administration

> Learn different ways of processing a database

> Understand the need for concurrency control, security, and backup and recovery

> Learn typical problems that can occur when multiple users process a database concurrently

> Understand the use of locking and the problem of deadlock

> Learn the difference between optimistic and pessimistic locking

> Know the meaning of *ACID transaction*

> Learn the four 1992 ANSI standard isolation levels

> Understand the need for security and specific tasks for improving database security

> Know the difference between recovery via reprocessing and recovery via rollback/rollforward

> Understand the nature of the tasks required for recovery using rollback/rollforward

> Know basic administrative and managerial DBA functions

This chapter describes the major tasks of an important business function called **database administration (DBA)**. This function involves managing a database so that its value to an organization is maximized.

Usually, this means balancing the conflicting goals of protecting the database and maximizing its availability and benefit to users.

All databases need database administration, although the tasks to be accomplished vary with the size and complexity of the database and its applications. For example, for a personal database, individuals follow simple procedures for backing up their data, and they keep minimal records for documentation. In this case, the person who uses the database also performs the DBA functions, even though the user is probably unaware of that term.

For multiuser database applications, database administration becomes more important and more difficult at the same time. Consequently, it generally receives formal recognition. One or two people are given this function on a part-time basis for some applications, but for large Internet or intranet databases, database administration responsibilities are often too time-consuming and too varied to be handled even by a single full-time person.

Supporting a database with hundreds or thousands of users requires considerable time, as well as technical knowledge and managerial and diplomatic skills. Such databases normally are supported by an office of database administration. The manager of the office is often known as the database administrator; the acronym *DBA* refers in this case to either the office or the manager.

If the only databases you have seen are small, single-user databases created in Access or some other desktop DBMS, it might be difficult for you to understand the need for database administration. Therefore, we will begin by surveying the database application-processing environment. Then we will describe three important database administration functions: concurrency control, security, and backup and recovery. After that, we will summarize the need for configuration change management.

▶ THE DATABASE PROCESSING ENVIRONMENT

Databases vary considerably in size and scope, from single-user databases to large, interorganizational databases such as an airline reservation system. As shown in Figure 6-1, they also vary in the way they are processed. Some databases have only a few forms and reports. Others are processed by applications using Internet technology such as **Active Server Pages (ASPs)** and **Java Server Pages (JSPs)**. Still others are processed by ancient COBOL application programs (for all their ugliness, may we all deliver that much value over the course of our lives!) or by more recent programs coded in Visual Basic, Java, C#, or

FIGURE 6-1

**Database Processing
Environment**

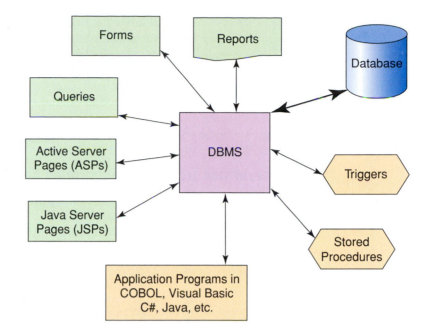

another language. Still other databases are processed by stored procedures and triggers. Let's consider each of these types.

Queries, Forms, and Reports

This book has focused on the use of a DBMS to build and process databases. For example, it has covered the need to specify rules such as cascading updates or deletions. However, think about some of the tasks that the DBMS—say Access—needs to be doing in the background to implement the database processing commands.

Suppose, for example, that you create a delete query on a table that has a 1:N relationship to a second table with On Delete Cascade permission. Suppose further that the second table has a 1:N relationship to a third table having Enforce Referential Integrity but without On Delete Cascade. When running your delete query, Access needs to delete rows from the first and second tables consistent with these relationship properties.

The situation is even more complicated if a second user is creating a report on these three tables as your delete query is operating. What should Access do? Should it show the report with whatever data remain as your query runs? Or should Access protect the report from your deletions and not make any of them until the report is finished? Should it deny your query, or do something else completely?

For a simpler example, suppose you create a form that has data from one table in the main section and data from a second table in a subform. Now suppose a user makes changes in five rows in the subform, then makes changes to some of the data in the first form, then presses the Escape key. Which of these changes will actually be made to the database? None? Changes to the subform data only? Or some other option?

Even in the case of simple queries, forms, and reports, management of the background functions is complex. You can change properties in your database to govern some of Access's behavior in these cases, but you need to know the implications of such changes. Organizational DBMS products such as Oracle, DB2, and SQL Server provide many more features and functions that let the developer change DBMS behavior for such cases. We will discuss many of these in the concurrency control section of this chapter.

Internet Application Processing

Figure 6-1 also shows the processing of a database using Internet technology such as Active Server Pages and Java Server Pages. ASPs are combinations of HTML and

VBScript or JScript that can read and write database data and transmit it over public and private networks using Internet protocols. Similarly, JSPs are combinations of HTML and Java that accomplish the same function by compiling pages into Java servlets.

We are not going to explain this technology here, but we will investigate it briefly in the next chapter. For now, realize that such pages can include application logic that involves the reading, updating, inserting, and deleting of rows from several or even many tables. Especially in the case of the Internet, these functions occur in a wild environment where it is normal for users to start transactions and walk away.

Client/Server and Traditional Application Processing

Organizational database processing began in the early 1970s. Since then, thousands if not millions of databases have been processed by application programs written in COBOL, Basic, C, C++, Visual Basic, Java, and C#. All of these languages embed SQL statements or their equivalent into programs written in these standard languages.

For example, to process an online order, an application needs to perform the following functions.

> Communicate with a user to obtain customer and salesperson identifiers.
> Read CUSTOMER data.
> Read SALESPERSON data.
> Present an order entry form to a user.
> Obtain ordered ITEMs and quantities.
> Verify stock levels for ITEMs.
> Remove ITEMs from inventory.
> Schedule backorders as necessary.
> Schedule inventory picking and shipping.
> Update CUSTOMER, SALESPERSON, ORDER, and LINE-ITEM data.

The application will be written to respond to exceptions such as data not present, data in error, communication failure, and dozens of other potential problems.

In addition, an order-processing application program will be written so that it can be utilized by many users concurrently. We will address this issue in more detail in the next section; for now, just understand that 50 to 100 users might be trying to run such an application at the same time.

Stored Procedures and Triggers

Organizational DBMS products such as Oracle, DB2, and SQL Server include features to allow developers to create modules of logic and database actions called stored procedures and triggers. A stored procedure is akin to a subroutine or function that performs database activity. An example is a stored procedure to schedule a backorder. Such a procedure is stored within the database. Application programs, ASPs or JSPs, and interactive query users can invoke the stored procedure, pass parameters to it, and receive results.

Stored procedures and triggers are written in languages provided by the DBMS. Oracle has developed a language called PL/SQL, and SQL Server has a language called TRANSACT-SQL. These are programming languages into which a developer can embed SQL statements for database activity.

Figure 6-2 shows an example of an Oracle stored procedure. The details of this procedure are beyond our discussion; just observe that after the BEGIN statement, SQL statements such as SELECT COUNT(*) and INSERT INTO CUSTOMER are embedded into logic coded in a programming language.

A trigger is similar to a stored procedure, except that it is written to be invoked by the DBMS when specified events occur. For example, Oracle supports BEFORE, AFTER, and INSTEAD OF triggers. A BEFORE trigger is called by the DBMS before

FIGURE 6-2

Example of an Oracle Stored Procedure

```
CREATE OR REPLACE PROCEDURE Customer_Insert
        (
        newname              IN        char,
        newareacode          IN        char,
        newphone             IN        char,
        artistnationality    IN        char
        )

AS

        rowcount integer(4);

        CURSOR        artistcursor IS
                      SELECT ArtistID
                      FROM ARTIST
                      WHERE Nationality=artistnationality;

BEGIN

        SELECT        Count (*) INTO rowcount
        FROM          CUSTOMER
        WHERE         Name=newname AND Area_Code=newareacode AND
                      Phone_Number = newphone;

        IF rowcount > 0 THEN
              BEGIN
                      DBMS_OUTPUT.PUT_LINE ('Customer Already Exists -- No Action Taken');
                      RETURN;
              END;
        END IF;

        INSERT INTO CUSTOMER
                (CustomerID, Name, Area_Code, Phone_Number)
                VALUES
                (CustID.NextVal, newname, newareacode, newphone);

        FOR artist IN artistcursor
              LOOP
                      INSERT INTO CUSTOMER_ARTIST_INT
                      (CustomerID, ArtistID)
                      VALUES
                      (CustID.CurrVal, artist.ArtistID);
              END LOOP;

        DBMS_OUTPUT.PUT_LINE ('New Customer Successfully Added') ;
END;
/
```

inserting, updating, or deleting data. A good use of such a trigger could be to process a business rule before an event occurs. AFTER triggers are used after such events occur, and INSTEAD OF triggers are used in place of DBMS insert, update, or delete actions.

The Need for Control, Security, and Reliability

Examine Figure 6-1 again. It is possible for every one of the application elements in this figure to be operating at the same time. Queries, forms, and reports can be generated while ASPs and JSPs access the database, possibly invoking stored procedures.

Traditional application programs can be processing transactions on the database. All of this activity can cause triggers to be invoked—and the actions in triggers might force yet other triggers to be fired, causing cascading triggers. While all of this is occurring, constraints such as those on referential integrity must be enforced. Finally, hundreds or even thousands of people might be using the system, and they might want to process the database 24 hours a day, seven days a week.

Three database administration functions are necessary to bring order to this potential chaos. First, the actions of concurrent users must be controlled to ensure that results are consistent with what is expected. Second, security measures must be in place and enforced so that only authorized users can take authorized actions at appropriate times. Finally, backup and recovery techniques and procedures must be operating to protect the database in case of failure and to recover it as quickly and accurately as possible when necessary. We will consider each of these in turn.

▶ CONCURRENCY CONTROL

The purpose of concurrency control is to ensure that one user's work does not inappropriately influence another user's work. In some cases, these measures ensure that a user gets the same result when processing with other users as that person would have received if processing alone. In other cases, it means that the user's work is influenced by other users but in an anticipated way.

For example, in an order-entry system, a user should be able to enter an order and get the same result regardless of whether there are no other users or hundreds of other users. On the other hand, a user who is printing a report of the most current inventory status might want to obtain in-process data changes from other users, even if those changes might later be canceled.

Unfortunately, no concurrency control technique or mechanism is ideal for all circumstances; they all involve trade-offs. For example, a user can obtain strict concurrency control by locking the entire database, but while that person is processing no other user will be able to do anything. This is robust protection, but it comes at a high cost. As you will see, other measures are available that are more difficult to program and enforce but that allow more throughput. Still other measures are available that maximize throughput but for a low level of concurrency control. When designing multiuser database applications, developers need to choose among these trade-offs.

The Need for Atomic Transactions

In most database applications, users submit work in the form of **transactions**, which are also known as *logical units of work (LUWs)*. A transaction (or LUW) is a series of actions to be taken on a database such that all of them are performed successfully or none of them are performed at all, in which case the database remains unchanged. Such a transaction is sometimes called **atomic**, because it is performed as a unit. Consider the following sequence of database actions that could occur when recording a new order.

1. Change the customer record, increasing the value of Amount Owed.
2. Change the salesperson record, increasing the value of Commission Due.
3. Insert the new order record into the database.

Suppose the last step failed, perhaps because of insufficient file space. Imagine the confusion that would ensue if the first two changes were made but the third one was not. The customer would be billed for an order that was never received, and a salesperson would receive a commission on an order that was never sent to the customer. Clearly, these three actions need to be taken as a unit—either all of them should be done or none of them should be done.

Figure 6-3 compares the results of performing these activities as a series of independent steps (Figure 6-3(a)) and as an atomic transaction (Figure 6-3(b)). Notice that when the steps are carried out atomically and one fails, no changes are made in the database. Also note that the commands Start Transaction, Commit Transaction, or Rollback Transaction must be issued by the application program to mark the boundaries of the transaction logic. The particular form of these commands varies from one DBMS product to another.

Concurrent Transaction Processing

When two transactions are being processed against a database at the same time, they are termed *concurrent transactions*. Although it might appear to the users that concurrent transactions are being processed simultaneously, this cannot be true because the central processing unit (CPU) of the machine processing the database can execute only one instruction at a time. Usually transactions are interleaved, which means the operating system switches CPU services among tasks so that some portion of each of them is carried out in a given interval. This switching among tasks is done so quickly that two people seated at browsers side by side, processing against the same database, might believe that their two transactions are completed simultaneously. However, in reality the two transactions are interleaved.

FIGURE 6-3

Comparison of the Results of Applying Serial Actions Versus a Multiple-Step Transaction; (a) Two Out of Three Activities Successfully Completed, Resulting in Database Anomalies, and (b) No Change Made Because Entire Transaction Not Successful

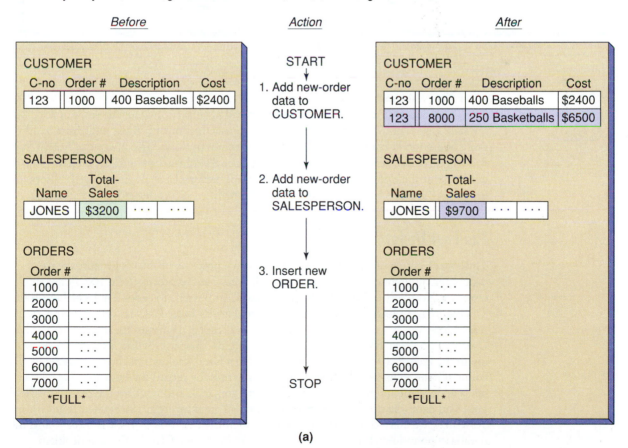

(a)

FIGURE 6-3

(continued)

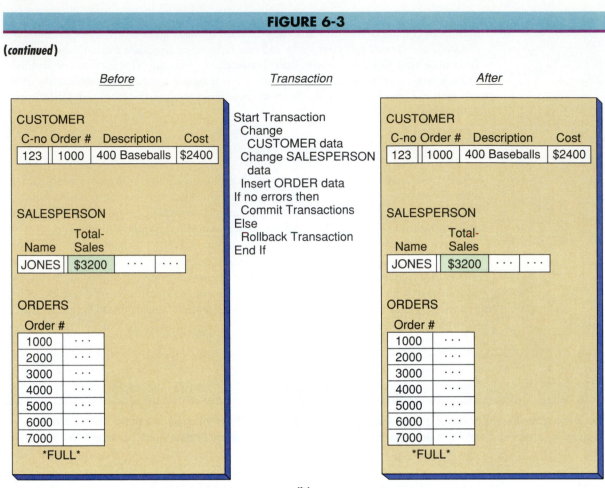

(b)

Figure 6-4 shows two concurrent transactions. User A's transaction reads Item 100, changes it, and rewrites it in the database. User B's transaction takes the same actions but on Item 200. The CPU processes User A's transaction until it must wait for a read or write operation to complete or for some other action to finish. The operating system then shifts control to User B. The CPU processes User B's transaction until an interruption, at which point the operating system passes control back to User A. Again, to the users the processing appears to be simultaneous, but in reality it is interleaved, or concurrent.

The Lost Update Problem

The concurrent processing illustrated in Figure 6-4 poses no problems because the users are processing different data. Now suppose both users want to process Item 100. For example, User A wants to order 5 units of Item 100, and User B wants to order 3 units of Item 100.

Figure 6-5 illustrates the problem. User A reads Item 100's record, which is transferred into a user work area. According to the record, 10 items are in inventory. Then User B reads Item 100's record, and it goes into another user work area. Again, according to the record, 10 items are in inventory. Now User A takes 5 of them, decrements the count of items in its user work area to 5, and rewrites the record for Item 100. Then User B takes 3, decrements the count in its user work area to 7, and rewrites the record for Item 100. The database now shows, incorrectly, that 7 units of Item 100 remain in inventory. To review, we started with 10 in inventory, then User A took 5, User B took 3, and the database wound up showing that 7 were left in inventory. Clearly, this is a problem.

FIGURE 6-4

Example of Concurrent Processing of Two Users' Tasks

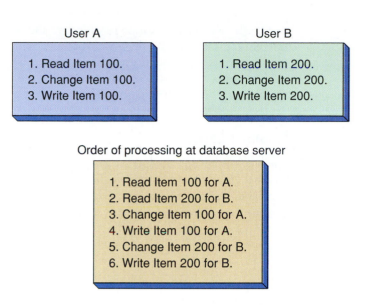

User A

1. Read Item 100.
2. Change Item 100.
3. Write Item 100.

User B

1. Read Item 200.
2. Change Item 200.
3. Write Item 200.

Order of processing at database server

1. Read Item 100 for A.
2. Read Item 200 for B.
3. Change Item 100 for A.
4. Write Item 100 for A.
5. Change Item 200 for B.
6. Write Item 200 for B.

Both users obtained data that were correct at the time they obtained it. However, when User B read the record, User A already had a copy that it was about to update. This situation is called the lost update problem, or the concurrent update problem. Another similar problem is called the inconsistent read problem. In this situation, User A reads data that have been processed by only a portion of a transaction from User B. As a result, User A reads incorrect data.

Concurrency Problems: Dirty Reads, Inconsistent Reads, and Phantom Reads

The problems that can occur due to concurrent processing have standardized names. Specifically, a dirty read occurs when one transaction reads a changed record that has not been committed to the database. This can occur, for example, if one transaction reads a row changed by a second transaction, and this second transaction later cancels its changes.

A nonrepeatable read occurs when a transaction rereads data it has previously read and finds modifications or deletions caused by another transaction. Finally, a phantom

FIGURE 6-5

Example of a Lost Update Problem

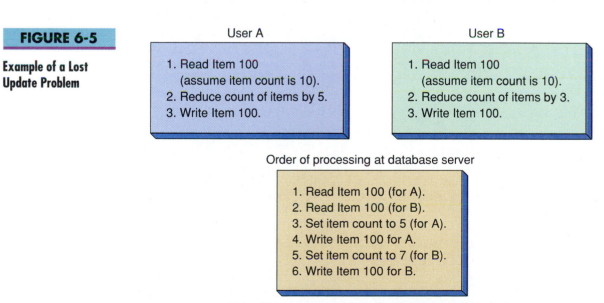

User A

1. Read Item 100
   (assume item count is 10).
2. Reduce count of items by 5.
3. Write Item 100.

User B

1. Read Item 100
   (assume item count is 10).
2. Reduce count of items by 3.
3. Write Item 100.

Order of processing at database server

1. Read Item 100 (for A).
2. Read Item 100 (for B).
3. Set item count to 5 (for A).
4. Write Item 100 for A.
5. Set item count to 7 (for B).
6. Write Item 100 for B.

Note: The change and write in Steps 3 and 4 are lost.

read occurs when a transaction rereads data and finds new rows that were inserted by a different transaction since the prior read.

One remedy for the inconsistencies caused by concurrent processing is to prevent multiple applications from obtaining copies of the same rows or tables when those rows or tables are about to be changed. This remedy is called resource locking.

Resource Locking

One way to prevent concurrent processing problems is to disallow sharing by locking data that are retrieved for update. Figure 6-6 shows the order of processing using a lock command. Because of the lock, User B's transaction must wait until User A is finished with the Item 100 data. Using this strategy, User B can read Item 100's record only after User A has completed the modification. In this case, the final item count stored in the database is 2, which is as it should be. (We started with 10, then A took 5 and B took 3, leaving 2.)

Locks can be placed automatically by the DBMS or by a command issued to the DBMS from the application program or query user. Locks placed by the DBMS are called implicit locks; those placed by command are called explicit locks.

In the preceding example, the locks were applied to rows of data; however, not all locks are applied at this level. Some DBMS products lock at the page level, some at the table level, and some at the database level. The size of a lock is referred to as the **lock granularity**. Locks with large granularity are easy for the DBMS to administer but frequently cause conflicts. Locks with small granularity are difficult to administer (the DBMS has many more details to keep track of and check), but conflicts are less common.

Locks also vary by type. An exclusive lock locks an item from access of any type. No other transaction can read or change the data. A shared lock locks an item from being changed but not from being read. That is, other transactions can read the item as long as they do not attempt to alter it.

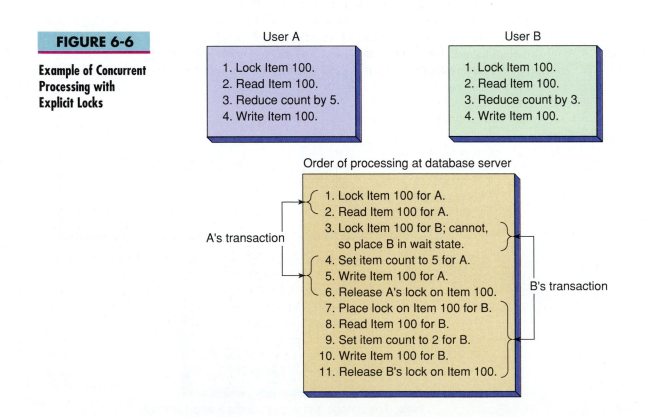

FIGURE 6-6

Example of Concurrent Processing with Explicit Locks

User A
1. Lock Item 100.
2. Read Item 100.
3. Reduce count by 5.
4. Write Item 100.

User B
1. Lock Item 100.
2. Read Item 100.
3. Reduce count by 3.
4. Write Item 100.

Order of processing at database server

A's transaction
1. Lock Item 100 for A.
2. Read Item 100 for A.
3. Lock Item 100 for B; cannot, so place B in wait state.
4. Set item count to 5 for A.
5. Write Item 100 for A.
6. Release A's lock on Item 100.
7. Place lock on Item 100 for B.
8. Read Item 100 for B.
9. Set item count to 2 for B.
10. Write Item 100 for B.
11. Release B's lock on Item 100.

B's transaction

Serializable Transactions

When two or more transactions are processed concurrently, the results in the database should be logically consistent with the results that would have been achieved had the transactions been processed in an arbitrary serial fashion. A scheme for processing concurrent transactions in this way is said to be serializable.

Serializability can be achieved by a number of different means. One way is to process the transaction using two-phased locking. With this strategy, transactions are allowed to obtain locks as necessary, but once the first lock is released, no other lock can be obtained. Transactions thus have a growing phase in which the locks are obtained, and a shrinking phase in which the locks are released.

A special case of two-phased locking is used with a number of DBMS products. With it, locks are obtained throughout the transaction, but no lock is released until the COMMIT or ROLLBACK command is issued. This strategy is more restrictive than two-phase locking requires, but it is easier to implement.

Consider an order-entry transaction that involves processing data in the CUSTOMER, SALESPERSON, and ORDER table. To make sure the database will suffer no anomalies due to concurrency, the order-entry transaction issues locks on CUSTOMER, SALESPERSON, and ORDER as needed; makes all the database changes; and then releases all its locks.

Deadlock

Although locking solves one problem, it causes another. Consider what might happen when two users want to order two items from inventory. Suppose User A wants to order some paper, and if she can get the paper, she also wants to order some pencils. Suppose also that User B wants to order some pencils, and if he can get the pencils, he also wants to order some paper. The order of processing could be that shown in Figure 6-7.

In this figure, Users A and B are locked in a condition known as deadlock, sometimes called the deadly embrace. Each is waiting for a resource that the other person has locked. Two common ways of solving this problem are preventing the deadlock from occurring or allowing the deadlock to occur and then breaking it.

Deadlock can be prevented in several ways. One way is to allow users to issue only one lock request at a time; in essence, users must lock all the resources they want at once.

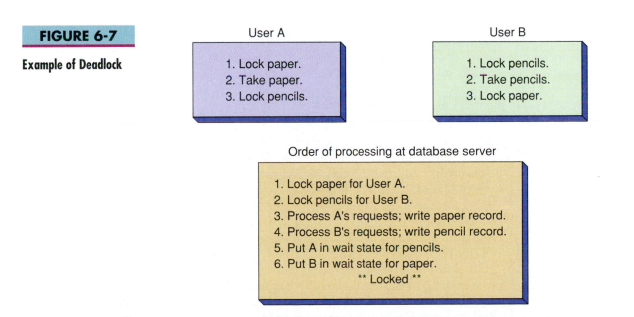

FIGURE 6-7

Example of Deadlock

User A

1. Lock paper.
2. Take paper.
3. Lock pencils.

User B

1. Lock pencils.
2. Take pencils.
3. Lock paper.

Order of processing at database server

1. Lock paper for User A.
2. Lock pencils for User B.
3. Process A's requests; write paper record.
4. Process B's requests; write pencil record.
5. Put A in wait state for pencils.
6. Put B in wait state for paper.
       ** Locked **

If User A in the illustration had locked both the paper and the pencil records at the beginning, the deadlock would not have occurred. A second way to prevent deadlock is to require all application programs to lock resources in the same order.

Almost every DBMS has algorithms for detecting deadlock. When deadlock occurs, the normal solution is to roll back one of the transactions to remove its changes from the database.

Optimistic Versus Pessimistic Locking

Locks can be invoked in two basic styles. With optimistic locking, the assumption is made that no conflict will occur. Data are read, the transaction is processed, updates are issued, and then a check is made to see if conflict occurred. If not, the transaction is finished. If so, the transaction is repeated until it processes with no conflict. With pessimistic locking, the assumption is made that conflict will occur. First locks are issued, then the transaction is processed, and then the locks are freed.

Figure 6-8 shows an example of each style for a transaction that is reducing the quantity of the pencil row in the PRODUCT table by five. Figure 6-8(a) shows optimistic locking. First, the data are read and the current value of Quantity of pencils is saved in the variable OldQuantity. The transaction is then processed, and assuming that all is OK, a lock is obtained on PRODUCT. The lock might be only for the pencil row, or it might be at a larger level of granularity. In any case, a SQL statement is issued to update the pencil row with a WHERE condition that the current value of Quantity equals OldQuantity. If no other transaction has changed the Quantity of the pencil row, then this UPDATE will be successful. If another transaction has changed the Quantity of the pencil row, the UPDATE will fail and the transaction will need to be repeated.

Figure 6-8(b) shows the logic for the same transaction using pessimistic locking. In this case, a lock is obtained on PRODUCT (at some level of granularity) before any work is begun. Then values are read, the transaction is processed, the UPDATE occurs, and PRODUCT is unlocked.

The advantage of optimistic locking is that the lock is obtained only after the transaction has processed. Thus, the lock is held for less time than with pessimistic locking. If the transaction is complicated or if the client is slow (due to transmission delays or to the user doing other work, getting a cup of coffee, or shutting down without exiting the application), the lock will be held for considerably less time. This advantage will be even more important if the lock granularity is large—say, the entire PRODUCT table.

The disadvantage of optimistic locking is that if a lot of activity is occurring on the pencil row, the transaction might have to be repeated many times. Thus, transactions that involve a lot of activity on a given row (purchasing a popular stock, for example) are poorly suited for optimistic locking.

Declaring Lock Characteristics

Concurrency control is a complicated subject; some of the decisions about lock types and strategy have to be made on the basis of trial and error. For this and other reasons, database application programs generally do not explicitly issue locks. Instead, the programs mark transaction boundaries and then declare the type of locking behavior they want the DBMS to use. In this way, if the locking behavior needs to be changed, the application need not be rewritten to place locks in different locations in the transaction. Instead, the lock declaration is changed.

Figure 6-9 shows the pencil transaction with transaction boundaries marked with BEGIN TRANSACTION, COMMIT TRANSACTION, and ROLLBACK TRANSACTION statements. These boundaries provide the essential information that the DBMS needs in order to enforce different locking strategies. If the developer later declares (via a system parameter or similar means) a desire for optimistic locking, the DBMS will implicitly set the locks in the correct place for that locking style. If the developer changes

FIGURE 6-8

Examples of
(a) Optimistic Locking,
and (b) Pessimistic
Locking

```
SELECT      PRODUCT.Name, PRODUCT.Quantity
FROM        PRODUCT
WHERE       PRODUCT.Name = 'Pencil'

OldQuantity = PRODUCT.Quantity

Set NewQuantity = PRODUCT.Quantity – 5

{process transaction – take exception action if NewQuantity < 0, etc.

Assuming all is OK:}

LOCK PRODUCT {at some level of granularity}

UPDATE      PRODUCT
SET         PRODUCT.Quantity = NewQuantity
WHERE       PRODUCT.Name = 'Pencil'
        AND PRODUCT.Quantity = OldQuantity

UNLOCK   PRODUCT

{check to see if update was successful;
if not, repeat transaction}
```

(a)

```
LOCK        PRODUCT {at some level of granularity}

SELECT      PRODUCT.Name, PRODUCT.Quantity
FROM        PRODUCT
WHERE       PRODUCT.Name = 'Pencil'

Set NewQuantity = PRODUCT.Quantity – 5

{process transaction – take exception action if NewQuantity < 0, etc.

Assuming all is OK:}

UPDATE      PRODUCT
SET         PRODUCT.Quantity = NewQuantity
WHERE       PRODUCT.Name = 'Pencil'

UNLOCK   PRODUCT

{no need to check if update was successful}
```

(b)

tactics again and requests pessimistic locking, the DBMS will implicitly set the locks in a different place.

Consistent Transactions

Sometimes the acronym *ACID* is applied to transactions. An **ACID transaction** is one that is atomic, consistent, isolated, and durable. *Atomic* and *durable* are easy to define. An atomic transaction is one in which all of the database actions occur or none of them do. A durable transaction is one in which all committed changes are permanent. The

FIGURE 6-9

Example of Marking Transaction Boundaries

```
BEGIN TRANSACTION:

SELECT      PRODUCT.Name, PRODUCT.Quantity
FROM        PRODUCT
WHERE       PRODUCT.Name = 'Pencil'

Old Quantity = PRODUCT.Quantity

Set NewQuantity = PRODUCT.Quantity – 5

{process part of transaction – take exception action if NewQuantity < 0, etc.}

UPDATE      PRODUCT
SET         PRODUCT.Quantity = NewQuantity
WHERE       PRODUCT.Name = 'Pencil'

{continue processing transaction} . . .



IF transaction has completed normally        THEN

        COMMIT TRANSACTION

ELSE

        ROLLBACK TRANSACTION

END IF

Continue processing other actions not part of this transaction . . .
```

DBMS will not remove such changes, even in the case of failure. If the transaction is durable, the DBMS will provide facilities to recover the changes of all committed actions when necessary.

The terms *consistent* and *isolated* are not as definitive as the terms *atomic* and *durable*. Consider the following SQL update command.

UPDATE   CUSTOMER

SET   AreaCode = '425'

WHERE   ZipCode = '98050';

Suppose the CUSTOMER table has 500,000 rows and 500 of them have a ZipCode value equal to 98050. It will take some time for the DBMS to find all 500 rows. During that time, will other transactions be allowed to update the AreaCode or ZipCode fields of CUSTOMER? If the SQL statement is consistent, such updates will be disallowed. The update will apply to the set of rows as they existed at the time the SQL statement started. Such consistency is called *statement level consistency*.

Now consider a transaction that contains two SQL update statements.

BEGIN TRANSACTION

UPDATE CUSTOMER

SET AreaCode = '425'

WHERE ZipCode = '98050';

{other transaction work}

. . .

UPDATE CUSTOMER

SET Discount = 0.05

WHERE AreaCode = '425';

{other transaction work}

…

COMMIT TRANSACTION

In this context, what does *consistent* mean? Statement level consistency means that each statement independently processes consistent rows, but changes from other users to these rows might be allowed during the interval between the two SQL statements. Transaction level consistency means that all rows impacted by either of the SQL statements are protected from changes during the entire transaction.

However, observe that for some implementations of transaction level consistency, a transaction will not see its own changes. In this example, the second SQL statement might not see rows changed by the first SQL statement.

Thus, when you hear the term *consistent*, look further to determine which type of consistency is intended. Be aware as well of the potential trap of transaction level consistency. The situation is even more complicated for the term *isolated,* which we will consider next.

Transaction Isolation Level

The 1992 ANSI SQL standard defines four isolation levels that specify which of the concurrency control problems are allowed to occur. The goal is for the application programmer to be able to declare the type of isolation level desired and then to have the DBMS manage locks to achieve that level of isolation.

As shown in Figure 6-10, read uncommitted isolation allows dirty reads, nonrepeatable reads, and phantom reads to occur. With read committed isolation, dirty reads are disallowed. The repeatable reads isolation level disallows both dirty reads and non-repeatable reads. The serializable isolation level will not allow any of these three.

Generally, the more restrictive the level is, the less throughput occurs, though much depends on the workload and how the application programs were written. Moreover, not all DBMS products support all of these levels. Products also vary in the manner in which they are supported and in the burden they place on the application programmer.

FIGURE 6-10

Summary of Isolation Levels

		Isolation Level			
		Read Uncommitted	Read Committed	Repeatable Read	Serializable
Problem Type	Dirty Read	Possible	Not Possible	Not Possible	Not Possible
	Nonrepeatable Read	Possible	Possible	Not Possible	Not Possible
	Phantom Read	Possible	Possible	Possible	Not Possible

▶ DATABASE SECURITY

The goal of database security is to ensure that only authorized users can perform authorized activities at authorized times. This goal is difficult to achieve, and to make any progress at all the database development team must determine the processing rights and responsibilities of all users. These security requirements can then be enforced using the security features of the DBMS, as well as the additions to those features written into the application programs.

Processing Rights and Responsibilities

Consider, for example, the needs of Heather Sweeney Designs, discussed in Chapter 4. The company has three types of users: administrative assistants, management (Heather), and a systems administrator (Heather's consultant). Figure 6-11 summarizes the processing rights that Heather determined were appropriate for her business.

Administrative assistants can read, insert, and change data in all tables. However, they can delete data only from SEMINAR-CUSTOMER and LINE-ITEM. This means administrative assistants can disenroll customers from seminars and can remove items from an order. Management can take all actions on all tables except delete CUSTOMER data. Heather believes that for as hard as she works to get a customer, she does not want to ever run the risk that she could accidentally delete one.

Finally, the system administrator can assign permissions to other users but can take no action on data. The system administrator is not a user and so should not be allowed

FIGURE 6-11

Processing Rights at Heather Sweeney Designs

	Administrative Assistants	Management	System Administrator
SEMINAR	Read, Insert, Change	Read, Insert, Change, Delete	Define permissions
CUSTOMER	Read, Insert, Change	Read, Insert, Change	Define permissions
SEMINAR-CUSTOMER	Read, Insert, Change, Delete	Read, Insert, Change, Delete	Define permissions
CONTACT	Read, Insert, Change	Read, Insert, Change, Delete	Define permissions
PRODUCT	Read, Insert	Read, Insert, Change, Delete	Define permissions
INVOICE	Read, Insert, Change	Read, Insert, Change, Delete	Define permissions
LINE-ITEM	Read, Insert, Change, Delete	Read, Insert, Change, Delete	Define permissions

access to user data. This limitation might seem weak. After all, if the system administrator can assign permissions, he or she can get around the security system by changing the permissions to take whatever action is desired, make the data changes, and then change the permissions back. This is true, but it would leave an audit trail in the DBMS logs. That coupled with the need to make the security system changes will dissuade the administrator from unauthorized activity. It is certainly better than allowing the administrator to have user data access permissions with no effort.

The permissions in this table are given to user groups or roles and not to individuals. This is typical but not required. It would be possible, for example, to say that the user identified as Benjamin Franklin has certain processing rights. Note, too, that when groups are used, it is necessary to have a means for allocating users to groups. When Mary Smith signs onto the computer, some means must to be available to determine which group or groups she belongs to. We will cover this further in the next section.

In this discussion, we have used the phrase *processing rights and responsibilities*. As this phrase implies, responsibilities go with processing rights. If, for example, the systems administrator deletes CUSTOMER data, it is that person's responsibility to ensure that these deletions do not adversely impact the company's operation, accounting, and so forth.

Processing responsibilities cannot be enforced by the DBMS or the database applications. Responsibilities are, instead, encoded in manual procedures and explained to users during systems training. These are topics of a systems development book, and we will not consider them further here except to reiterate that responsibilities go with rights. Such responsibilities must be documented and enforced.

The DBA has the task of managing processing rights and responsibilities. As this implies, these rights and responsibilities will change over time. As the database is used and as changes are made to the applications and to the DBMS's structure, the need for new or different rights and responsibilities will arise. The DBA is a focal point for the discussion of such changes and for their implementation.

After processing rights have been defined, they can be implemented at many levels: operating system, network, Web server, DBMS, and application. The next two sections will consider the DBMS and application aspects. The others are beyond the scope of this book.

DBMS Security

Figure 6-12 lists security guidelines for the DBMS. First, the DBMS should be run behind a firewall. In most cases, no communication with the DBMS or database applications should be allowed to be initiated from outside the organization's network. However, if the DBMS supports e-commerce applications, then this rule cannot be followed. In this case though, the DBMS should support only the e-commerce applications. All other database applications should be managed by a different DBMS on a different machine behind a firewall.

Second, service packs and fixes for the operating system and the DBMS must be applied as soon as possible. In the spring of 2003, the slammer worm exploited a security hole in SQL Server, bringing major organizational database applications to their knees. Microsoft had published a patch that eliminated the hole, so any organization that applied that patch was not affected by the worm.

A third protection is to limit the capabilities of the DBMS to only those features and functions that the applications need. For example, Oracle can support many different

FIGURE 6-12

DBMS Security Guidelines

- Run the DBMS behind a firewall
- Apply the latest operating system and DBMS service packs and fixes
- Limit DBMS functionality to needed features
- Protect the computer that runs the DBMS
- Manage accounts and passwords

communications protocols. To improve security, any Oracle-supported protocol that is not used should be removed or disabled. Similarly, every DBMS ships with hundreds of system-stored procedures. Any procedure that is not used should be removed from operational databases.

Another important security measure is to protect the computer that runs the DBMS. No users should be allowed to work on the DBMS computer, and that computer should reside in a separate facility behind locked doors. Visits to the room housing the DBMS should be logged with date and time.

Finally, user accounts and passwords should be managed carefully. The terminology, features, and functions of DBMS account and password security depend on the DBMS product used. Basically, though, all such products provide facilities that limit certain actions on certain objects to certain users. A general model of DBMS security is shown in Figure 6-12.

According to this figure, a user can be assigned to one or more roles, and a role can have one or more users. Users, roles, and objects (used in a generic sense) have many permissions. Each permission pertains to one user or role and one object.

When a user signs onto the database, the DBMS limits the person's actions to the defined permissions for that user and to the permissions for roles to which that user has been assigned. Determining whether someone is who he or she claims to be is, in general, a difficult task. All commercial DBMS products use some version of a user name and password system, even though such security is readily circumvented if users are careless with their identities.

A user can enter a name and password, or in some applications, the name and password is entered on behalf of the user. For example, the Windows 2000 user name and password can be passed directly to SQL Server. In other cases, an application program provides the user name and password.

Internet applications usually define a group such as Unknown Public and assign anonymous users to that group when they sign on. In this way, companies that conduct e-commerce with unknown customers need not enter every such customer into their security system by name and password.

The security systems used by Oracle, DB2, and SQL Server are variations on the model shown in Figure 6-13. The terminology used might vary from this, but the essence of their security systems is the same.

Application Security

Although DBMS products such as Oracle, DB2, and SQL Server do provide substantial database security capabilities, by their very nature they are generic. If the application requires specific security measures, such as disallowing users to view a row of a table or of a join of a table that has an employee name other than the user's own, the DBMS facilities will not be adequate. In these cases, the security system must be augmented by features in database applications.

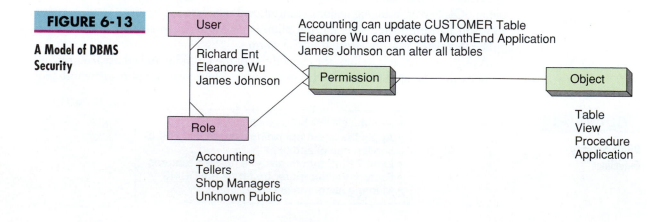

FIGURE 6-13

A Model of DBMS Security

For example, application security in Internet applications often is provided on the Web server computer. Executing application security on this server means that sensitive security data need not be transmitted over the network.

To understand this better, suppose an application is written such that when users click a particular button on a browser page, the following query is sent to the Web server and then to the DBMS.

SELECT   *

FROM   EMPLOYEE;

This statement will return all EMPLOYEE rows. If the application security allows employees to access only their own data, then a Web server could add the following WHERE clause to this query.

SELECT   *

FROM   EMPLOYEE

WHERE   EMPLOYEE.Name = '<%SESSION("EmployeeName")%>';

As you will learn when you study Internet applications technology, an expression like this will cause the Web server to fill in the employee's name for the WHERE clause. For a user signed on under the name Benjamin Franklin, the following statement results from this expression.

SELECT   *

FROM   EMPLOYEE

WHERE   EMPLOYEE.Name = 'Benjamin Franklin';

Because the name is inserted by a program on the Web server, the browser user does not know it is occurring and cannot interfere with it.

Such security processing can be done as shown here on a Web server, but it also can be done within the application programs themselves, or written as stored procedures or triggers to be executed by the DBMS at the appropriate times.

This idea can be extended by storing additional data in a security database that is accessed by the Web server, and also by using stored procedures and triggers. That security database could contain, for example, the identities of users paired with additional values of WHERE clauses. For example, suppose the users in the personnel department can access more than just their own data. The predicates for appropriate WHERE clauses could be stored in the security database, read by the application program, and appended to SQL SELECT statements as necessary.

Many other possibilities exist for extending DBMS security with application processing. In general, you should use the DBMS security features first. Only if they are inadequate for the requirements should you add to them with application code. The closer the security enforcement is to the data, the less chance there is for infiltration. Also, using the DBMS security features is faster, cheaper, and probably produces higher-quality results than if you develop your own.

▶ DATABASE BACKUP AND RECOVERY

Computer systems fail. Hardware breaks. Programs have bugs. Procedures written by humans contain errors, and people make mistakes. All of these failures can and do occur in database applications. Because a database is shared by many people, and because it often is a key element of an organization's operations, it is important to recover it as soon as possible.

Several problems must be addressed. First, from a business standpoint, business functions must continue. For example, customer orders, financial transactions, and packing lists must be completed manually. Later, when the database application is operational again, the new data can be entered. Second, computer operations personnel must restore the system to a usable state as quickly as possible and as close as possible to what it was when the system crashed. Third, users must know what to do when the system becomes available again. Some work might need to be reentered, and users must know how far back they need to go.

When failures occur, it is impossible simply to fix the problem and resume processing. Even if no data are lost during a failure (which assumes that all types of memory are nonvolatile—an unrealistic assumption), the timing and scheduling of computer processing are too complex to be accurately re-created. Enormous amounts of overhead data and processing would be required for the operating system to be able to restart processing precisely where it was interrupted. It is simply not possible to roll back the clock and put all the electrons in the same configuration they were in at the time of the failure. However, two other approaches are possible: recovery via reprocessing and recovery via rollback/rollforward.

Recovery via Reprocessing

Because processing cannot be resumed at a precise point, the next-best alternative is to go back to a known point and reprocess the workload from there. The simplest form of this type of recovery involves periodically making a copy of the database (called a database save) and keeping a record of all transactions that were processed since the save. Then, when failure occurs, the operations staff can restore the database from the save and reprocess all the transactions.

Unfortunately, this simple strategy normally is not feasible. First, reprocessing transactions takes the same amount of time as did processing them in the first place. If the computer is heavily scheduled, the system might never catch up.

Second, when transactions are processed concurrently, events are asynchronous. Slight variations in human activity, such as a user reading an e-mail message before responding to an application prompt, could change the order of the execution of concurrent transactions. Therefore, whereas Customer A got the last seat on a flight during the original processing, Customer B might get the last seat during reprocessing. For these reasons, reprocessing is normally not a viable form of recovery from failure in multiuser systems.

Recovery via Rollback and Rollforward

A second approach involves periodically making a copy of the database (the database save) and keeping a log of the changes made by transactions against the database since the save. Then, when a failure occurs, one of two methods can be used. In the first method, called rollforward, the database is restored using the saved data, and all valid transactions since the save are reapplied. (We are not reprocessing the transactions, as the application programs are not involved in the rollforward. Instead, the processed changes, as recorded in the log, are reapplied.)

The second method is called rollback, in which we correct mistakes caused by erroneous or partially processed transactions by undoing the changes they made in the database. Then the valid transactions that were in process at the time of the failure are restarted.

As stated, both of these methods require that a log of the transaction results be kept. This log contains records of the data changes in chronological order. Note that transactions must be written to the log before they are applied to the database. That way, if the system crashes between the time a transaction is logged and the time it is applied, then at worst there is a record of an unapplied transaction. If transactions were applied before being logged, it would be possible (and undesirable) to change the database without having a record of the change. If this happens, an unwary user might reenter an already-completed transaction.

In the event of a failure, the log is used to undo and redo transactions, as shown in Figure 6-14. To undo a transaction, the log must contain a copy of every database record before it was changed. Such records are called before-images. A transaction is undone by applying before-images of all its changes to the database.

To redo a transaction, the log must contain a copy of every database record (or page) after it was changed. These records are called after-images. A transaction is redone by applying after-images of all its changes to the database. Possible data items of a transaction log are shown in Figure 6-15(a).

For this example log, each transaction has a unique name for identification purposes. Furthermore, all images for a given transaction are linked together with pointers. One pointer points to the previous change made by this transaction (the reverse pointer), and the other points to the next change made by this transaction (the forward pointer). A zero in the pointer field means that this is the end of the list. The DBMS recovery subsystem uses these pointers to locate all records for a particular transaction. Figure 6-15(b) shows an example of the linking of log records.

Other data items in the log are: the time of the action; the type of operation (START marks the beginning of a transaction and COMMIT terminates a transaction, releasing all locks that were in place); the object acted upon, such as record type and identifier; and, finally, the before-images and after-images. Given a log with before-images and after-images, the undo and redo actions are straightforward. To undo the transaction in

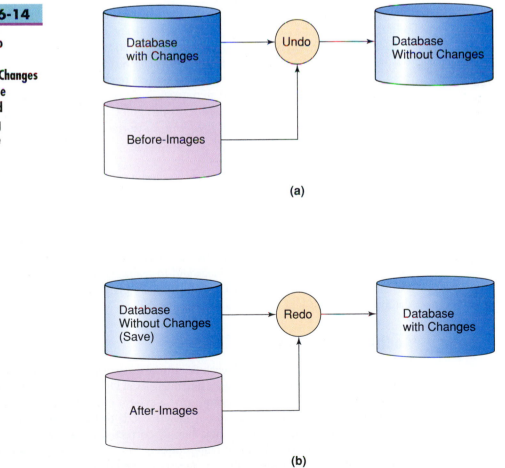

FIGURE 6-14

Undo and Redo Transactions: (a) Removing Changes in the Database (Rollback), and (b) Reapplying Changes in the Database (Rollforward)

Database with Changes → Undo → Database Without Changes

Before-Images

(a)

Database Without Changes (Save) → Redo → Database with Changes

After-Images

(b)

FIGURE 6-15

Example Transaction Log

Relative Record Number	Transaction ID	Reverse Pointer	Forward Pointer	Time	Type of Operation	Object	Before-Image	After-Image
1	OT1	0	2	11:42	START			
2	OT1	1	4	11:43	MODIFY	CUST 100	(old value)	(new value)
3	OT2	0	8	11:46	START			
4	OT1	2	5	11:47	MODIFY	SP AA	(old value)	(new value)
5	OT1	4	7	11:47	INSERT	ORDER 11		(value)
6	CT1	0	9	11:48	START			
7	OT1	5	0	11:49	COMMIT			
8	OT2	3	0	11:50	COMMIT			
9	CT1	6	10	11:51	MODIFY	SP BB	(old value)	(new value)
10	CT1	9	0	11:51	COMMIT			

Figure 6-16, the recovery processor simply replaces each changed record with its before-image. When all before-images have been restored, the transaction is undone. To redo a transaction, the recovery processor starts with the version of the database at the time the transaction started and applies all after-images. As stated, this action assumes that an earlier version of the database is available from a database save.

Restoring a database to its most recent save and reapplying all transactions might require considerable processing. To reduce the delay, DBMS products sometimes use checkpoints. A checkpoint is a point of synchronization between the database and the transaction log. To perform a checkpoint, the DBMS refuses new requests, finishes processing outstanding requests, and writes its buffers to disk. The DBMS then waits until the operating system notifies it that all outstanding write requests to the database and to the log have been completed successfully. At this point, the log and the database are synchronized. A checkpoint record is then written to the log. Later, the database can be recovered from the checkpoint, and only after-images for transactions that started after the checkpoint need to be applied.

Checkpoints are inexpensive operations, and it is feasible to make three or four (or more) per hour. In this way, no more than 15 or 20 minutes of processing needs to be recovered. Most DBMS products automatically checkpoint themselves, making human intervention unnecessary.

You will need to learn much more about backup and recovery if you work in database administration using products such as Oracle, DB2, or SQL Server. For now, you just need to understand the basic ideas and to realize that it is the responsibility of the DBA to ensure that adequate backup and recovery plans have been developed and that database saves and logs are generated as required.

Additional DBA Responsibilities

Concurrency control, security, and reliability are the three major concerns of database administration. However, other administrative and managerial DBA functions are also important.

For one, the DBA needs to ensure that a system exists to gather and record user-reported errors and other problems. A means needs to be devised to prioritize those errors and problems and to ensure that they are corrected accordingly. In this regard, the DBA works with the development team not only to resolve these problems, but also to evaluate features and functions of new releases of the DBMS.

FIGURE 6-16

Example of a Recovery
Strategy: (a) ORDER
Transaction and
(b) Recovery
Processing to Undo an
ORDER Record

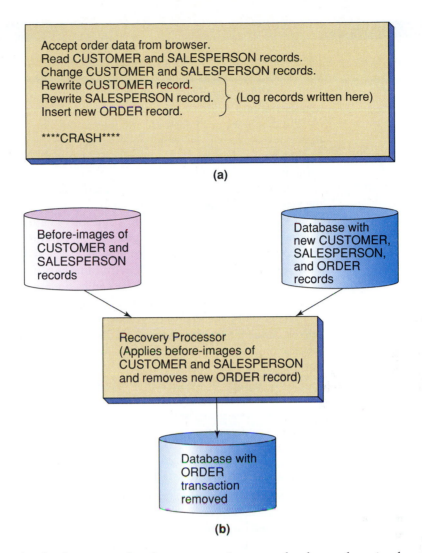

Accept order data from browser.
Read CUSTOMER and SALESPERSON records.
Change CUSTOMER and SALESPERSON records.
Rewrite CUSTOMER record.
Rewrite SALESPERSON record. } (Log records written here)
Insert new ORDER record.

****CRASH****

(a)

Before-images of CUSTOMER and SALESPERSON records

Database with new CUSTOMER, SALESPERSON, and ORDER records

Recovery Processor
(Applies before-images of
CUSTOMER and SALESPERSON
and removes new ORDER record)

Database with
ORDER
transaction
removed

(b)

As the database is used and as new requirements develop and are implemented, requests for changes to the structure of the database will occur. Changes to an operational database need to be made with great care and thoughtful planning. Because databases are shared resources, a change to the structure of a database to implement features desired by one user or group can be detrimental to the needs of other users or groups.

Therefore, the DBA needs to create and manage a process for controlling the database configuration. Such a process includes procedures for recording change requests, conducting user and developer reviews of such requests, and creating projects and tasks for implementing changes that are approved. All of these activities need to be conducted with a community-wide view.

Finally, the DBA is responsible for ensuring that appropriate documentation is maintained about database structure, concurrency control, security, backup and recovery, applications use, and a myriad of other details that concern the management and use of the database. Some vendors provide tools for recording such documentation. At a minimum, the DBMS will have its own metadata that it uses to process the database. Some products augment these metadata with facilities for storing and reporting application metadata, as well as operational procedures.

The DBA has significant responsibilities in the management and administration of a database. These responsibilities vary with the database type and size, the number of users, and the complexity of applications. However, the responsibilities are important for all databases. You should know about the need for DBA services and consider the material in this chapter even for the smallest, most personal database.

SUMMARY

Database administration is a business function that involves managing a database in a way that maximizes its value to an organization. The conflicting goals of protecting the database and maximizing its availability and benefit to users must be balanced via good administration.

All databases need database administration. The database administration for small, personal databases is informal; database administration for large, multiuser databases can involve an office and many people. The acronym *DBA* can stand for database administration or database administrator.

Databases vary not only in size and scope and in their number of users, but also in the way they are processed. Some databases are processed just by queries, forms, and reports; some are processed by ASPs and JSPs that use Internet technology to publish database applications; some are processed by traditional application programs; and some are processed by stored procedures and triggers. Other databases are processed by all of these types of applications, with hundreds or thousands of concurrent users. Because of the complexity of database applications, three database administration functions are necessary: concurrency control, security, and backup and recovery.

The goal of concurrency control is to ensure that one user's work does not inappropriately influence another user's work. No single concurrency control technique is ideal for all circumstances. Trade-offs need to be made between the level of protection and throughput.

A transaction, or logical unit of work, is a series of actions taken against a database that occur as an atomic unit; either all of them occur or none of them do. The activity of concurrent transactions is interleaved on the database server. In some cases, updates can be lost if concurrent transactions are not controlled. Another concurrency problem concerns inconsistent reads.

A dirty read occurs when one transaction reads a changed record that has not been committed to the database. A nonrepeatable read occurs when one transaction rereads data it has previously read and finds modifications or deletions caused by another transaction. A phantom read occurs when a transaction rereads data and finds new rows that were inserted by a different transaction.

To avoid concurrency problems, database elements are locked. Implicit locks are placed by the DBMS; explicit locks are issued by the application program. The size of the locked resource is called lock granularity. An exclusive lock prohibits other users from reading the locked resource; a shared lock allows other users to read the locked resource, but they cannot update it.

Two transactions that run concurrently and generate results that are consistent with the results that would have occurred if the transactions had run separately are referred to as serializable transactions. Two-phased locking, in which locks are acquired in a growing phase and released in a shrinking phase, is one scheme for serializability. A special case of two-phase locking is to acquire locks throughout the transaction but not to free any lock until the transaction is finished.

Deadlock, or "the deadly embrace," occurs when two transactions are each waiting on a resource that the other transaction holds. Deadlock can be prevented by requiring transactions to acquire all locks at the same time. Once deadlock occurs, the only way to cure it is to abort one of the transactions and back out partially completed work.

Optimistic locking assumes that no transaction conflict will occur and then deals with the consequences if it does. Pessimistic locking assumes that conflict will occur and so prevents it ahead of time with locks. In general, optimistic locking is preferred for the Internet and for many intranet applications.

Most application programs do not explicitly declare locks. Instead, they mark transaction boundaries with BEGIN, COMMIT, and ROLLBACK transaction statements and declare the concurrent behavior they want. The DBMS then places locks for the application that will result in the desired behavior. An ACID transaction is one that is atomic, consistent, isolated, and durable. *Durable* means that database changes are permanent. *Consistency* can mean either statement level or transaction level consistency. With transaction level consistency, a transaction may not see its own changes.

The 1992 SQL standard defines four transaction isolation levels: read uncommitted, read committed, repeatable read, and serializable. The characteristics of each are summarized in Figure 6-10.

The goal of database security is to ensure that only authorized users can perform authorized activities at authorized times. To develop effective database security, the processing rights and responsibilities of all users must be determined.

DBMS products provide security facilities. Most involve the declaration of users, groups, objects to be protected, and permissions or privileges on those objects. Almost all DBMS products use some form of user name and password security. DBMS security can be augmented by application security.

In the event of system failure, the database must be restored to a usable state as soon as possible. Transactions in process at the time of the failure must be reapplied or restarted. Although in some cases recovery can be done by reprocessing, the use of logs and before-images and after-images with rollback and rollforward is almost always preferred. Checkpoints can be taken to reduce the amount of work that needs to be done after a failure.

In addition to concurrency control, security, and backup and recovery, the DBA needs to ensure that a system exists to gather and record errors and problems. The DBA works with the development team to resolve such problems on a prioritized basis and also to evaluate features and functions of new releases of the DBMS. Additionally, the DBMS needs to create and manage a process for controlling the database configuration so that changes to the database structure are made with a community-wide view. Finally, the DBA has the responsibility of ensuring that appropriate documentation is maintained about database structure, concurrency control, security, backup and recovery, and other details that concern the management and use of the database.

REVIEW QUESTIONS

6.1   What is the purpose of database administration?

6.2   Explain how database administration tasks vary with the size and complexity of the database.

6.3   What are two interpretations of the acronym *DBA?*

6.4   Describe five different ways databases can be processed (use Figure 6-1).

6.5   Summarize the issues involved in processing a form as described in this chapter.

6.6   What do the acronyms *ASPs* and *JSPs* stand for?

6.7   Describe in your own words the nature of traditional database processing applications.

6.8   What is a stored procedure and how is it used?

6.9   What is a trigger and how is it used?

6.10 Name three types of triggers.

6.11 What is the purpose of concurrency control?

6.12 What is the goal of a database security system?

6.13 Explain the meaning of the word *inappropriately* in the phrase "one user's work does not inappropriately influence another user's work."

6.14 Explain the trade-off that exists in concurrency control.

6.15 Describe what an atomic transaction is and explain why atomicity is important.

6.16 Explain the difference between concurrent transactions and simultaneous transactions. How many CPUs are required for simultaneous transactions?

6.17 Give an example, other than the one in this text, of the lost update problem.

6.18 Define the terms *dirty read, nonrepeatable read*, and *phantom read*.

6.19 Explain the difference between an explicit and an implicit lock.

6.20 What is lock granularity?

6.21 Explain the difference between an exclusive lock and a shared lock.

6.22 Explain two-phased locking.

6.23 How does releasing all locks at the end of a transaction relate to two-phase locking?

6.24 What is deadlock? How can it be avoided? How can it be resolved once it occurs?

6.25 Explain the difference between optimistic and pessimistic locking.

6.26 Explain the benefits of marking transaction boundaries, declaring lock characteristics, and letting the DBMS place locks.

6.27 Explain the use of the BEGIN, COMMIT, and ROLLBACK TRANSACTION statements.

6.28 Explain the meaning of the expression *ACID transaction*.

6.29 Describe statement level consistency.

6.30 Describe transaction level consistency. What disadvantage can exist with it?

6.31 What is the purpose of transaction isolation levels?

6.32 Explain what read uncommitted isolation level is. Give an example of its use.

6.33 Explain what read committed isolation level is. Give an example of its use.

6.34 Explain what repeatable read isolation level is. Give an example of its use.

6.35 Explain what serializable isolation level is. Give an example of its use.

6.36 Explain the necessity of defining processing rights and responsibilities. How are such responsibilities enforced?

6.37 Explain the relationships of users, groups, permission, and objects for a generic database security system.

6.38 Describe the advantages and disadvantages of DBMS-provided security.

6.39 Describe the advantages and disadvantages of application-provided security.

6.40 Explain how a database could be recovered via reprocessing. Why is this generally not feasible?

6.41 Define the terms *rollback* and *rollforward*.

6.42 Why is it important to write to the log before changing the database values?

6.43 Describe the rollback process. Under what conditions should rollback be used?

6.44 Describe the rollforward process. Under what conditions should rollforward be used?

6.45 What is the advantage of taking frequent checkpoints of a database?

6.46 Summarize the DBA's responsibilities for managing database user problems.

6.47 Summarize the DBA's responsibilities for configuration control.

6.48 Summarize the DBA's responsibilities for documentation.

EXERCISES

6.49 To respond to the following, open Microsoft Access and search in Access Help for "sharing an Access database."

    A. Summarize the ways in which an Access database can be shared.

    B. Summarize Access locking facilities.

C.   Summarize the facilities for setting options on shared Access databases.

D.   Search in Help for "backup and restore." Summarize the backup and recovery options available with Microsoft Access.

6.50   If you have access to SQL Server, search its Help site to answer the following questions.

A.   Does SQL Server support stored procedures? If so, what language(s) is (are) used to write them?

B.   What types of triggers does SQL Server support? Give an example of the use of each type.

C.   Is it the case that SQL Server supports both optimistic and pessimistic locking?

D.   What levels of transaction isolation are available?

E.   How does the security model for SQL Server differ from that shown in Figure 6-13?

F.   Summarize the types of SQL Server backup.

G.   Summarize the SQL Server recovery models.

6.51   If you have access to Oracle, search its Help site to answer the following questions.

A.   Does Oracle support stored procedures? If so, what language(s) is (are) used to write them?

B.   What types of triggers does Oracle support? Give an example of the use of each type.

C.   Explain why it is not possible to make dirty reads when using Oracle.

D.   What levels of transaction isolation are available?

E.   How does the security model for Oracle differ from that shown in Figure 6-13?

F.   Summarize in broad terms how Oracle performs recovery from instance failure.

G.   Summarize in broad terms how Oracle performs recovery from media failure.

GARDEN GLORY PROJECT QUESTIONS

Assume that office personnel at Garden Glory use a database application to record services and related data changes. The service-recording application reads a row from the following PROPERTY table and another row from the following EMPLOYEE table. It then creates a new row in service and updates TotalHoursWorked in EMPLOYEE by adding the HoursWorked value in the new SERVICE record to TotalHoursWorked. This operation is referred to as a Service Update Transaction.

PROPERTY (PropertyID, Street, City, State, Zip, *OwnerID*)

EMPLOYEE (Initials, Name, CellPhone, ExperienceLevel, TotalHoursWorked)

SERVICE (PropertyID, *Initials*, Date, HoursWorked)

In some cases, the employee record does not exist before the service is recorded. In this case, a new EMPLOYEE row is created and then the service is recorded. This is termed a Service Update for New Employee Transaction.

A. Explain why it is important for the changes made by the Service Update Transaction to be atomic.

B. Describe a scenario in which an update of TotalHoursWorked could be lost during a Service Update Transaction.

C. Assume that many Service Update Transactions and many Service Update for New Employee Transactions are processed concurrently. Describe a scenario for a non-repeatable read and a scenario for a phantom read.

D. Explain how locking could be used to prevent the lost update in your answer to question B.

E. Is it possible for deadlock to occur between two Service Update Transactions? Why or why not? Is it possible for deadlock to occur between a Service Update and a Service Update for New Employee Transaction? Why or why not?

F. Do you think optimistic or pessimistic locking would be better for the Service Update Transactions?

G. Suppose Garden Glory identifies three groups of users: managers, administrative personnel, and system administrators. Suppose further that the only job of administrative personnel is to make Service Update Transactions. Managers can make Service Update Transactions and Service Updates for New Employee Transactions. System administrators have unrestricted access to the tables. Describe processing rights that you think would be appropriate for this situation. Use Figure 6-11 as an example. What problems might this security system have?

H. Garden Glory has developed the following procedure for backup and recovery. The company backs up the database from the server to a second computer on its network each night. Once a month, it copies the database to a CD and stores it at a manager's house. It keeps paper records of all services provided for an entire year. If it ever loses its database, it plans to restore it from a backup and reprocess all service requests.

Do you think this backup and recovery program is sufficient for Garden Glory? What problems might occur? What alternatives exist? Describe any changes you think the company should make to this system.

JAMES RIVER JEWELRY PROJECT QUESTIONS

Assume that office personnel at James River use a database application to record consignment data. The following two tables are used to maintain owner data, to record the negotiated sales price and commission percentage for each item of jewelry accepted on consignment, and to record the actual sales price.

OWNER (<u>OwnerID</u>, Name, Phone, Email, AmountOwed)

JEWELRY_ITEM (<u>ItemNumber</u>, DateReceived, DateSold, NegotiatedSalesPrice, ActualSalesPrice, ComissionPercentage, *OwnerID*)

When an item is received on consignment, owner data are stored if the owner is new; otherwise existing owner data are used. A new JEWELRY_ITEM row is created, and data are stored for all columns except DateSold and ActualSalesPrice. James River personnel refer to these actions as an Acceptance Transaction. Later, if the jewelry item does not sell, the NegotiatedSalesPrice and CommissionPercentage values may be reduced. This is called a Price Adjustment Transaction. Finally, when an item sells, the DateSold and ActualSalesPrice fields for the item are given values, and the AmountOwed value in OWNER is updated by increasing AmountOwed by the owner's percentage of the ActualSalesPrice value. This third transaction is called a Sales Transaction.

A. Explain why it is important for the changes made by each of these transactions to be atomic.

B. Describe a scenario in which an update of AmountOwed could be lost.

C. Describe a scenario for a nonrepeatable read and a scenario for a phantom read.

D. Explain how locking could be used to prevent the lost update in your answer to question B.

E. Is it possible for deadlock to occur between two Acceptance Transactions? Why or why not? Is it possible for deadlock to occur between two Sales Transactions? Why or why not? Is it possible for deadlock to occur between an Acceptance Transaction and a Sales Transaction? Why or why not?

F. For each of these three types of transaction, describe whether you think optimistic or pessimistic locking would be better. Explain the reasons for your answer.

G. Suppose James River identifies three groups of users: managers, administrative personnel, and system administrators. Suppose further that managers and administrative personnel can perform Acceptance and Sales Transactions, but only managers can perform Price Adjustment Transactions. Describe processing rights that you think would be appropriate for this situation. Use Figure 6-11 as an example.

H. James River has developed the following procedure for backup and recovery. The company backs up the database from the server to a second computer on its network each night. Once a month, it copies the database to a CD and stores it at a manager's house. It keeps paper records of all services provided for an entire year. If it ever loses its database, it plans to restore it from a backup and reprocess all service requests. Do you think this backup and recovery program is sufficient for James River? What problems might occur? What alternatives exist? Describe any changes you think the company should make to this system.

MID-WESTERN UNIVERSITY CHEMISTRY DEPARTMENT

The computer that stores the magnet scheduling database is infected by a virus, and the database file is destroyed. No backup exists. All upcoming appointment data and all records of past magnet utilization are lost. For several weeks, magnet scheduling is chaotic. Several principal investigators complain to the department chair about missing important deadlines because of the scheduling problems. In addition, historical usage data that could have been used to justify the need for another magnet have been lost.

Someone tells the department chair that the database needs a database administrator. The department chair does not know what this term means or what the job involves. Assume she asks you to prepare a one- to two-page memo that explains what database administration is and how it would pertain to the magnet scheduling database. Include specific tasks in your memo, and describe the qualifications needed by the person(s) who will serve as the DBA.

Advanced Topics

Understand the nature, need, and importance of the following topics:

> Web database processing
> Database processing with XML
> Distributed database processing
> OLAP and data mining
> Object-relational database management

This chapter introduces topics that build upon the fundamentals you learned in the prior six chapters. Here we present the goals and purpose, fundamental ideas, and advantages and disadvantages of five topics. This knowledge will add to your database literacy, as well as introduce you to ideas that you might find interesting and about which you might want to learn more on your own.

▶ WEB DATABASE PROCESSING

Figure 7-1 shows the typical Web database processing environment. Client computers run browsers that process the database via a Web server. The Web server computer processes the Hypertext Transfer Protocol HTTP protocol to communicate with the browsers. In most cases, database applications also run on the Web server. Such applications are normally a mixture of Hypertext Markup Language HTML and application logic coded in scripting languages like JavaScript, VBScript, and Hypertext Preprocessor PHP; in some cases, full-blown programming languages like Java, C#, and VisualBasic.Net are used as well. The DBMS and database are the final components.

If the Web server and the DBMS can run on the same computer, the system has **two-tier** architecture. (One tier is for the browsers and one is for the Web server/DBMS computer.) Alternatively, the Web server and DBMS can run on different computers in which the system has **three-tier** architecture. High-performance applications might use many Web server computers, and in some systems, several computers can run the DBMS, as well. In the latter case, if the DBMS computers are processing the same databases, the system is referred to as a **distributed database**. (See the discussion starting on page 175.)

Web Processing with Active Server Pages

If the computer hosting the Web server runs Windows, the Web server software is usually **Internet Information Server (IIS)**, a Web server that is built in to Windows NT and Windows XP Professional. IIS processes HTTP and provides other features and functions that support server programs. In particular, IIS can process **Active Server Pages (ASPs)**, which are blends of HTML and program statements that are executed on the Web server.

Figure 7-2 shows a typical ASP. In this figure, the statements included between <% and %> are program code that is to be executed on the Web server computer. All other ASP code is HTML that is generated and sent to the browser client. In Figure 7-2, the statements:

```
<HTML>

<HEAD>

<META HTTP-EQUIV="Content-Type"
CONTENT="text/html;charset=windows-1252">

<TITLE>Artist</TITLE>

</HEAD>

<!--#include virtual="ADOExamples/adovbs.inc"-->

<BODY>
```

are normal HTML. When sent to the browser, they set the title of the browser window to Artist and cause other HTML-related actions. The next group of statements:

```
<%
    Dim objConn, objRecordSet, varSql
    If IsObject(Session("_conn")) Then ' if already have a connection, use it
        Set objConn = Session("_conn")
    Else
        Set objConn = Server.CreateObject("ADODB.connection") ' get
        connection
```

FIGURE 7-1

Web Database Processing Environment

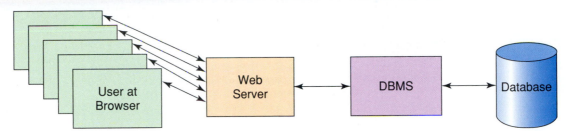

objConn.open "ViewRidgeSS" ' open VRG database using operating system authentication

objConn.IsolationLevel = adXactReadCommitted ' avoid dirty reads

Set Session("_conn") = objConn

End If

Set objRecordSet = Server.CreateObject("ADODB.Recordset") ' create the record set object

varSql = "SELECT Name, Nationality FROM ARTIST" ' set up SQL command

objRecordSet.Open varSql, objConn, adOpenStatic, adLockReadOnly ' static with no need to update

%>

are included between <% and %> and thus are code that will be executed by IIS on the Web server computer. For example, notice the second-from-last statement.

varSql = "SELECT Name, Nationality FROM ARTIST" ' set up SQL command

This statement is setting a variable to a SQL select statement. In the next statement, that variable is passed to the Open method of a record set object that causes the select statement to be executed.

The remainder of the ASP causes the result of the SQL query statement to be displayed on the Web page. The result of this ASP is shown in Figure 7-3.

ASP can contain only scripting language statements. However, such scripts can call COM objects written in languages like C# and C++. Thus, some Web database applications are a mixture of logic encoded in scripting languages along with calls to compiled objects.

We do not have sufficient space here to describe the meaning of all of the statements in this ASP. Strive instead to understand that such pages are mixtures of HTML and scripting statements. This example is taken from Chapter 12 of *Database Processing,* 9th edition.[1] See that text for an explanation of the details.

The latest Web server offering from Microsoft is ASP.NET. This is a new version of ASP; with it, Web pages are blends of HTML and object-oriented programming statements. Whereas ASP pages are interpreted, ASP.NET pages are compiled; hence, ASP.NET pages are faster than ASP pages. ASP.NET pages also segregate HTML from programming statements so they are easier to understand and maintain.

---

[1]David Kroenke, *Database Processing,* 9th edition (Upper Saddle River, NJ: Prentice Hall, 2004).

FIGURE 7-2

Example of an Active Java Server Page (ASP)

```
<HTML>
<HEAD>
<META HTTP-EQUIV="Content-Type" CONTENT="text/html;charset=windows-1252">
<TITLE>Artist</TITLE>
</HEAD>
<!--#include virtual="ADOExamples/adovbs.inc"-->
<BODY>
<%
Dim objConn, objRecordSet, varSql

        If IsObject(Session("_conn")) Then ' if already have a connection, use it
            Set objConn = Session("_conn")
        Else
            Set objConn = Server.CreateObject("ADODB.connection") ' get connection
            objConn.open "ViewRidgeSS"  ' open VRG database using operating system authentication
            objConn.IsolationLevel = adXactReadCommitted ' avoid dirty reads
            Set Session("_conn") = objConn
        End If

        Set objRecordSet = Server.CreateObject("ADODB.Recordset") ' create the record set object

        varSql = "SELECT Name, Nationality FROM ARTIST" ' set up SQL command
        objRecordSet.Open varSql, objConn, adOpenStatic, adLockReadOnly ' static with no need to update
%>

<TABLE BORDER=1 BGCOLOR=#ffffff CELLSPACING=5><FONT FACE="Arial" COLOR=#000000><CAPTION><B>ARTIST
</B></CAPTION></FONT>
<THEAD>
<TR>
<TH BGCOLOR=#c0c0c0 BORDERCOLOR=#000000 ><FONT SIZE=2 FACE="Arial" COLOR=#000000>Name</FONT></TH>
<TH BGCOLOR=#c0c0c0 BORDERCOLOR=#000000 ><FONT SIZE=2 FACE="Arial" COLOR=#000000>Nationality</FONT>
</TH>

</TR>
</THEAD>
<TBODY>
<%
On Error Resume Next
objRecordSet.MoveFirst
do while Not objRecordSet.eof
 %>
<TR VALIGN=TOP>
<TD BORDERCOLOR=#c0c0c0 ><FONT SIZE=2 FACE="Arial" COLOR=#000000><%=Server.HTMLEncode(objRecordSet
("Name"))%><BR></FONT></TD>
<TD BORDERCOLOR=#c0c0c0 ><FONT SIZE=2 FACE="Arial" COLOR=#000000><%=Server.HTMLEncode(objRecordSet
("Nationality"))%><BR></FONT></TD>

</TR>
<%
objRecordSet.MoveNext
loop%>
</TBODY>
<TFOOT></TFOOT>
</TABLE>
</BODY>
</HTML>
```

Web Processing with JSP

In the Linux and Unix worlds, the most commonly used Web server is Apache. Apache fulfills a role similar to that for IIS; it processes HTTP and provides support for the processing of logic in Web pages. The scripting language PHP is frequently used in conjunction with Apache. The structure and content of PHP pages is conceptually similar to that of ASP pages.

FIGURE 7-3

Results of ASP in
Figure 7-2

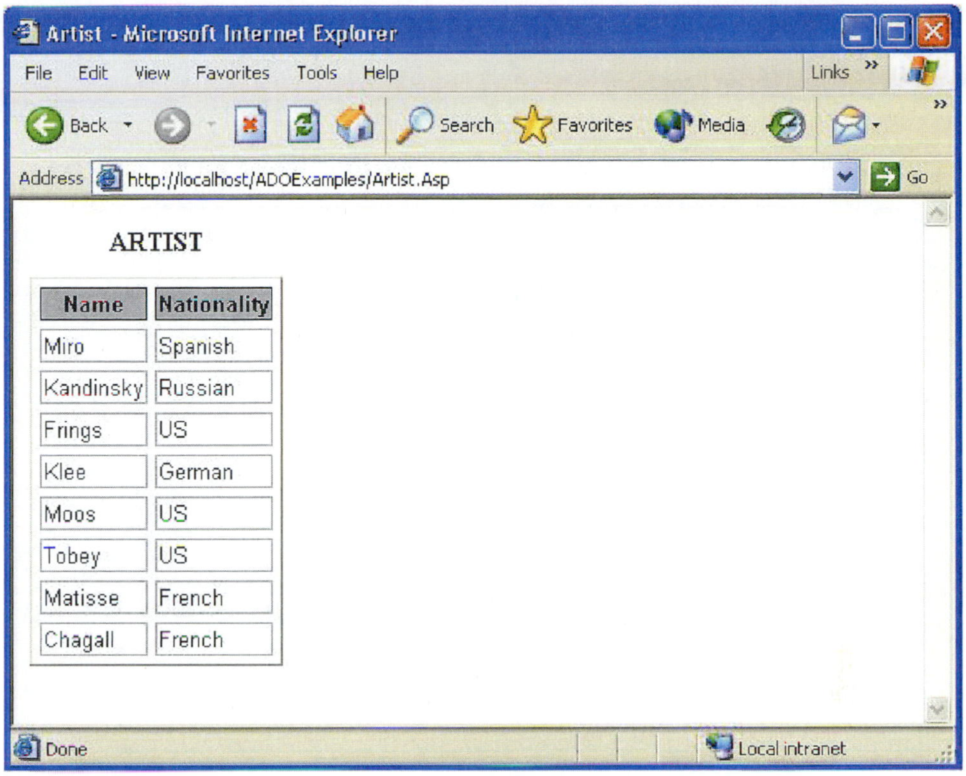

Another alternative for processing databases with Apache is **Java Server Pages (JSPs)**. Unlike ASPs, which are interpreted during execution, JSPs are compiled into Java executables called **servlets**. Thus, they are generally faster than equivalent ASP pages. In addition, any valid Java statement or structure can be included in a JSP. JSPs are akin to ASP.NET pages. Figure 7-4 summarizes these products.

Figure 7-5 shows a typical JSP page. The page appears deceptively similar to the ASP page in Figure 7-2. The important difference is that the statements included between <% . . . %> are Java statements. Any valid Java statement can be included in them. This means the capabilities of a full-blown programming language are available to the Web page author. In addition, this page, unlike the ASP page in Figure 7-2, will be compiled into executable code. The result of this JSP is shown in Figure 7-6. These examples are taken from Chapter 14 of *Database Processing,* 9th edition. You can see that text for an explanation of the details.

This example uses a DBMS program called MySQL. MySQL does not have as many features as products like Oracle and SQL Server, but it is easier to use. Also, for non-commercial applications, it is license-free under the GPL license agreement. See the Web site **www.MySQL.com** for more information about MySQL.

FIGURE 7-4

Comparison of Popular
Web Server Products

	Windows	Linux or Unix
Scripting Languages (interpreted)	IIS/ASP pages with VBScript or JavaScript	Apache with PHP
Object Oriented Languages (compiled)	IIS/ASP.NET with VisualBasic.Net, C#, or C++	JSP with Java

FIGURE 7-5

Example of a Java Server Page (JSP)

```
<!DOCTYPE HTML PUBLIC "-//W3C//DTD HTML 4.0 Transitional//EN">
<!-- Example of Database Access from a JSP Page -->
<%@ page import="java.sql.*" %>
<HTML>
<HEAD>
<TITLE>Table Display Using JDBC and MySQL</TITLE>
<META NAME="author" CONTENT="David Kroenke">
<META NAME="keywords"
      CONTENT="JSP,JDBC,Database Access">
<META NAME="description"
      CONTENT="An example of displaying a table using JSP.">
<LINK REL=STYLESHEET HREF="JSP-Styles.css" TYPE="text/css">
</HEAD>
<BODY>
<H2>Database Access Example</H2>
<% String varTableName= request.getParameter("Table");
   varTableName = varTableName.toUpperCase(); %>
<H3>Showing Data from MySQL Database vr1</H3>
<%
try    {
    // Load the Mark Mathew MySQL JDBC Drivers
    Class.forName("org.gjt.mm.mysql.Driver").newInstance();

    // Connect to vr1 with user dk1
    String connString = "jdbc:mysql://localhost/" + "vr1" + "?user=dk1";
        Connection conn = DriverManager.getConnection(connString);

    // Get rs and rsMeta for the SELECT statement
    Statement stmt = conn.createStatement();
    String varSQL = "SELECT * FROM " + varTableName;
    ResultSet rs = stmt.executeQuery(varSQL);
    ResultSetMetaData rsMeta = rs.getMetaData();
%>
<TABLE BORDER=1 BGCOLOR=#ffffff CELLSPACING=5><FONT FACE="Arial" COLOR=#000000
><CAPTION><B><%=varTableName%></B></CAPTION></FONT>
<THEAD>
<TR><%
    String varColNames ="";
    int varColCount = rsMeta.getColumnCount();
    for (int col =1; col <= varColCount; col++) {
        %><TH BGCOLOR=#c0c0c0 BORDERCOLOR=#000000 ><FONT SIZE=2 FACE ="Arial" COLOR=#000000
        ><%=rsMeta.getColumnName(col)%></FONT> </TH>
<%  }%>
</TR>
</THEAD>
<TBODY><%
    while (rs.next()) {
        %><TR VALIGN=TOP><%
            for (int col = 1; col <= varColCount; col++) {
        %><TD BORDERCOLOR=#C0C0C0 ><FONT SIZE=2 FACE="Arial" COLOR=#000000
            ><%=rs.getString(col)%><BR></FONT></TD>
<%      }
    }

    // Clean up
    rs.close();
    stmt.close();
    conn.close();
}
catch (ClassNotFoundException e) {
    out.println("Driver Exception  " + e);
}%>
</TR>
</TBODY>
<TFOOT</TFOOT>
</TABLE>
</BODY>
</HTML>
```

FIGURE 7-6

Results of JSP in
Figure 7-5

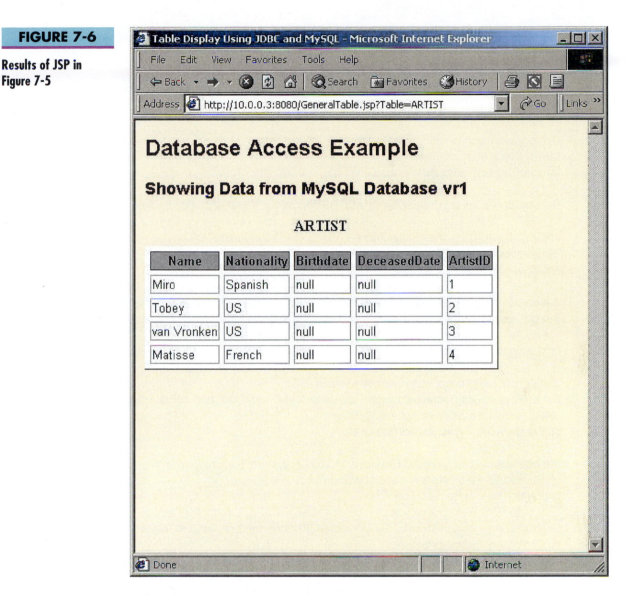

ODBC and JDBC

Every DBMS product has an **application program interface (API)**. An API is a collection of objects, methods, and properties for executing DBMS functions from program code. Unfortunately, each DBMS has its own API, and the APIs vary from one DBMS product to another. To save programmers from having to learn to use many different interfaces, the computer industry developed two standards for database access.

The **Open Database Connectivity (ODBC)** standard is the older and more popular of these two standards. Using ODBC, a programmer codes instructions using ODBC standard statements. These instructions are passed to an ODBC driver, which translates them into the API of the particular DBMS in use. The driver receives results back from the DBMS and translates those results into a form that is part of the ODBC standard.

Figure 7-7 shows a portion of an ASP that has a code segment that calls a stored procedure named Customer_Insert. The stored procedure is coded to receive four parameters: Name, AreaCode, PhoneNumber, and Nationality. The purpose of the code in Figure 7-7 is to obtain values for the four parameters from the Web page that has just been submitted and then to set up and call the DBMS to execute the Customer_Insert stored procedure using those values.

FIGURE 7-7

Example Use of ODBC in ASP Page

```
<%

Dim objConn, objCommand, objParam, oRs
Dim objRecordSet, objField
Dim varI, varSql, varNumCols, varValue

Set objConn = Server.CreateObject("ADODB.connection") 'stored procedure sets isolation level

objConn.open "DSN=ViewRidgeOracle2;UID=DK1;PWD=Sesame"
'objConn.open "ViewRidgeSS", could use this to update via SQL Server
Set Session("_conn") = objConn

Set objCommand = Server.CreateObject("ADODB.Command") 'create a command object
Set objCommand.ActiveConnection = objConn 'set the command objects connection

objCommand.CommandText="{call Customer_Insert (?, ?, ?, ?)}" 'setup call to stored procedure

'Set up four parameters with necessary values
Set objParam = objCommand.CreateParameter("NewName", adChar, adParamInput, 50)
objCommand. Parameters.Append objParam
objParam.Value = Request.Form("text1")

Set objParam = objCommand.CreateParameter("AreaCode", adChar, adParamInput, 5)
objCommand. Parameters.Append objParam
objParam.Value = Request.Form("text2")

Set objParam = objCommand.CreateParameter("PhoneNumber", adChar, adParamInput, 8)
objCommand. Parameters.Append objParam
objParam.Value = Request.Form("text3")

Set objParam = objCommand.CreateParameter("Nationality", adChar, adParamInput, 25)
objCommand. Parameters.Append objParam
objParam.Value = Request.Form("text4")

'Fire the Stored Proc

set oRs = ojbCommand.Execute

%>
```

This code is remarkable because, with the exception of one statement, it can process either an Oracle or a SQL Server database. The fifth line of this procedure sets up a connection to an Oracle database. The sixth line, which is commented out (like Visual Basic, an apostrophe at the beginning of a line indicates a comment), would, if it were active, set up a connection to a SQL Server database. Other than these two lines, the rest of the ASP code is identical, regardless of which DBMS product is in use.

Behind the scenes, ODBC drivers are translating the ODBC calls into syntax that is acceptable to the Oracle or SQL Server APIs, whichever is in use. Although these two

APIs are very different, the application program is protected from that difference because it uses the ODBC standard.

A similar standard, called **JDBC**, has been developed for use with Java. JDBC is used primarily on computers that run Linux or Unix. The concept of JDBC is the same as for ODBC. Namely, the programmer writes Java code to a standard interface, and JDBC programs translate the standard interface commands into instructions for a particular DBMS. JDBC programs receive results back from the DBMS and pass them according to the standard interface, back to the calling program. The implementation of JDBC is different than that for ODBC, but the overall concept is the same.

The JDBC interface was developed and promulgated by the company Sun, which states that JDBC does *not* stand for Java Database Connectivity; in fact, it is not an acronym for anything.

Challenges for Web Database Processing

Web database application processing is complicated by an important characteristic of HTTP. Specifically, HTTP is stateless; it has no provision for maintaining sessions between requests. Using HTTP, a client at a browser makes a request of a Web server. The server services the client request, sends results back to the browser, and forgets about the interaction with that client. A second request from that same client is treated as a new request from a new client. No data are kept to maintain a session or connection with the client.

This characteristic poses no problem for serving content, either static Web pages or responses to queries of a database. However, it is not acceptable for applications that require multiple database actions in an atomic transaction. Recall from Chapter 6 that in some cases, a group of database actions needs be grouped into a transaction with all of them committed to the database or none of them committed to the database. In this case, the Web server or other program must augment the base capabilities of HTTP.

For example, IIS provides features and functions for maintaining data about sessions between multiple HTTP requests and responses. Using these features and functions, the application program on the Web server can save data to and from the browser. A particular session will be associated with a particular set of data. In this way, the application program can start a transaction, conduct multiple interactions with the user at the browser, make intermediate changes to the database, and finally, commit or roll back all changes when ending the transaction.

Other means are used to provide for sessions and session data with Apache. In some cases, the application programs must create their own methods for tracking session data. PHP4 includes limited support for sessions that will likely be extended in the future.

The particulars of session management are beyond the scope of the present discussion. However, you should be aware that HTTP is stateless, and regardless of the Web server, additional code must be added to database applications to enable transaction processing.

▶ DATABASE PROCESSING AND XML

The **Extensible Markup Language (XML)** is becoming a standard means for defining the structure of documents and for transmitting documents from one computer to another. XML is important for database processing because it provides a standardized means of submitting data to a database and for receiving results back from the database. XML is a large, complicated subject that requires several books to explain fully. Here we will touch on the fundamentals and further explain why XML is important for database processing.

XML is a markup language like HTML, but it is much more, as well. Consider the XML document in Figure 7-8, which contains data about an artist. Like HTML, it has tags that identify content. For example, the tag <Name> … </Name> identifies the data item Miro. The tag <Nationality> … </Nationality> identifies the data value Spanish. Other tags identify Birthdate and DeceasedDate.

FIGURE 7-8

Example XML Document

```
<Artist xmlns:xsi="http://www.w3.org/2001/XMLSchema-instance"
        xsi:noNamespaceSchemaLocation="C:\DB9e\First Draft\Chapter 13\XML Docs\Artist1.xsd"
        ArtStyle="Modern">
   <Name>Miro</Name>
   <Nationality>Spanish</Nationality>
   <Birthdate>1893</Birthdate>
   <DeceasedDate>1983</DeceasedDate>
</Artist>
```

XML Schema Documents

HTML has a fixed set of tags that was determined by the developers of that language. In contrast, with XML, the author of a document type can create his or her own set of tags. That is the meaning of the term *extensible* in Extensible Markup Language—the developer can extend the basic XML tags. Even more, the author of a document type can declare the relationships the tags have to one another. Thus, with XML, one can declare that a document called INVOICE will have a tag named Customer. Within that tag, there must be at least a Name and a Phone number; within Phone, there must be an AreaCode and a LocalNumber.

The allowable tags and their relationships to one another are defined in an **XML schema document**. The XML Schema document in Figure 7-9 defines the structure of the document in Figure 7-8. Without worrying about the particulars, notice the relationship of the tags in Figure 7-8 to their definition in Figure 7-9.

An XML document can declare the name and location of the schema document that defines the tags it uses. When this is done, a validation program can verify that the document does, in fact, conform to its schema. Every browser today, as well as hundreds of other programs, contains a schema validation program. You can submit an XML document and its schema to Internet Explorer, for example, and it will verify whether the document conforms to its schema or is **schema-valid document**.

XML schema documents are themselves XML documents. This means that they, too, can be validated against their schema, which is a schema of schemas. That document is maintained by the World Wide Web Consortia (W3C) on its Web site at **www.W3C.org**. That Web site contains much more information as well, including a number of excellent tutorials.

The ability of an automated process to validate documents means enormous cost savings. For example, a large corporation such as Wal-Mart can publish XML schemas for all of the documents that it exchanges with its vendors. In particular, suppose they publish an XML schema for invoice documents. Any vendor that wishes to submit an invoice to

FIGURE 7-9

Document for the XML Document in Figure 7-8

```
<xsd:schema xmlns:xsd="http://www.w3.org/2001/XMLSchema">
   <xsd:element name="Artist">
      <xsd:complexType>
         <xsd:sequence>
            <xsd:element name="Name"/>
            <xsd:element name="Nationality"/>
            <xsd:element name="Birthdate" minOccurs="0"/>
            <xsd:element name="DeceasedDate" minOccurs="0"/>
         </xsd:sequence>
         <xsd:attribute name="ArtStyle"/>
      </xsd:complexType>
   </xsd:element>
</xsd:schema>
```

Wal-Mart can first obtain the schema to determine how to prepare the invoice. (The schema documents are placed in a publicly accessible location on the Web.) The vendor can then prepare an invoice accordingly and can check its work by validating the invoice before sending it. When Wal-Mart receives the invoice, it validates it against the schema to ensure that the vendor sent a correctly formatted invoice. Thus, once the document has been created, the validation is automated. This might not sound important, but it can save tens of thousands of clerical hours for a corporation like Wal-Mart.

XML and Database Processing

What does all of this have to do with database processing? Notice the next-to-last sentence in the prior paragraph: "Once the document has been created, the validation is automated." The question is, how are the XML documents to be generated in the first place? In addition, once a company has received and validated a document, how does it place the data in that document into its database?

The answer is to use database applications. Such applications can be written to generate XML documents that conform to an XML schema document, and they can be written to accept such documents and extract that data for storage in the database.

The means by which this is done is currently under development. One way is to extend SQL to cause the results from a SQL statement to be produced in XML format. For example, using SQL Server, the SQL statement:

```
SELECT    *

FROM      ARTIST

          FOR XML AUTO, ELEMENTS;
```

will generate the XML document shown in Figure 7-10.

In truth, this solution is not satisfactory for a number of reasons. It works for certain data structures but not for all. Other means are currently being developed by Oracle, Microsoft, and additional companies. ADO.NET, for example, is Microsoft's leading solution for the transformation of XML documents to and from databases.

XML Web Services

The use of XML for the transmission of database data is even more important because of the development of a new standard called **XML Web Services**. Actually, XML Web Services involves several new standards including SOAP, WSDL, UDDI, and others. In essence, XML Web Services is a means for exposing elements of program functionality over the Web.

For example, suppose you have created a database application that converts currencies. Your program will receive the amount of money stated in one currency and convert it into a second currency. You can convert U.S. dollars into Mexican pesos, or Japanese yen into euros, and so on. Using XML Web Services, you can publish your database application over the Web in such a way that other programs can consume your program as if it were on their own machine. It will appear to them as if they are using a local program even though your program might be on the other side of the world.

Perhaps you have heard the statement "The Internet is the computer." That statement becomes a reality when different computers, connected via Internet plumbing, can share programs as if they are all on the same machine.

When database applications are written as XML Web Services, any computer in the world can access the database applications using standard interfaces, and it will appear

FIGURE 7-10

Output from For XML SQL Statement

```xml
<MyData>
    <ARTIST>
        <ArtistID>3</ArtistID>
        <Name>Miro            </Name>
        <Nationality>Spanish            </Nationality>
        <Birthdate>1870</Birthdate>
        <DeceasedDate>1950</DeceasedDate>
    </ARTIST>
    <ARTIST>
        <ArtistID>4</ArtistID>
        <Name>Kandinsky        </Name>
        <Nationality>Russian            </Nationality>
        <Birthdate>1854</Birthdate>
        <DeceasedDate>1900</DeceasedDate>
    </ARTIST>
    <ARTIST>
        <ArtistID>5</ArtistID>
        <Name>Frings            </Name>
        <Nationality>US            </Nationality>
        <Birthdate>1700</Birthdate>
        <DeceasedDate>1800</DeceasedDate>
    </ARTIST>
    <ARTIST>
        <ArtistID>6</ArtistID>
        <Name>Klee            </Name>
        <Nationality>German            </Nationality>
        <Birthdate>1900</Birthdate>
    </ARTIST>
    <ARTIST>
        <ArtistID>8</ArtistID>
        <Name>Moos            </Name>
        <Nationality>US            </Nationality>
    </ARTIST>
    <ARTIST>
        <ArtistID>14</ArtistID>
        <Name>Tobey            </Name>
        <Nationality>US            </Nationality>
    </ARTIST>
    <ARTIST>
        <ArtistID>15</ArtistID>
        <Name>Matisse            </Name>
        <Nationality>French            </Nationality>
    </ARTIST>
    <ARTIST>
        <ArtistID>16</ArtistID>
        <Name>Chagall            </Name>
        <Nationality>French            </Nationality>
    </ARTIST>
</MyData>
```

as if the applications are local to the machine that uses those applications. Thus, Wal-Mart can publish its ordering application as an XML Web Service, and its vendors can write programs to consume that ordering application. The particulars are beyond the scope of this discussion. Realize, however, that Web Services are going to be important in the future, and learning about them could be advantageous.

▶ DISTRIBUTED DATABASE PROCESSING

A distributed database is a database that is stored and processed on more than one computer. Depending on the type of database and the processing that is allowed, distributed databases can present significant problems. Consider first the types of distributed databases.

Types of Distributed Databases

A database can be distributed by **partitioning**, which means to break the database into pieces and to store the pieces on multiple computers; by **replication**, which means to store the copies of the database on multiple computers; or by replication and partitioning combined.

Figure 7-11 illustrates these alternatives. Figure 7-11(a) shows a nondistributed database with four pieces labeled W, X, Y, and Z. In Figure 7-11(b), the database has been partitioned but not replicated. Portions W and X are stored and processed on Computer 1, and portions Y and Z are stored and processed on Computer 2. Figure 7-11(c) shows a database that has been replicated but not partitioned. The entire database is stored and processed on Computers 1 and 2. Finally, Figure 7-11(d) shows a database that is partitioned and replicated. Portion Y of the database is stored and processed on Computers 1 and 2.

The portions to be partitioned or replicated can be defined in many different ways. A database that has five tables (say, for example, CUSTOMER, SALESPERSON, INVOICE, LINE-ITEM, and PART) could be partitioned by assigning CUSTOMER to portion W, SALESPERSON to portion X, INVOICE AND LINE-ITEM to portion Y, and PART to portion Z. Alternatively, different rows of each of these five tables could be assigned to different computers, or different columns of each of these tables could be assigned to different computers.

Databases are distributed for two major reasons: performance and control. Having the database on multiple computers can improve throughput, either because multiple computers are sharing the workload or because communications delays can be reduced by placing the computers closer to their users. Distributing the database can improve control by segregating different portions of the database to different computers, each of which can have its own set of authorized users and permissions.

Challenges of Distributed Databases

Significant challenges must be overcome when distributing a database, and those challenges depend on the type of distributed database and on the activity that is allowed. In the case of a fully replicated database, if only one computer is allowed to make updates on one of the copies, then the challenges are not too great. All update activity occurs on that single computer, and copies of that database are sent periodically to the replication sites. The challenge is to ensure that only a logically consistent copy of the database is distributed (no partial or uncommitted transactions, for example), and to ensure that the sites understand that they are processing data that might not be current, because changes could have been made to the updated database after the local copy was made.

If multiple computers can make updates to a replicated database, then difficult problems arise. Specifically, if two computers are allowed to process the same row at the same time, they can cause three types of error: They can make inconsistent changes, one computer can delete a row that another computer is updating, or the two computers can make changes that violate uniqueness constraints.

FIGURE 7-11

Types of Distributed Databases (a) Nonpartitioned, Nonreplicated Alternative; (b) Partitioned, Nonreplicated Alternative; (c) Nonpartitioned, Replicated Alternative; and (d) Partitioned, Replicated Alternative

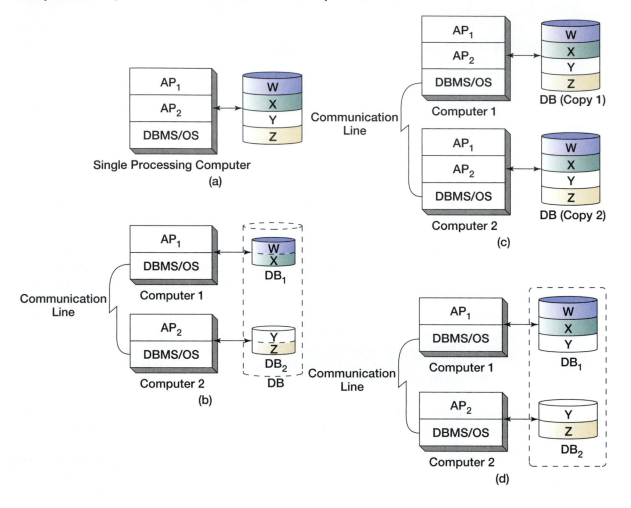

To prevent these problems, some type of record locking is required. Because multiple computers are involved, standard record locking will not work. Instead, a far more complicated locking scheme, called **distributed two-phase locking**, must be used. The specifics of that scheme are beyond the scope of this discussion; however, implementing this algorithm is difficult and expensive. For now, simply be aware that if multiple computers can process multiple replications of a distributed database, then significant problems must be solved.

If the database is partitioned but not replicated (Figure 7-11(b)), then problems will occur if any transaction updates data that span two or more distributed partitions. For example, suppose the CUSTOMER and SALESERSON tables are placed on a partition on one computer and that INVOICE, LINE-ITEM, and PART tables are placed on a second computer. Further suppose that when recording a sale, all five tables are updated in an atomic transaction. In this case, a transaction must be started on both computers, and it can be allowed to commit on one computer only if it can be allowed to commit on both computers. In this case, distributed two-phase locking also must be used.

If the data are partitioned in such a way that no transaction requires data from both partitions, then regular locking will work. However, in this case, the databases are actually two separate databases, and some would argue that they should not be considered a distributed database.

If the data are partitioned in such a way that no transaction updates data from both partitions but that one or more transactions read data from one partition and update data on a second partition, then problems might or might not result with regular locking. If dirty reads are possible, then some form of distributed locking will be required; otherwise, regular locking should work.

If the database is partitioned and at least one of those partitions is replicated, then locking requirements are a combination of those just described. If the replicated portion is updated, if transactions span the partitions, or if dirty reads are possible, then distributed two-phase locking is required; otherwise, regular locking might suffice.

Distributed processing is complicated and can create substantial problems. Except for replicated, read-only databases, only experienced teams with a substantial budget and significant time to invest should attempt distributed databases. Such databases also require data communications expertise. Distributed databases are not for the faint of heart.

▶ OLAP AND DATA MINING

As stated throughout this text, databases are created to keep track of something. Often, they serve as the core of transaction processing systems such as order entry, customer resource management, enterprise resource planning, supply chain management, and other operational systems. After months or years of such activity, databases become the repository of significant portions of the organization's history, customers, suppliers, requirements, and the like. As such, a significant amount of information can be found in operational databases that could be useful for organizational analysis, planning, marketing, and other management activities.

Two styles of analyzing database data are popular today: OLAP and data mining. We will briefly consider each.

OLAP

OnLine Analytical Processing (OLAP) is a technique for slicing and dicing database data in a dynamic fashion. OLAP is a tool to use when you don't know the second question to ask until you see the answer to the first question.

Figure 7-12 shows an OLAP analysis of student project data. The body of the table shows the **measures** of the analysis, which in this case are the average of student project scores and the total number of students. If you look in the bottom, right-hand corner of this table, you can see that the average total points for all students was 522. You also can see that the analysis was performed on a total of 120 students.

A **dimension** in an OLAP analysis is a characteristic associated with the measures. Figure 7-12 shows three measures: Major (shown in rows), Sex, and Year (shown in columns). The values of the majors are coded; the user of this analysis knows the meanings of these values. For your interpretation, the value O-E-ACCTG means a business college accounting major, the value O-E-B A means a general business administration major, the value O-E I S means a business college information systems major, and so forth.

The values of the Sex dimension are F (female) and M (male), and the values of the Year dimension are 1 (freshman), 2 (sophomore), 3 (junior), and 4 (senior). If you examine this table, you can see the results of average project scores broken down by the dimensions. Looking along the right-hand margin, you can see, for example, that a total of 37 accounting students averaged 540 points on the projects. The 52 business administration students averaged 513 points.

Looking along the bottom of the grid you can see that a total of 71 females and 49 males are counted in the data, including eight sophomore females, 46 junior females, and 17 senior females. You can see the average for each of these categories, as well.

One of the advantages of OLAP is that the dimensions can easily be switched and combined in different ways. Figure 7-13 shows the same data, but this time broken down first by grade level and second by sex. The analysis in Figure 7-12 was changed to

FIGURE 7-12

OLAP Analysis of Student Assignment Scores

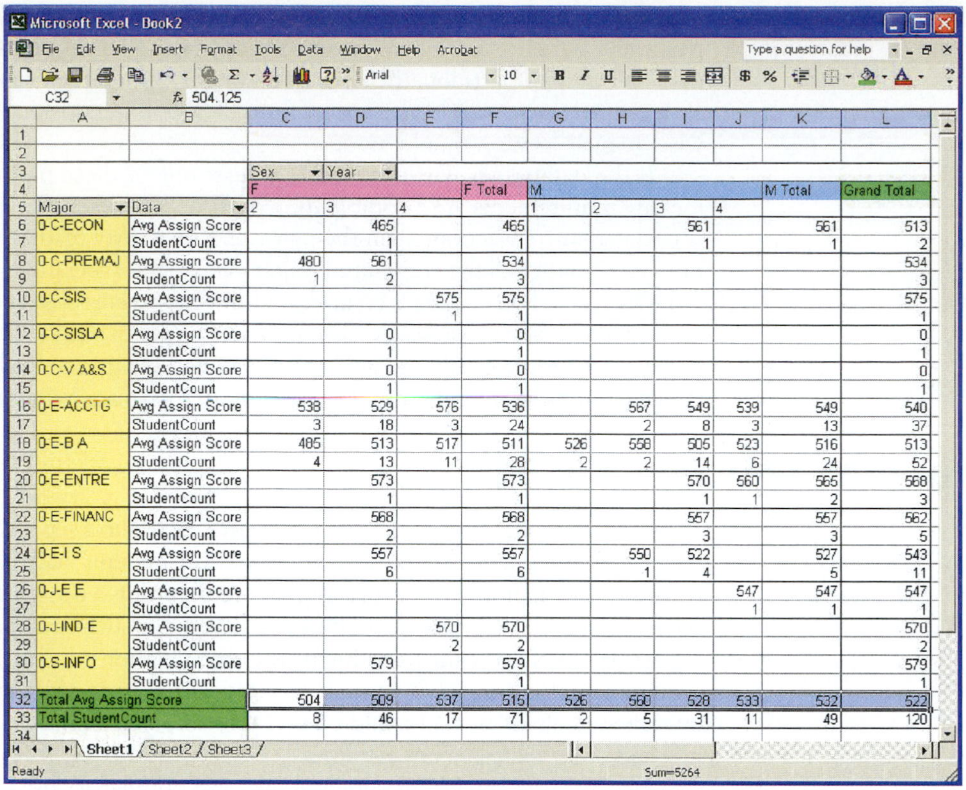

Microsoft Excel - Book2

Major	Data	Sex F / Year 2	3	4	F Total	M 1	2	3	4	M Total	Grand Total
0-C-ECON	Avg Assign Score		465		465			561		561	513
	StudentCount		1		1			1		1	2
0-C-PREMAJ	Avg Assign Score	480	561		534						534
	StudentCount	1	2		3						3
0-C-SIS	Avg Assign Score			575	575						575
	StudentCount			1	1						1
0-C-SISLA	Avg Assign Score		0		0						0
	StudentCount		1		1						1
0-C-V A&S	Avg Assign Score		0		0						0
	StudentCount		1		1						1
0-E-ACCTG	Avg Assign Score	538	529	576	536			567	549	539	549	540
	StudentCount	3	18	3	24		2	8	3	13	37
0-E-B A	Avg Assign Score	485	513	517	511	526	558	505	523	516	513
	StudentCount	4	13	11	28	2	2	14	6	24	52
0-E-ENTRE	Avg Assign Score		573		573			570	560	565	568
	StudentCount		1		1			1	1	2	3
0-E-FINANC	Avg Assign Score		568		568			557		557	562
	StudentCount		2		2			3		3	5
0-E-I S	Avg Assign Score		557		557		550	522		527	543
	StudentCount		6		6		1	4		5	11
0-J-E E	Avg Assign Score								547	547	547
	StudentCount								1	1	1
0-J-IND E	Avg Assign Score			570	570						570
	StudentCount			2	2						2
0-S-INFO	Avg Assign Score		579		579						579
	StudentCount		1		1						1
Total Avg Assign Score		504	509	537	515	526	560	528	533	532	522
Total StudentCount		8	46	17	71	2	5	31	11	49	120

C32 = 504.125   Sum=5264

FIGURE 7-13

Alternative OLAP Analysis of Student Assignment Scores

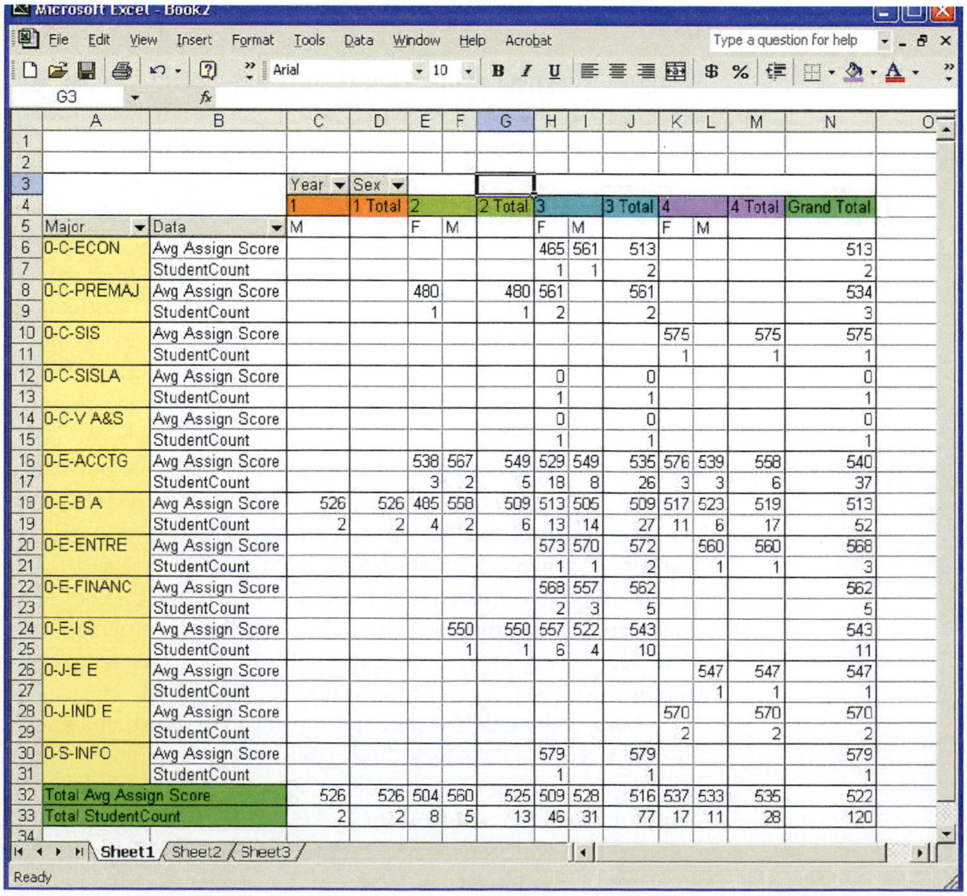

Microsoft Excel - Book2

Major	Data	Year 1 (M)	1 Total	2 (F)	2 (M)	2 Total	3 (F)	3 (M)	3 Total	4 (F)	4 (M)	4 Total	Grand Total
0-C-ECON	Avg Assign Score						465	561	513				513
	StudentCount						1	1	2				2
0-C-PREMAJ	Avg Assign Score			480		480	561		561				534
	StudentCount			1		1	2		2				3
0-C-SIS	Avg Assign Score									575		575	575
	StudentCount									1		1	1
0-C-SISLA	Avg Assign Score						0		0				0
	StudentCount						1		1				1
0-C-V A&S	Avg Assign Score						0		0				0
	StudentCount						1		1				1
0-E-ACCTG	Avg Assign Score			538	567	549	529	549	535	576	539	558	540
	StudentCount			3	2	5	18	8	26	3	3	6	37
0-E-B A	Avg Assign Score	526	526	485	558	509	513	505	509	517	523	519	513
	StudentCount	2	2	4	2	6	13	14	27	11	6	17	52
0-E-ENTRE	Avg Assign Score						573	570	572		560	560	568
	StudentCount						1	1	2		1	1	3
0-E-FINANC	Avg Assign Score						568	557	562				562
	StudentCount						2	3	5				5
0-E-I S	Avg Assign Score				550	550	557	522	543				543
	StudentCount				1	1	6	4	10				11
0-J-E E	Avg Assign Score									547		547	547
	StudentCount									1		1	1
0-J-IND E	Avg Assign Score									570		570	570
	StudentCount									2		2	2
0-S-INFO	Avg Assign Score						579		579				579
	StudentCount						1		1				1
Total Avg Assign Score		526	526	504	560	525	509	528	516	537	533	535	522
Total StudentCount		2	2	8	5	13	46	31	77	17	11	28	120

G3

that in Figure 7-13 by simply dragging and dropping the Year label on top of the Sex label. Using the analysis in Figure 7-13, you can now see, for example, that the average scores and number of students for freshmen, sophomores, juniors, and seniors were, respectively (526, 2), (525, 13), (516, 77), and (535, 28). Other breakouts on this data would be to show Major with Year, Year within Major, Major within Sex, and Sex within Major.

Figures 7-12 and 7-13 show an analysis with three dimensions. In fact, the number of dimensions in an OLAP analysis is unlimited. It is possible to have as many dimensions as are available from the underlying data.

Figure 7-14 shows the Cube Editor window for the Analysis Services (OLAP) processor that is part of SQL Server. The right-hand pane shows the structure of the two tables used to generate Figures 7-12 and 7-13. The Sex, Year, and Major columns of STUDENT were used for the dimensions. The TotalGrade column of AssignmentGrade6 (which is actually a join and not a table in the underlying database) was used to provide the measure. If desired, other columns of STUDENT could generate other dimensions. LabSection, for example, would make a good dimension.

Figures 7-12 and 7-13 are two-dimensional projections of the three dimensions of data. If this table were shown as a cube, it would include a Major axis, a Year Axis, and a Sex axis. If a LabSection dimension were included, then we would have a four-dimensional display.

Because a cube has three dimensions and because three dimensions are the most that can be shown in a display, an OLAP analysis like that in Figure 7-12 is called an **OLAP cube**. Such terminology is misleading because the display is a table, and the table is not restricted to three dimensions; regardless, such displays are called OLAP cubes. Hence, the display in Figure 7-14 is called the Cube Editor.

FIGURE 7-14

OLAP Cube Editor for Data Used in Figures 7-12 and 7-13

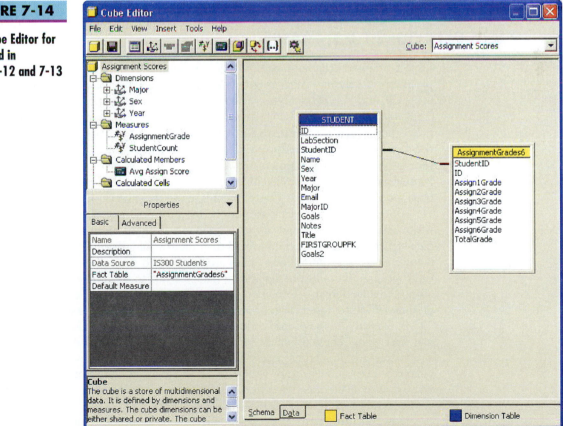

OLAP is a powerful analytical tool that is easy to learn to use, at least for basic analyses. Much untapped information undoubtedly lies in operational databases. Learning to use OLAP could be an excellent career builder for you.

Data Mining

Data mining is another form of analysis of database data. Whereas OLAP consists of the analysis of sums, averages, and other simple arithmetic measures, data mining involves the statistical processing of data, usually involving complicated mathematical and statistical techniques.

Cluster analysis is one form of data mining. With it, the underlying data are processed to search for non-normal (in the statistical sense, as in a non-Gaussian distribution) groupings in the data. For example, the data shown in Figure 7-12 might be analyzed to determine that junior, female accounting majors and senior, male information systems majors have a similar, non-normal pattern of project scores. A cluster analysis is so named because it results in descriptions of the data points that tend to cluster together.

Other forms of data mining involve regression analysis, time-series analysis, factor analysis, and more sophisticated fitting techniques such as nonparametric Monte Carlo analysis. Each of these techniques is used to search for patterns in the database data.

Data mining is used increasingly in science, where it is causing some debate and consternation among traditional scientists. When using data mining, researchers gather data and use statistical techniques to find patterns. After those patterns are found, the researchers look for explanations in science. This flies in the face of traditional research, in which hypotheses are formed and then experiments are designed to test those hypotheses. Traditional scientists would say that using data mining is allowing the throw of the dice to determine the theory. On the contrary, proponents of data mining say that data mining is just a way of using the immense computational power of the modern computer to facilitate the growth in scientific knowledge.

▶ OBJECT-RELATIONAL DATABASES

Object-oriented programming (OOP) is a technique for designing and writing computer programs. Today, most new program development is done using OOP techniques. Java, C++, C#, and VisualBasic.Net are object-oriented computer programs.

Objects have methods, which are computer programs that perform some task, and properties, which are data items particular to that object. All objects of a given class have the same methods, but each has its own set of data items. When using an OOP, the properties of the object are created and stored in main memory. Storing the values of properties of an object is called **object persistence**. Many different techniques have been used for object persistence. One of them is to use some variation of database technology.

Although relational databases can be used for object persistence, doing so requires substantial work on the part of the programmer. The problem is that, in general, object data structures are more complicated than the row of a table. Typically, several or even many rows of several different tables are required to store object data. This means the OOP programmer must design a mini database just to store objects. Many objects usually are involved in an information system, so many different mini databases need to be designed and processed. That prospect is so undesirable that it is seldom used.

In the early 1990s, several vendors developed special-purpose DBMS products for storing object data. These products, which were called **object-oriented DBMS (OODBMS)**, never achieved commercial success. The problem was that by the time they were introduced, billions of bytes of data already were stored in relational DBMS format, and no organization wanted to convert their data to OODBMS format to be able to use an OODBMS. Consequently, such products failed in the marketplace.

However, the need for object persistence did not disappear. Some vendors, most notably Oracle, added features and functions to their relational database DBMS products. These features and functions are basically add-ons to a relational DBMS that facilitate object persistence. Using them, object data can be stored more readily than with a pure relational database. However, an object-relational database can at the same time still process relational data.

Object-relational databases have seen some use in industry, but they have not gained significant market share. The rise of the Internet has made XML important, and because XML is extensible, it can be readily used to provide object persistence. Many experts today believe that object-relational databases will be supplanted by the use of XML.

If you wish to learn more about object-relational databases, check the Oracle Web site at **www.Oracle.com**. Also, search for OODBMS and ODBMS on the Web.

SUMMARY

This chapter introduces five advanced topics: Web database processing, XML and database processing, distributed database processing, OLAP and data mining, and object-relational database management.

Web database processing systems consist of users who employ browsers that connect via HTTP to a Web server that processes communications and database applications. The database applications process the database via the DBMS. In a two-tiered system, the Web server and DBMS reside on the same computer. In a three-tiered system, the Web server and DBMS reside on different computers. Higher-capacity systems employ more than one Web server.

If the Web server host runs Windows, the Web server software is usually IIS. IIS processes the HTTP protocol and Active Server Pages. These pages are blends of HTML and scripting code. HTML is processed and sent to the users' browsers. Any scripting code enclosed in <% . . . %> is executed on the Web server. Database application logic is often processed using such scripts. Scripts also can call COM objects written in full programming languages.

Microsoft's latest Web server offering is ASP.NET. With it, object-oriented programming languages like VisualBasic.Net, C#, and C++ can be used. ASP.NET pages are compiled and not interpreted.

If the Web server host runs Linux or Unix, then the Web server software is normally Apache. Apache processes HTTP and also serves as a host to other facilities, such as the scripting language PHP. A PHP page is a blend of HTML and script code, similar to ASP. JSPs are mixtures of Java and HTML. Unlike ASPs, which are interpreted, JSPs are compiled servlets. They also contain Java statements, which means that the capabilities of a full-blown OOP language are available to the JSP programmer.

Every DBMS has it own API. To simplify DBMS access, the computer industry supports two major standards: ODBC and JDBC. ODBC, which stands for Open Database Connectivity, is the older of the two and is more popular. Using ODBC, the programmer invokes database functions using standard ODBC commands. Behind the scenes, an ODBC driver transforms those commands into the API of a particular DBMS product. JDBC, which does not stand for Java Database Connectivity, is similar in concept and was developed for use with Java.

Web database processing is complicated by the fact that HTTP is stateless. When processing atomic transactions, application programs must include logic to provide for session state. The means by which this is done depends on the Web server and language in use.

XML is becoming a standard means for defining documents and transmitting them from one computer to another. Increasingly, it is used to transmit data to and from database applications. XML tags are not fixed but can be extended by document designers. An XML schema is a document that defines the structure of another document. XML schema documents are themselves XML documents; their structure is defined by a schema document at **www.w3c.org**. A document that conforms to its schema is a schema-valid document. Hundreds of programs are available that can determine schema validity.

The ability to use automated means to verify document correctness means substantial labor savings to organizations.

Database applications can create XML documents. One means for doing this is via extensions to SQL like the *For XML* expression in SQL Server. Other means are currently in development at Oracle, Microsoft, and other vendors. ADO.NET is one such means.

XML Web Services include several standards that enable program functionality to be published, or consumed, over the Web. Using XML Web Services, a database application can be utilized by computer programs across the Web as if those programs were on the local machine. XML Web Services enable the Internet to become one large computer.

A distributed database is a database that is stored and processed on more than one computer. A replicated database is one in which multiple copies of some or all of the database are stored on different computers. A partitioned database is one in which different pieces of the database are stored on different computers. A distributed database can be replicated and distributed.

Distributed databases pose processing challenges. If the database is updated on a single computer, then the challenge is simply to ensure that the copies of the database are logically consistent when they are distributed. However, if updates are to be made on more than one computer, the challenges become significant. If the database is partitioned and not replicated, then challenges occur if transactions span data on more than one computer. If the database is replicated and if updates occur to the replicated portions, then some form of a special locking algorithm called distributed two-phase locking is required. Implementing this algorithm can be difficult and expensive.

Operational databases contain records of significant portions of an organization's history. Such databases can be analyzed to provide information for management and planning. Two analytical approaches are common. With OLAP, measures of data are summed and averaged, and other simple arithmetic operations are performed. The measures are broken down by dimensions in the data. Exchanging the dimensions is easily done, and OLAP provides a flexible analytic tool.

Data mining involves the statistical processing of data, usually involving complicated mathematical and statistical techniques. Cluster analysis searches for groupings in the data. Data mining tools also include regression analysis, time-series analysis, factor analysis, and other more sophisticated techniques.

The use of data mining has increased in science, where it is used to identify patterns and trends in data. Data mining flies in the face of traditional hypothesis testing, and its use is causing debate among scientists.

Objects consist of methods and properties or data values. All objects of a given class have the same methods, but they have different property values. Object persistence is the process of storing object property values. Relational databases are difficult to use for object persistence. Some specialized products called object-oriented DBMS were developed in the 1990s but never received commercial acceptance. Oracle and others have extended the capabilities of their relational DBMS products to provide support for object persistence. Such databases are referred to as object-relational databases. In the future, XML is likely to be used for object persistence and probably will replace the use of object-relational databases.

REVIEW QUESTIONS

7.1   Name the three major components of a Web database application.

7.2   As explained in this chapter, what are the two major functions of the Web server?

7.3   Explain the difference between two-tier and three-tier architecture.

7.4   What is IIS and what functions does it serve?

7.5   What is ASP and what functions does it serve?

7.6   What is the significance of the symbols <% and %> in an ASP?

7.7   What languages are used in ASPs?

7.8 What is ASP.NET?

7.9 In the Windows world, what type of Web pages are interpreted and what type are compiled?

7.10 What is Apache and what functions does it serve?

7.11 What is PHP and what function does it serve?

7.12 What is a JSP and what functions does it serve?

7.13 Explain the differences between an ASP and a JSP.

7.14 Explain the differences between ASP.NET and JSP.

7.15 What is MySQL, and how does it differ from Oracle and SQL Server?

7.16 What does *API* stand for and, with respect to a DBMS, what does it mean?

7.17 What does *ODBC* stand for and what is its purpose?

7.18 What does *JDBC* stand for and what is its purpose?

7.19 Explain what is remarkable about the code in Figure 7-7.

7.20 With respect to HTTP, what does *stateless* mean?

7.21 Under what circumstances does stateless-ness pose a problem for database processing?

7.22 In general terms, how are sessions managed by database applications when using HTTP?

7.23 What does *XML* stand for?

7.24 How does XML differ from HTML?

7.25 Explain why XML is extensible.

7.26 What is the purpose of an XML schema document?

7.27 How is an XML document validated?

7.28 How is an XML schema document validated?

7.29 Explain an advantage of automated schema validation.

7.30 In general terms, explain why XML is important for database processing.

7.31 What is the purpose of the FOR XML expression in a SQL statement?

7.32 Name one of the purposes of ADO.NET.

7.33 What is the purpose of XML Web Services?

7.34 Explain how XML Web Services enable the Internet to be the computer.

7.35 Define *distributed database*.

7.36 Explain one way to partition a database that has three tables: T1, T2, and T3.

7.37 Explain one way to replicate a database that has three tables: T1, T2, and T3.

7.38 Explain what must be done when fully replicating a database but allowing only one computer to process updates.

7.39 If more than one computer can update a replicated database, what three problems can occur?

7.40 What solution is used to prevent the problems in question 7.39?

7.41 Explain what problems can occur in a distributed database that is partitioned but not replicated.

7.42 What organizations should consider using a distributed database?

7.43 Explain the statement "Databases can become the repository of significant portions of an organization's history."

7.44 What does *OLAP* stand for and what is its purpose?

7.45 Give an example of a measure of an OLAP analysis.

7.46 Give three examples of a dimension of an OLAP analysis.

7.47 Explain the essential difference between the OLAP cube in Figure 7-12 and the one in Figure 7-13.

7.48 Explain the meaning of the term *OLAP cube*.

7.49 How does data mining differ from OLAP?

7.50 What is the purpose of cluster analysis?

7.51 Summarize the philosophical problem when using data mining for scientific research.

7.52 Explain the meaning of the term *object persistence*.

7.53 In general terms, explain why relational databases are difficult to use for object persistence.

7.54 What does *OODBMS* stand for and what is its purpose?

7.55 According to this chapter, why were OODBMSs not successful?

7.56 What is an object-relational database?

EXERCISES

7.57 Search the Web for the terms *PHP Tutorial* and *ASP Tutorial*. Find examples of PHP and ASP that will enable you to compare and contrast them.

7.58 Go to **www.w3c.org** and read tutorials on XML and XML schema. Develop an XML schema for a document that has basic student data including Name, Phone, Email, Address, Major, and possibly many values of Activity. Give three example XML documents for your schema. Use Internet Explorer (or any other program you find) to validate your three XML documents against your schema document.

7.59 Search the Web for the terms *ADO Tutorial* and *ADO.NET Tutorial*. Find out the purposes of ADO and ADO.NET. How are they similar and how are they different?

7.60 Search the Web for the term *distributed two-phase locking*. Find a tutorial on that topic and explain, in general terms, how this locking algorithm works.

7.61 Install SQL Server Analysis services, start Analysis services, and click Analysis Manager Concepts and Tutorial. Work through the first two chapters of this tutorial: QuickStart and Basic functions. Explain in general terms the process for creating an OLAP cube.

7.62 Go to **www.Oracle.com** and search for tutorial information on object-relational databases. Explain the terms *column object, nested tables,* and *row objects*.

Appendix

Database Processing with Microsoft Access

Learn how to use Microsoft Access to:

> Create tables
> Create relationships
> Create queries using the query design tool
> Create basic forms
> Create forms with lookup combo boxes
> Create basic reports
> Create parameterized reports

In this appendix, you will learn how to apply database concepts to develop portions of a desktop database application using Microsoft Access. We begin by creating tables and relationships, and then we will build SQL queries using Access's graphical query development tool. Next, we will learn how to develop simple forms and reports with Access.

The goal of this appendix is to illustrate how to use database concepts when working with a DBMS, not to teach Access specifically.

Access is a large, complicated product with many features and functions. The *Access 2000 Developer's Handbook, Volume 1* has more than 1,600 pages. (Imagine Volume 2!) We cannot hope to cover all of Access in a short appendix. Instead, this appendix will introduce you to the major Access components. This knowledge will get you started so that you can learn more on your own.

For this database, we will use the Carbon River Construction example introduced in Chapter 1. We begin with a discussion of the database schema for this application.

▶ DATABASE SCHEMA FOR CARBON RIVER CONSTRUCTION

A database schema is a design of database tables, relationships, and constraints. As explained in Chapter 4, schemas are developed by analyzing user requirements—particularly requirements for forms, queries, and reports—and then constructing a data model. That data model is then transformed into a schema using the normalization principles discussed in Chapters 2 and 5.

For now, we will assume that the design has been finished for Carbon River Construction and that the result is the following set of four tables:

PROJECT (<u>ProjectID</u>, Name, Owner, Phone)

ITEM (<u>ItemNumber</u>, Description, Category)

SUPPLIER (<u>SupplierID</u>, Supplier, Contact, Phone, Discount)

QUOTATION (<u>QuotationID</u>, *ProjectFK*, *ItemFK*, *SupplierFK*, Quantity, RetailPrice, QuoteDate)

with the following constraints.

ProjectFK must exist in ProjectID in PROJECT

ItemFK must exist in ItemNumber in ITEM

SupplierFK must exist in SupplierID in SUPPLIER

Review these four tables in the context of Figure 1-12 (see page 11), which is a list of price quotations for items. As we stated in Chapter 1, that list has four basic themes: projects, items, suppliers, and price quotations. Each of the tables represents one of these themes. We also can examine the tables in the context of normalization, which we described in Chapter 2. From that perspective, we can say that each of these tables is normalized because, in each of them, all columns functionally depend on the table's key. For example, in the SUPPLIER table, SupplierID → (Supplier, Contact, Phone, Discount).

Carbon River Schema Data Structure Diagram

Figure A-1 shows the relationships among these tables in a data structure diagram. Such a diagram shows the tables and their columns, and represents relationships with lines between the tables. For example, the line between PROJECT and QUOTATION represents the relationship of rows between these two tables. The crow's foot at the end of the line means that one row of PROJECT can be related to many rows of QUOTATION. This makes sense; a given project will have many possible parts quotes. The oval near the

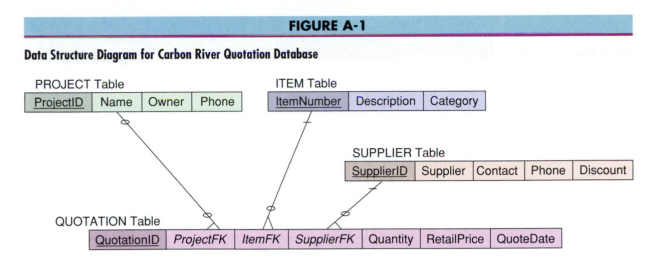

FIGURE A-1

Data Structure Diagram for Carbon River Quotation Database

bottom of this line means the relationship is optional; in other words, a PROJECT row can be stored in the database even if it has no relationship to a QUOTATION row. The oval at the top of the line between PROJECT and QUOTATION means that a QUOTATION row can be stored in the database even if it has no relationship to a PROJECT.

Examine the two other relationships shown in this diagram. An ITEM can be related to anywhere from zero to many QUOTATION rows. The straight line across the relationship line below ITEM means the relationship is required. In other words, a QUOTATION row must be related to an ITEM row. Because there is no crow's foot, a row in QUOTATION can be related to no more than one row of ITEM. Thus, a row in QUOTATION must be related to exactly one row in ITEM. This also makes sense; we cannot have a quotation without having an item for which the quote is made, and a quotation can pertain to only one item.

According to this data structure diagram, a row in SUPPLIER is related to anywhere from zero to many rows in QUOTATION, but a row in QUOTATION is related to exactly one row in ITEM. Again, these constraints make sense.

Column Design

Figure A-2 shows the design of the columns in the tables of the Carbon River database. Type shows the data type as it will be defined in Access. AutoNumber refers to a surrogate key data type; Access will provide a unique number for this column every time a row is created. As stated earlier, that column will have no meaning to the users. Other data types are as shown in Figure A-2.

In this figure, Key refers to whether the column is a primary key, a foreign key, or not a key at all. Required? indicates whether or not a null value is allowed, and Remarks contains comments about the column values as specified in the design.

Given this design, we are now ready to use Access to create the database structure.

▶ CREATING TABLES AND RELATIONSHIPS USING ACCESS

Figure A-3 shows the opening screen for Microsoft Access 2002. To create a new database, select Blank Database under the New section in the pane on the right-hand side of the screen. It also is possible to create a new database from a template, but because we have done our own database design, we need not consider that option. Other choices in this pane are beyond the scope of this appendix.

When you select Blank Database, Access displays the screen shown in Figure A-4. Because we have created our own database design, we need not use a wizard to create the tables. Instead, click Create table in Design view, and you will see the table design form in Figure A-5(a).

PROJECT Table

Column Name	Type	Key	Required?	Remarks
ProjectID	Autonumber	Primary	Yes	Surrogate Key
Name	Text (50)	No	Yes	
Owner	Text (50)	No	Yes	
Phone	Text (10)	No	No	Use input mask

ITEM Table

Column Name	Type	Key	Required?	Remarks
ItemNumber	Number (Long Integer)	Primary	Yes	User data, not surrogate key
Description	Text (100)	No	Yes	
Category	Text (12)	No	Yes	

SUPPLIER Table

Column Name	Type	Key	Required?	Remarks
SupplierID	AutoNumber	Primary	Yes	Surrogate Key
Supplier	Text (50)	No	Yes	
Contact	Text (50)	No	No	
Phone	Text (10)	No	Yes	
Discount	Number (Integer)	No	Yes	Entered as percentage

QUOTATION Table

Column Name	Type	Key	Required?	Remarks
QuotationID	Autonumber	Primary	Yes	Surrogate Key
ProjectFK	Number (Long Integer)	Foreign key to PROJECT	No	Can have a quote without a project
ItemFK	Number (Long Integer)	Foreign key to ITEM	Yes	
SupplierFK	Number (Long Integer)	Foreign key to SUPPLIER	Yes	
Quantity	Number (Long Integer)	No	Yes	
Retail Price	Currency	No	Yes	
QuoteDate	Date/Time (Medium Format)	No	Yes	Default to system date

Creating Tables

The first two fields at the top part of this form are used to enter the name and type of each column. The third field, Description, is used to enter optional comments for documentation purposes. The Description comments are ignored by Access. Notice that Access refers to columns as fields; we will continue to refer to them as columns because that is the more standard practice among database practitioners.

As shown in Figure A-5(a), you select the data type from a drop-down list. Here we are selecting AutoNumber, the data type you use in Access to create a surrogate key. After you select the data type, you can enter documentation comments.

Figure A-5(b) shows the PROJECT table after all of its columns have been defined. In this figure, the symbol of a key next to ProjectID indicates that the ProjectID column has been defined as the primary key. To define a column as the primary key, just highlight

FIGURE A-3

Opening Screen for
Microsoft Access 2002

FIGURE A-4

Table Creation Form for
Microsoft Access 2002

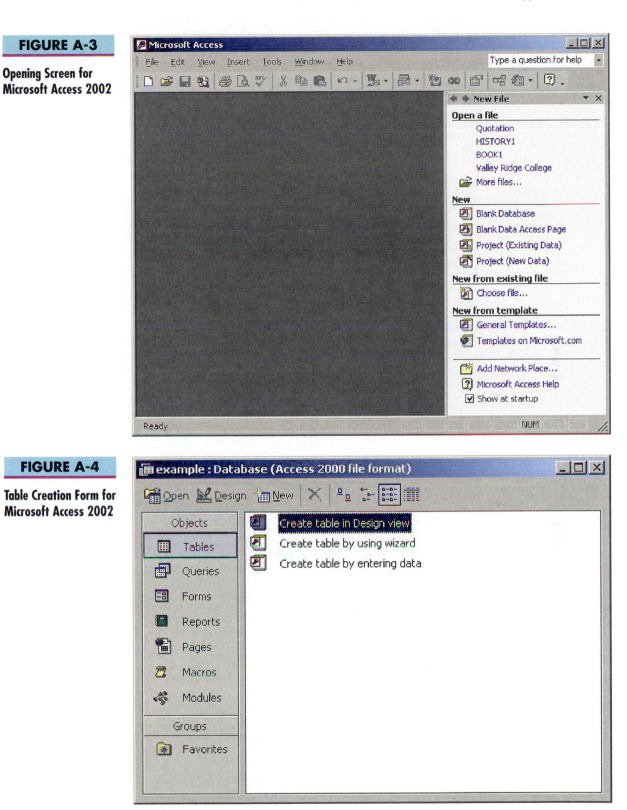

the key column (or columns, in the case of a composite key) and then click the key icon
in the toolbar at the top of the screen.

In this figure, the focus is on the Phone column. It has been defined as a Text data
type. In the bottom section of this form, note that the Field Size property has been set to
10. Notice also that the Required property has been set to No in accordance with the column design shown in Figure A-2. Also note that the Input Mask has been set to cause

FIGURE A-5(a)

Creating a Column in an Access Table

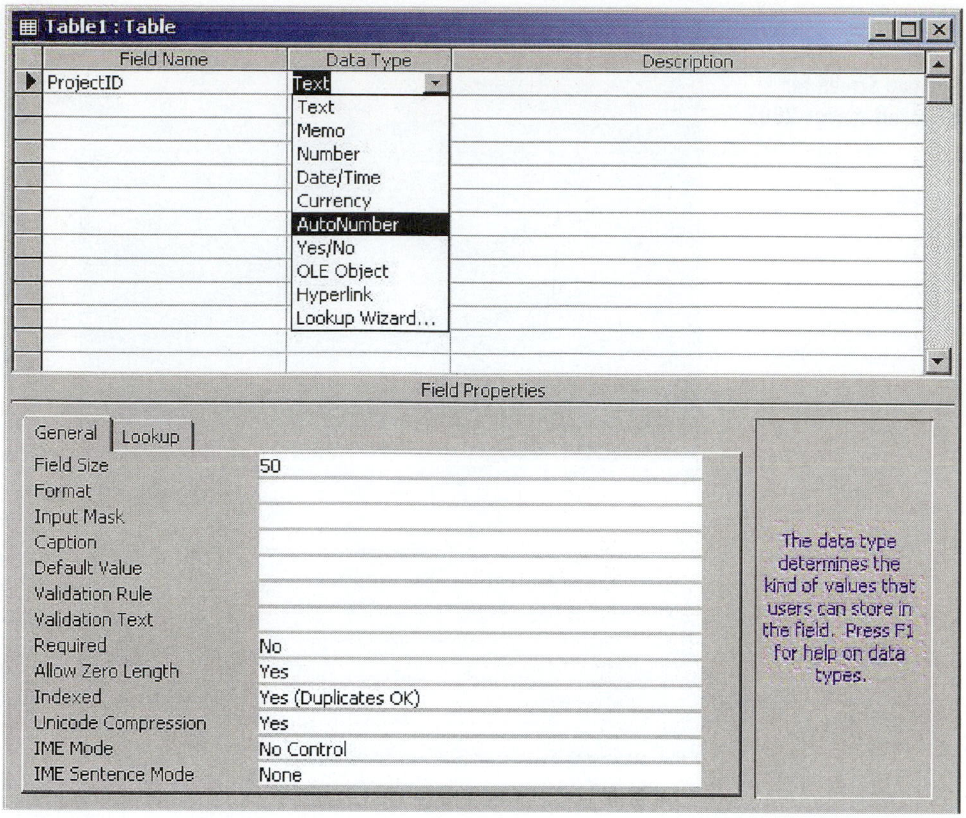

FIGURE A-5(b)

PROJECT Table with All Columns Defined

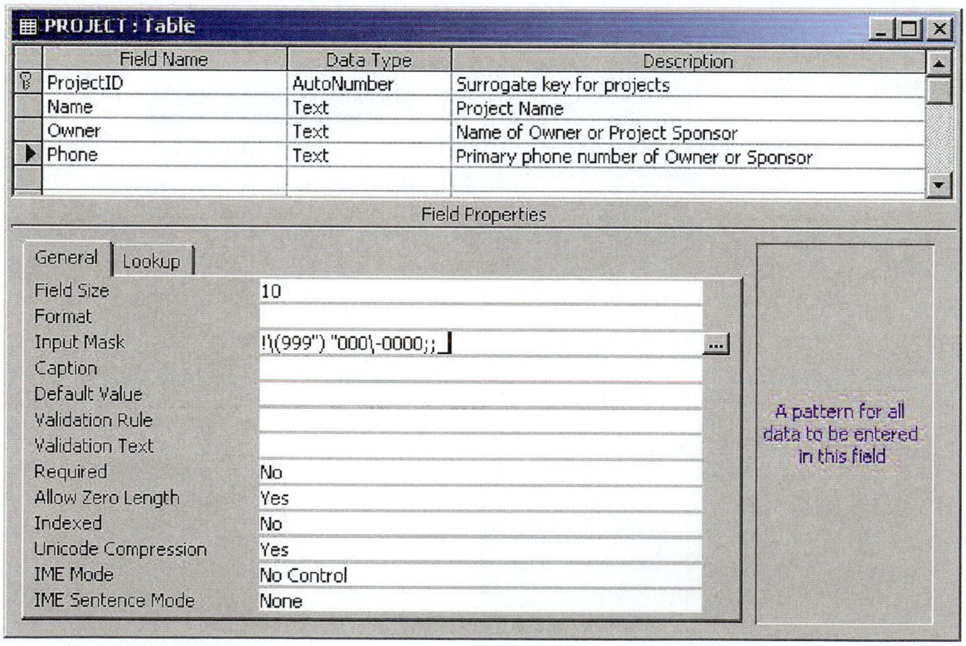

Access to place parentheses and a dash in the text boxes for entering phone data. This mask was created by running the wizard that pops up when you click the button with the ellipses (. . .) to the right of the Input Mask property. Try this on your own to see how it works.

The remaining three tables are defined to Access in a similar way. Figure A-6 shows the completed definition for the QUOTATION table. Notice that foreign keys are not defined in any special way in the table definition. All that need be done is to define the

**QUOTATION Table
Including Foreign Keys**

data type of a foreign key so that it corresponds to the data type of the primary key to which it refers. In Figure A-6, for example, the data type of ItemFK has been set to Number (Long Integer) because that is how ItemNumber is defined in ITEM (see Figure A-2). In Access, AutoNumber data types always use the Number (Long Integer) format, so any foreign key that references an AutoNumber primary key also should be defined as Number (Long Integer).

Creating Relationships

After the tables have been created, the next step is to define relationships. To do so, select Tools/Relationships . . . from the Access main menu. The Relationships window will open and the Show Table dialog box will be displayed, as shown in Figure A-7(a). Double-click each of the four table names, and all four tables will be added to the Relationships window. Close the Show Table dialog box. Drag and drop the QUOTATION window below the other three windows. Also, expand the QUOTATION window by pulling down on its lower border so that your screen appears like the one shown in Figure A-7(b).

To create a relationship, all you need to do is drag a primary key column and drop it on top of a foreign key column. In Figure A-7(b), for example, you would click ProjectID in PROJECT and drag and drop it on ProjectFK in QUOTATION. The dialog box shown in Figure A-8(a) will now appear. This dialog box shows that Access is going to relate ProjectID in PROJECT to ProjectFK in QUOTATION. At the bottom of this window, you can see that it is defining a one-to-many relationship. All of this is appropriate.

Before we can fill out the rest of this dialog box, we need to consider the design of the relationships in this database. Specifically, do we want Access to enforce referential integrity? If so, then Access will ensure that any value of a foreign key matches a value of a primary key. In addition, Access will not allow a null value for the foreign key.

For the example in Figure A-8(a), if we check Enforce Referential Integrity, Access will ensure that any value of ProjectFK (in QUOTATION) has a matching value of ProjectID (in PROJECT). In addition, Access will require a value of ProjectFK in every row of QUOTATION. However, according to Figure 4-1, a QUOTATION row does not necessarily need to relate to a PROJECT row; this means that null values of ProjectFK

FIGURE A-7(a)

Selecting Tables for
Relationship
Definitions

FIGURE A-7(b)

Four Tables in the
Relationship Definition
Window

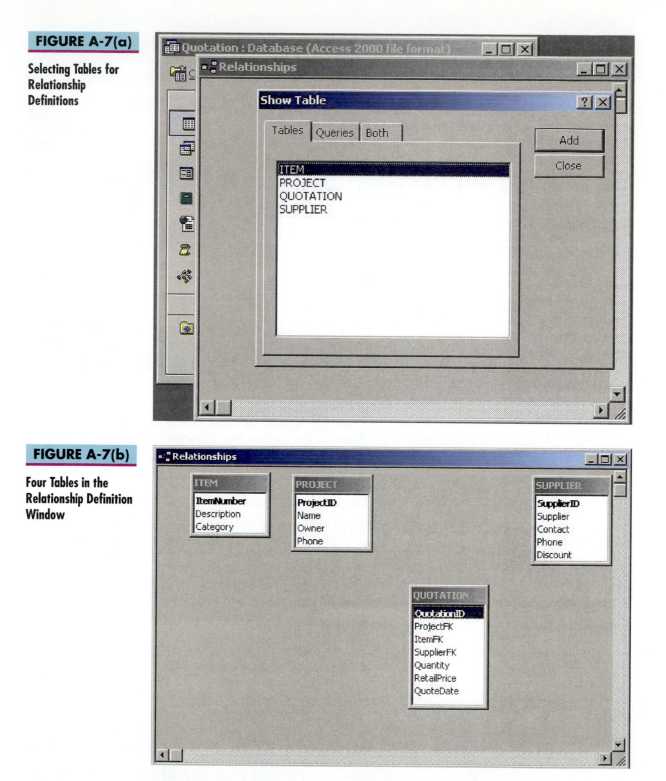

are to be allowed. Consequently, we should not check Enforce Referential Integrity on this relationship, and we can close the dialog box as it appears in Figure A-8(a).

(This does point out a design flaw in Access. We want ProjectFK to be optional, but if a value is supplied, we want Access to ensure that the value corresponds to a valid value in ProjectID of PROJECT. However, there is no way to declare this case to Access. The referential integrity constraint will need to be enforced by application code.)

Now consider the relationship between ITEM and QUOTATION. ItemFK is required, and we also want to ensure that all values of ItemFK correspond to values of

FIGURE A-8(a)

Defining the PROJECT-
QUOTATION
Relationship

FIGURE A-8(a)

Defining the PROJECT-
QUOTATION
Relationship

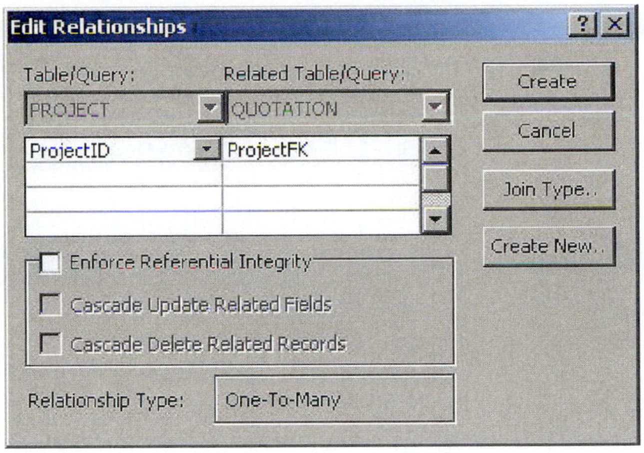

ItemNumber. Thus, as shown in Figure A-8(b), we will check Enforce Referential Integrity. When we do so, Access enables two other options: Cascade Update Related Fields and Cascade Delete Related Records. If the first option is selected, when the user changes a primary key value, Access will make corresponding changes in the foreign key of all related records. Thus, if the user changes a value of ItemNumber from 1000 to 5000, then Access will change all values of ItemFK from 1000 to 5000, as well. In this way, records that were related before the change in the ItemNumber value will remain related after the change.

If this option is not chosen but Enforce Referential Integrity is chosen, then if the user attempts to change a value of ItemNumber from 1000 to 5000, and if any row of QUOTATION has an ItemFK value of 1000, the update will be disallowed. If no row in QUOTATION has an ItemFK value of 1000, the update will be allowed.

This situation reveals one of the advantages of surrogate keys. If surrogate keys are used, no change to a surrogate key value can ever occur, and cascading updates will never be needed.

The Cascade Delete Related Records option is similar. If this option is chosen, then when a row in ITEM is deleted, all connected rows in QUOTATION will be deleted, as well. Thus, deleting an ITEM with an ItemNumber of 1000 will cause the deletion of QUOTATION rows that have an ItemFK value of 1000, as well. If this option is not chosen but Enforce Referential Integrity is chosen, then a row in ITEM cannot be deleted if it has any matching rows in QUOTATION.

Figure A-9 summarizes the cascade types for the relationships in the Carbon River database. As described, Enforce Referential Integrity is not selected for the PROJECT-QUOTATION relationship; however, that option is selected for the ITEM-QUOTATION and SUPPLIER-QUOTATION relationships. In addition, for the ITEM-QUOTATION

FIGURE A-8(b)

Defining the ITEM-
QUOTATION
Relationship

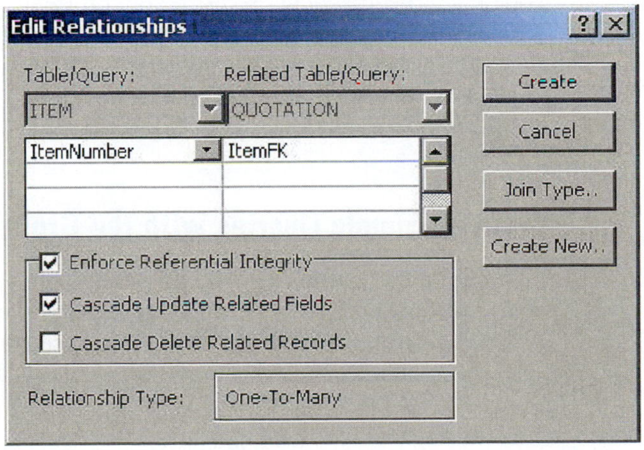

FIGURE A-9

Carbon River
Construction Quotation
Relationship Design

Parent Table	Child Table	Enforce Referential Integrity?	Cascade Type
PROJECT	QUOTATION	No	------
ITEM	QUOTATION	Yes	Update
SUPPLIER	QUOTATION	Yes	None

FIGURE A-10

Relationships Window
with All Relationships

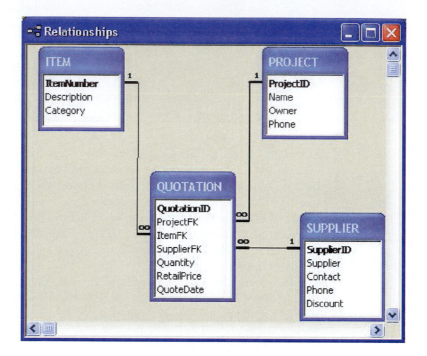

relationship, Cascade Update is selected but Cascade Delete is not. For the SUPPLIER-QUOTATION relationship, neither cascade update option is selected. Cascade update is not required for this third relationship because SupplierID is a surrogate key. Observe that no cascading deletions will be done for any relationship in this database. However, in some cases this is appropriate.

Figure A-10 shows the relationships window after all relationships have been defined.

▶ CREATING QUERIES AND SQL STATEMENTS

Microsoft Access provides a graphical tool for creating queries. This tool generates SQL statements that are subsequently processed. If desired, the developer can modify the SQL code that is generated by Access before processing it. For more advanced queries, this is sometimes easier than using the graphical tool alone, as you will see. It is also possible not to use the graphical tool at all and to enter complete SQL statements directly. Many developers use the graphical query tool to cause Access to write SQL statements and then modify that SQL code by hand, if necessary. We will illustrate this process as we proceed.

Creating Simple Queries with the Graphical Tool

To create a query in Access, click Queries in the left-hand pane of the database window, and then click Create query in Design view, as shown in Figure A-11. The query design tool will open the Show Table dialog box, as shown in Figure A-12. To add a table to the new query, highlight it and click Add (or double-click the table's name). In Figure A-12, the tables PROJECT and QUOTATION have been added. Click Close to dismiss the Show Table dialog.

FIGURE A-11

Opening the Query Design Window

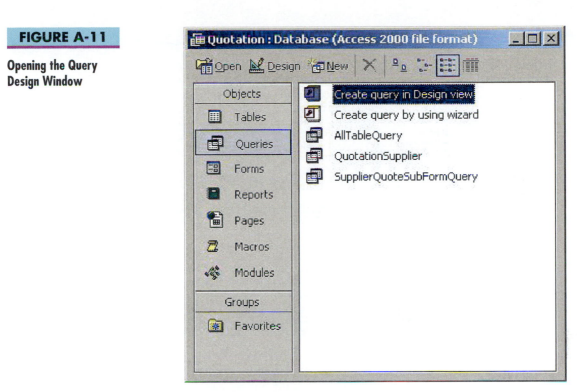

The query design window is shown in Figure A-13. It has two sections: The top section shows tables that have been added to the query; the bottom section is used to indicate the columns to appear in the query and also to add sorting and selection criteria. Note in Figure A-13 that Access shows a relationship line between ProjectID of PROJECT and ProjectFK of QUOTATION. Access knows to do this because the relationships were defined previously in the Relationships window.

FIGURE A-12

Adding Table to the Query

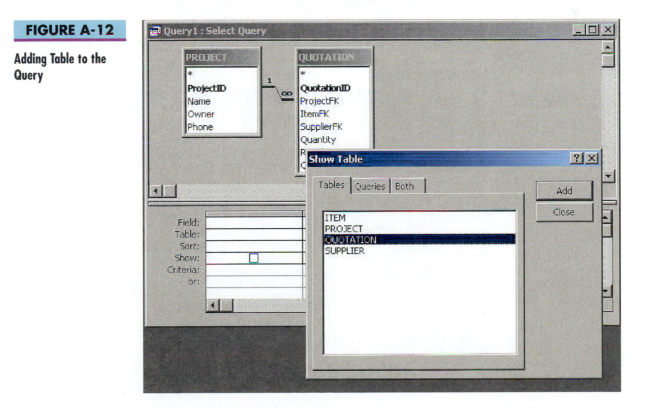

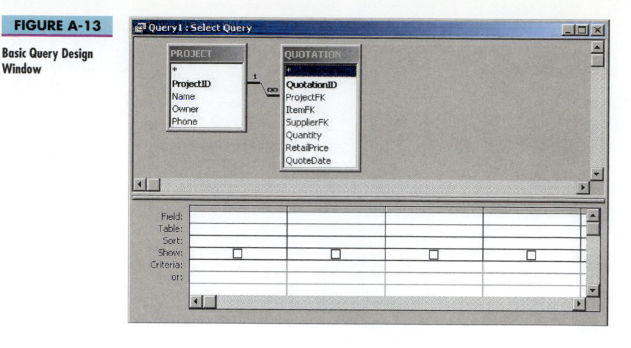

To add columns to the query, drag and drop them from the table list in the top section of the tool to a column space in the bottom half. In Figure A-14, this has been done for Name and Owner of PROJECT and for ItemFK and RetailPrice of ITEM. Now, to display the query results, click the View icon, which is the left-most button on the toolbar, right under the File menu command. (The button looks like a spreadsheet.) As an alternative, you can right-click any of the gray background in the upper portion of the query window and select Datasheet View, or you can select View from the main menu and then select Datasheet View.

Figure A-15 shows sample data for this database. The results of the query in Figure A-14 for the sample data in Figure A-15 are shown in Figure A-16.

To run this query, Access generated a SQL statement. To see the SQL code that was created, select View in the main menu, and then select SQL View. The window shown in Figure A-17 will be displayed. By default, Access uses a different format for the join

FIGURE A-15

Sample Quotation Database Data

QUOTATION : Table

QuotationID	ProjectFK	ItemFK	SupplierFK	Quantity	RetailPrice	QuoteDate
11	1	1100	1	1	$170.00	07-Aug-01
13	1	1200	1	3	$60.00	07-Aug-01
14	1	1300	1	0	$35.00	07-Aug-01
15	1	1400	1	15	$35.00	07-Aug-01
16	1	1500	2	200	$1.50	07-Aug-01
17	1	1550	2	300	$1.25	07-Aug-01
18	2	1600	3	35	$22.50	11-Aug-01
19	1	1400	2	10	$35.00	17-Aug-01
20	2	1700	3	28	$4.75	07-Sep-01
21	2	1800	3	100	$65.00	07-Sep-01
22	1	2000	4	15	$52.50	07-Sep-01
23	1	2100	4	15	$29.95	07-Sep-01
24	1	2200	4	15	$275.00	11-Oct-01
25	3	1100	1	1	$170.00	12-Oct-01
26	3	1200	1	2	$60.00	02-Nov-01
27	3	1300	1	5	$35.00	07-Nov-01
28	3	1400	1	20	$35.00	07-Nov-01
29	3	1500	1	150	$1.50	11-Nov-01
30	3	1550	4	300	$1.25	11-Nov-01
(AutoNumber)	0	0	0	0	$0.00	13-Aug-01

Record: 1 of 19

ITEM : Table

ItemNumber	Description	Category
1100	200 amp Panel	Electrical
1200	50 watt breaker	Electrical
1300	20 watt breaker	Electrical
1400	15 watt breaker	Electrical
1500	12 ga, 3 wire, per foot	Electrical
1550	14 ga, 3 wire, per foot	Electrical
1600	siding, 4x8	Exterior
1700	1x4x8	Exterior
1800	Cedar shingles, bundl	Exterior
2000	Door handle set	Interior
2100	Door hinge set	Interior
2200	Door	Interior
0		

Record: 1 of 12

PROJECT : Table

ProjectID	Name	Owner	Phone
1	Highland House	Elizabeth Barna	(555) 444-8899
2	Baker Remodel	John Stanley	(555) 787-8392
3	Hew Remodel	Ralph & Geri He	(555) 298-4244
(AutoNumber)			

Record: 1 of 3

SUPPLIER : Table

SupplierID	Supplier	Contact	Phone	Discount
1	NW Electric	James Gookin	(555) 786-9987	25
2	EB Supplies	Ely Glover	(555) 560-4492	15
3	Contractor, Inc.	Christine Smathers	(555) 897-3341	35
4	Interior, Inc.	Sybil Morchin	(555) 898-3422	15
(AutoNumber)				0

Record: 1 of 4

command than you learned in Chapter 3. However, you can enter statements in the format of that in Chapter 3 and Access will process them without problem.

Now consider the query in Figure A-18(a). Here, the ITEM table has been added to the query, and the query results have been sorted in ascending order of PROJECT Name. Also, only items having a RetailPrice value of more than four are to be displayed. ITEM was added by right-clicking the gray space in the top of the query form, selecting Show Table, and double-clicking ITEM. The sort order was specified by clicking the Sort row

FIGURE A-16

Result of Query in Figure A-14

Query1 : Select Query

Name	Owner	ItemFK	RetailPrice
Highland House	Elizabeth Barnaby	1100	$170.00
Highland House	Elizabeth Barnaby	1200	$60.00
Highland House	Elizabeth Barnaby	1300	$35.00
Highland House	Elizabeth Barnaby	1400	$35.00
Highland House	Elizabeth Barnaby	1500	$1.50
Highland House	Elizabeth Barnaby	1550	$1.25
Highland House	Elizabeth Barnaby	1400	$35.00
Highland House	Elizabeth Barnaby	2000	$52.50
Highland House	Elizabeth Barnaby	2100	$29.95
Highland House	Elizabeth Barnaby	2200	$275.00
Baker Remodel	John Stanley	1600	$22.50
Baker Remodel	John Stanley	1700	$4.75
Baker Remodel	John Stanley	1800	$65.00
Hew Remodel	Ralph & Geri Hew	1100	$170.00
Hew Remodel	Ralph & Geri Hew	1200	$60.00
Hew Remodel	Ralph & Geri Hew	1300	$35.00
Hew Remodel	Ralph & Geri Hew	1400	$35.00
Hew Remodel	Ralph & Geri Hew	1500	$1.50
Hew Remodel	Ralph & Geri Hew	1550	$1.25

Record: 1 of 19

Query1 : Select Query

```
SELECT PROJECT.Name, PROJECT.Owner, QUOTATION.ItemFK,
QUOTATION.RetailPrice
FROM PROJECT INNER JOIN QUOTATION ON PROJECT.ProjectID =
QUOTATION.ProjectFK;
```

under Name and choosing Ascending. The condition was created by typing ".4" in the Criteria row under RetailPrice. The result of this query is shown in Figure A-18(b).

Figure A-18(c) shows the SQL statement that Access generated for this query. Again, except for the join syntax, this SQL should be familiar. Note especially the condition after the WHERE clause and the sort specification after the ORDER BY clause. They are just as you learned them in Chapter 3.

To save a query, simply close the query window and Access will ask if you want to save. Click Yes and name the query in the resulting dialog box.

Action Queries

In Microsoft Access, any query that makes data changes is referred to as an action query. Such queries include those that modify and delete data, that append data to a table, and that create a new table from an existing one and add data to it. Here, we will consider only queries that modify and delete data.

The easiest way to generate an action query is to create the query as a SELECT query first and then change it to an action query. This process also allows you to see which rows you are about to update before changing them. Figure A-19(a) shows a query of SUPPLIER with the WHERE condition that Supplier is to equal EB Supplies. The query results can be displayed in the datasheet view to ensure that the query is correct so far.

To transform this into a modification query, from the design view click Query/Update Query in the main Access menu. In the line labeled Update To, enter the new value for Supplier; in this case it is New Supplies, as shown in Figure A-19(b). Now you can display the query in SQL View if you want, and you can execute it by clicking the red exclamation point on the toolbar.

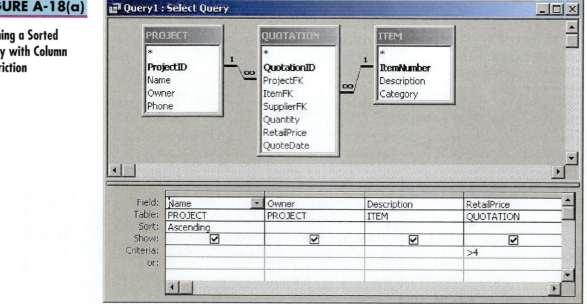

FIGURE A-18(b)

Result of Query in Figure A-18(a)

Name	Owner	Description	RetailPrice
Baker Remodel	John Stanley	Cedar shingles, bundle	$65.00
Baker Remodel	John Stanley	1x4x8	$4.75
Baker Remodel	John Stanley	siding, 4x8	$22.50
Hew Remodel	Ralph & Geri Hew	15 watt breaker	$35.00
Hew Remodel	Ralph & Geri Hew	20 watt breaker	$35.00
Hew Remodel	Ralph & Geri Hew	50 watt breaker	$60.00
Hew Remodel	Ralph & Geri Hew	200 amp Panel	$170.00
Highland House	Elizabeth Barnaby	Door	$275.00
Highland House	Elizabeth Barnaby	Door hinge set	$29.95
Highland House	Elizabeth Barnaby	Door handle set	$52.50
Highland House	Elizabeth Barnaby	15 watt breaker	$35.00
Highland House	Elizabeth Barnaby	15 watt breaker	$35.00
Highland House	Elizabeth Barnaby	20 watt breaker	$35.00
Highland House	Elizabeth Barnaby	50 watt breaker	$60.00
Highland House	Elizabeth Barnaby	200 amp Panel	$170.00

Record: 1 of 15

FIGURE A-18(c)

SQL for Query in Figure A-18(a)

Query1 : Select Query

```
SELECT PROJECT.Name, PROJECT.Owner, ITEM.Description, QUOTATION.RetailPrice
FROM ITEM INNER JOIN (PROJECT INNER JOIN QUOTATION ON PROJECT.ProjectID =
QUOTATION.ProjectFK) ON ITEM.ItemNumber = QUOTATION.ItemFK
WHERE (((QUOTATION.RetailPrice)>4))
ORDER BY PROJECT.Name;
```

FIGURE A-19(a)

The SELECT Query to Be Used to Form the Update Query

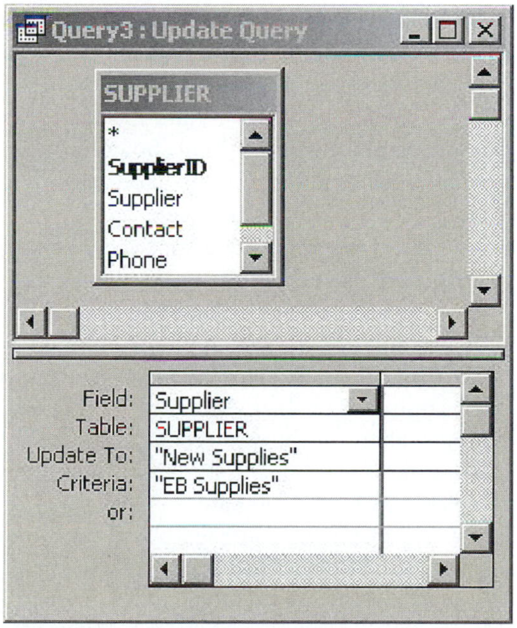

Query3 : Update Query

SUPPLIER

*
SupplierID
Supplier
Contact
Phone

Field:	Supplier	
Table:	SUPPLIER	
Update To:	"New Supplies"	
Criteria:	"EB Supplies"	
or:		

Similarly, if you want to delete rows with the Supplier value of EB Supplies, create the query as a SELECT query, but then click Query/Delete Query. In the line labeled Where, you can add criteria for the deleted rows.

As mentioned, Access also has Append and Make-table queries. We will not consider them here, but you can learn about them from Access's documentation.

FIGURE A-19(b)

Changing the SELECT
Query to an Update
Query

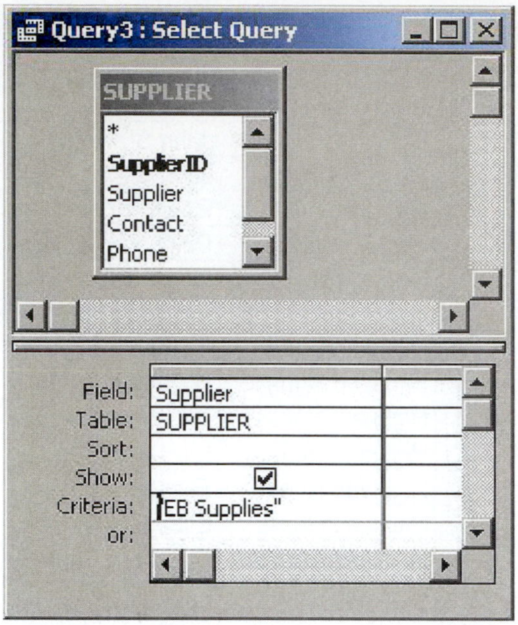

▶ CREATING ACCESS DATA ENTRY FORMS

A form is a graphical display for adding, updating, viewing, and deleting data from one or more tables. Access provides wizards to help generate forms. Wizards are good for creating basic forms, and they also can be used to generate a starting point for more advanced forms.

Creating a Simple Form

To create a form, click Forms in the database window, and then click Create form by using wizard. The window in Figure A-20(a) will be displayed. The combo box labeled Tables/Queries shows the tables and queries that exist in the database; pick one or more of these tables or queries, and then select the columns from that table or query to place on the form. Figure A-20(a) shows form generation for the PROJECT table at the point where ProjectID and Name have been selected, and where Owner and Phone are available but have not yet been selected.

If Owner and Phone are selected and Finish is clicked, the form in Figure A-20(b) will be displayed. This form can be used to modify data by typing new data values over existing values; a new phone for Elizabeth Barnaby, for example, can be entered by typing on top of her existing phone number. To add a new row to PROJECT, click the last button at the bottom of the form—the one with an arrow followed by an asterisk. When this button is clicked, Access clears the form and prepares to add a new row to the table. Type values for the new record in the form. To delete a row, choose Edit/Delete Record from the Access menu bar (not shown) and the row(s) that underlie the form will be deleted from the database.

ProjectID is a surrogate key; its values are supplied by Access and can never be changed. Because this is so, and because the values of surrogate keys have no meaning to the user, such keys are often hidden. To hide ProjectID in the form in Figure A-20(b), open it in design view by clicking the design icon (the left-most icon on the Access toolbar). Then, right-click the text box labeled ProjectID and select Properties. The property sheet will open as shown in Figure A-20(c). Set the third property under the Format tab, Visible, to No, and then reopen the form by clicking the View button (in the same left-most position on the Access toolbar [not shown]). Your form will appear as in Figure A-20(d); ProjectID is not visible, just as we intended.

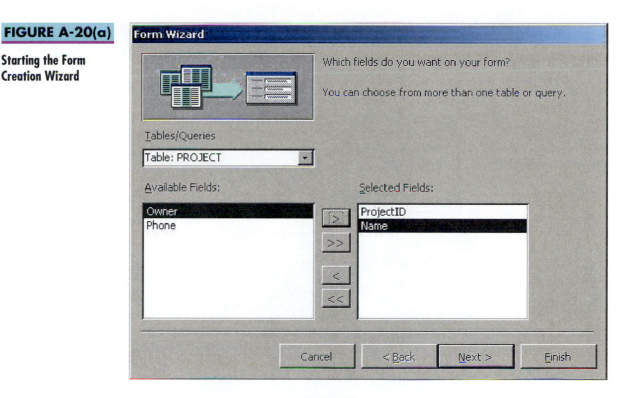

Using Default Values and Combo Boxes with Forms

If we follow the process just described for the QUOTATION table, Access will generate a form like that in Figure A-21. Although this form does represent all of the QUOTATION table columns (except the surrogate key QuotationID), it is difficult to use. For one, users do not know which values of ProjectFK or SupplierFK to enter. For another, users probably will not remember which values of ItemFK correspond to which parts. Finally, most likely the users will want to enter the current date in the QuoteDate field; it will be frustrating for them to have to enter it on every quote.

The QuoteDate problem is the easiest to solve, so we will address it first. In Access, every table column has a Default Value property. We can set this property for QuoteDate by opening the QUOTATION table in design view and placing the focus on the QuoteDate column. We can then specify that the Default Value should be the current date by setting this property to Now(). This has been done in Figure A-22. With this change, when the user opens the QUOTATION form for a new record, Access will supply the current system date as the default value.

Concerning the other problems, we can make the form in Figure A-21 much easier to use if we supply names for users to choose rather than requiring them to enter values. For example, we would like to show a list of project names and let the users choose from this list. Then, when the user selects a project name, we would like Access to store the ProjectID that corresponds to that name in the ProjectFK column of QUOTATION.

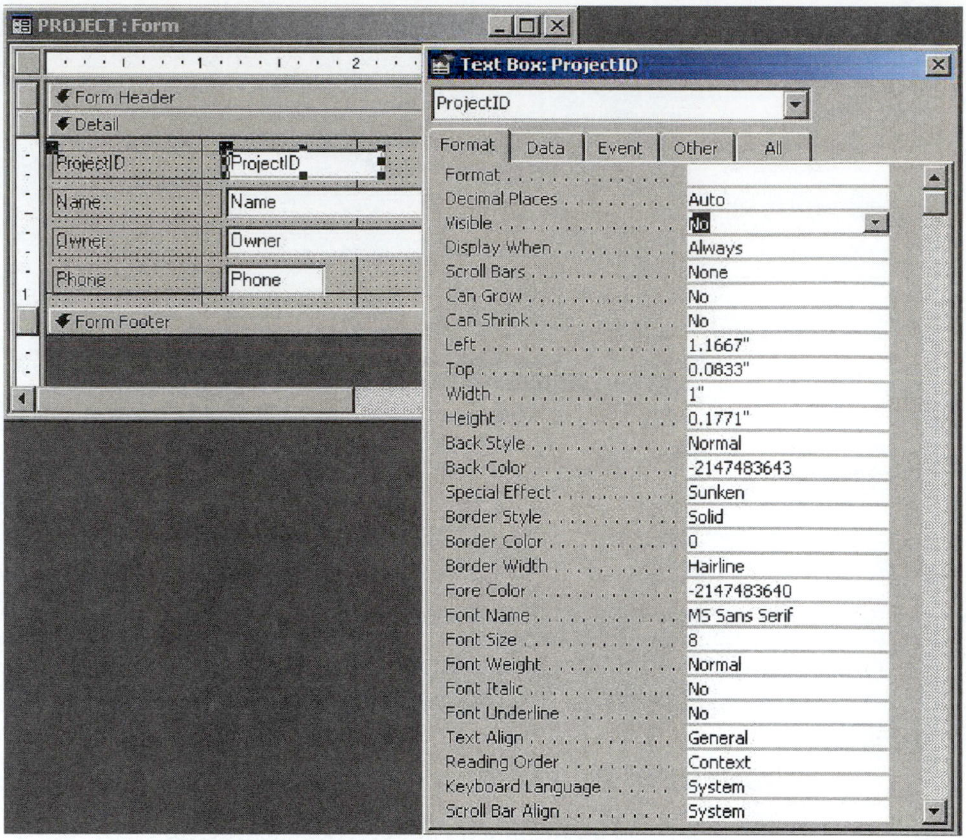

FIGURE A-20(c)

**Setting the ProjectID
Text Box Visible
Property to No**

FIGURE A-20(d)

**Form with ProjectID
Not Visible**

Microsoft created the Access combo box control to do exactly this. To create a combo box, we can open the QUOTATION form in design view and select the combo box tool from the toolbox. (If the toolbox is not open, click View/Toolbox to open it.) Now you can drag and draw a new combo box control over the QuotationID text box. Because QuotationID has been made invisible, this overlaying will not be apparent when the form is open in View mode. The form will appear as in Figure A-23(a).

When you drop the new combo box, Access opens a wizard with several screens. In the first screen, select "I want the combo box to look up . . . " as shown in Figure A-23(b). Click Next and select Table:PROJECT as the table to provide the values for the combo box. In the next screen, select Name to be included in the combo box, as shown in Figure A-23(c). (You can select more than one field to be shown in the drop-down box if you want.) Now, click Next twice, and in the screen that appears, select the second option and pick ProjectFK from the combo box next to it, as shown in Figure A-23(d). Now, click Finish.

Access will set up the properties of the combo box so that it will obtain its values from the PROJECT table, display the Name of projects in the drop-down list, and store the appropriate value of ProjectID in the ProjectFK field of QUOTATION. Figure A-24(a) shows the form as the user is selecting Hew Remodel for Name (of PROJECT). After this

FIGURE A-21

Simple Quotation Form

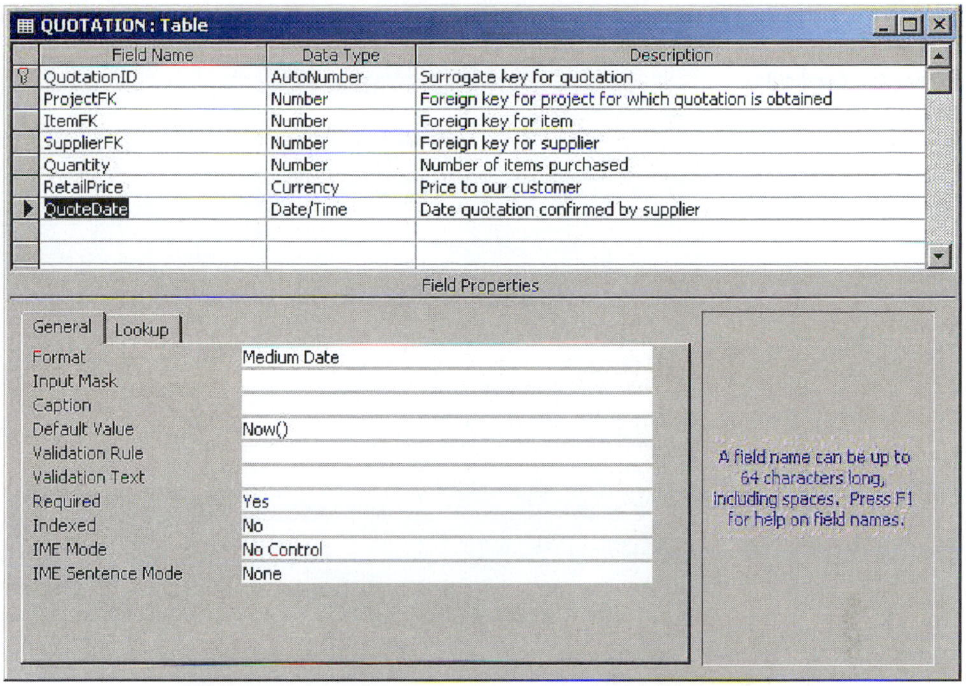

FIGURE A-22

Setting the Default Value of QuoteDate to Now

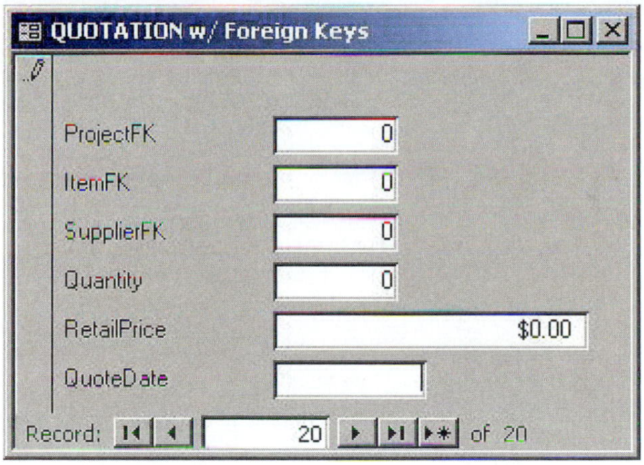

has been done, Access stores the value 3, which is the ProjectID value of the Hew Remodel row of PROJECT, in the ProjectFK field, as shown in Figure A-24(b).

Combo boxes like this make forms much easier to use. Note, too, that when Access opens a form on an existing QUOTATION row, it will use the value of ProjectFK to look up the Name value of the appropriate project in the PROJECT table. That value of Name will be displayed.

We can follow this same process for ITEM and SUPPLIER, as well. Because users need not know the values of the foreign keys, we can cover ProjectFK with the project lookup combo box, ItemFK with the item lookup combo box, and SupplierFK with the supplier lookup combo box. Figure A-24(c) shows the result of this. Notice that the combo box for suppliers contains two columns: Supplier and Discount. This occurs if you select two columns in the wizard screen shown in Figure A-23(c).

Looking Up Nonkey Data

The form in Figure A-24(c) is an improvement over the forms that expose foreign key values, but the result is not as satisfying as it could be. For example, if the user selects a particular supplier, the person cannot tell from the form in Figure A-24(c) what the supplier's

FIGURE A-23(a)

Placing the Combo Box on the Form

FIGURE A-23(b)

Causing the Combo Box to Be Filled with Lookup Data

Contact, Phone, or Discount are. An example of a better-designed form is shown in Figure A-25. Here, when the user selects from one of the combo boxes, Access looks up the rest of the data associated with the given foreign key. For example, when the user selects NW Electric from the Supplier combo box, Access automatically supplies the correct values for Contact, Phone, and Discount.

The form in Figure A-25 is a direct extension to the one in Figure A-24(c). To create it, we first need to create a query that includes all of the data from all tables. Figure A-26(a) shows such a query that has been saved with the name AllTableQuery. It is worth noting that we can place all of the columns of a table into the query by dragging the asterisk from the table at the top of the window into one of the columns in the bottom. This has been done for all four tables in Figure A-26(a).

FIGURE A-23(c)

Selecting Name as the
Column to Show in the
Combo Box

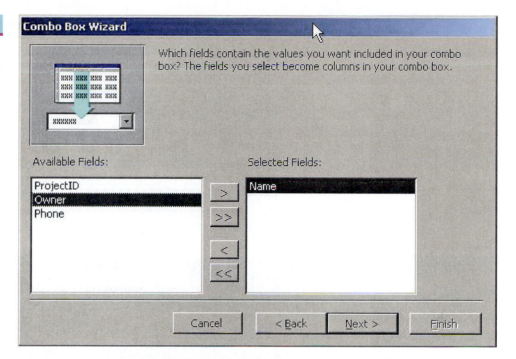

FIGURE A-23(d)

Storing the Looked Up
ProjectID Value in the
Foreign Key

To continue building the form, we run the Access form generation wizard and select AllTableQuery as the source of data for the form. Using the form shown in Figure A-26(b), select all the columns from the QUOTATION table, but only those columns. Click Finish. Now place combo boxes for Project, Item, and Supplier on the form as shown in the last section. Finally, add the nonkey fields from the PROJECT, ITEM, and SUPPLIER tables to the form.

To obtain the format in Figure A-25, hide QuotationID, ProjectFK, ItemFK, and SupplierFK by setting their Visible property to No. Rearrange the text boxes, place a rectangle around items from the same table, change the background color of nonkey items, and voilá! You have the form in Figure A-25. Access will fill in the appropriate text boxes automatically as the user makes selections from the combo box.

FIGURE A-24(a)

Selecting a PROJECT by Name

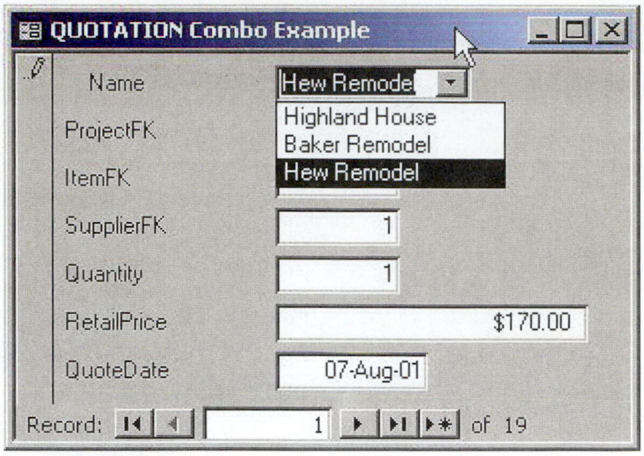

FIGURE A-24(b)

Proper Value Is Stored in ProjectFK

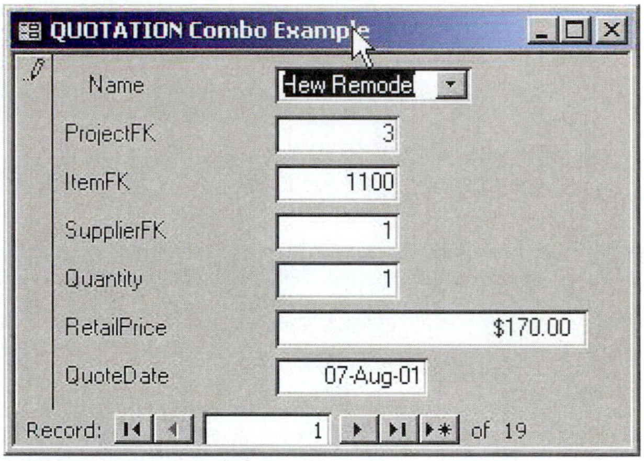

FIGURE A-24(c)

SUPPLIER Combo Box with Two Columns

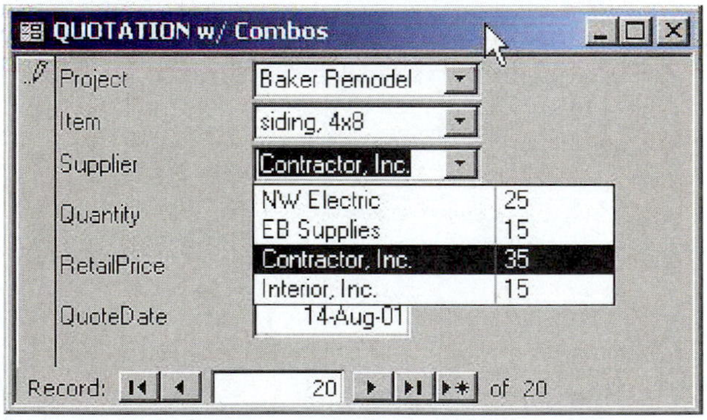

Microsoft Access forms have many, many more features and functions, but we will not address them here. If you want to learn more, a good place to start is to learn about using subforms. Search for the topic in Access Help to get started.

▶ CREATING ACCESS REPORTS

A report is a formatted display of data. Access reports can be as simple as the output of a query or as complicated as those that reformat themselves depending on the report's content. Because this is a database book and not a book on systems development, the focus is on the database concepts that underlie report generation.

To create a report in Access, click Reports in the database window. As with queries and forms, you can then either open the report design window or create a report with a

FIGURE A-25

Looking Up Data Associated with Foreign Keys

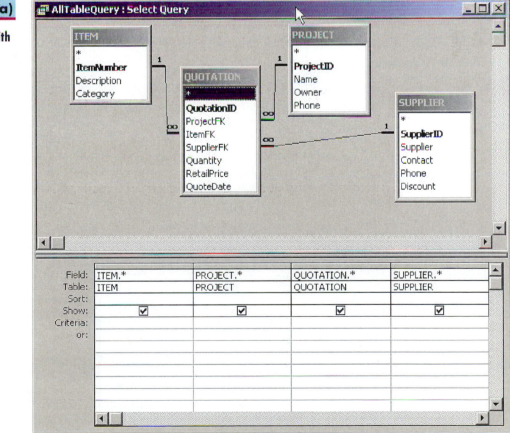

wizard. Usually, it is worthwhile to use the wizard, even if all it does is create a starting point from which you can begin customizing. Because using the report wizard is similar to that for queries and forms, we will not discuss its use here. Instead, we will discuss three important reporting concepts.

Banded Report Writers

Figure A-27 shows the design of a query of the Carbon River quotation database, and Figure A-28(a) and Figure A-28(b) show two different presentations of the query's data. The only difference in these presentations is the format; the data are the same. Figure A-28(a)

FIGURE A-26(a)

Creating a Query with All Columns of All Tables

FIGURE A-26(b)

Using the Query in
Figure 1-26(a) as the
Basis for a New Form

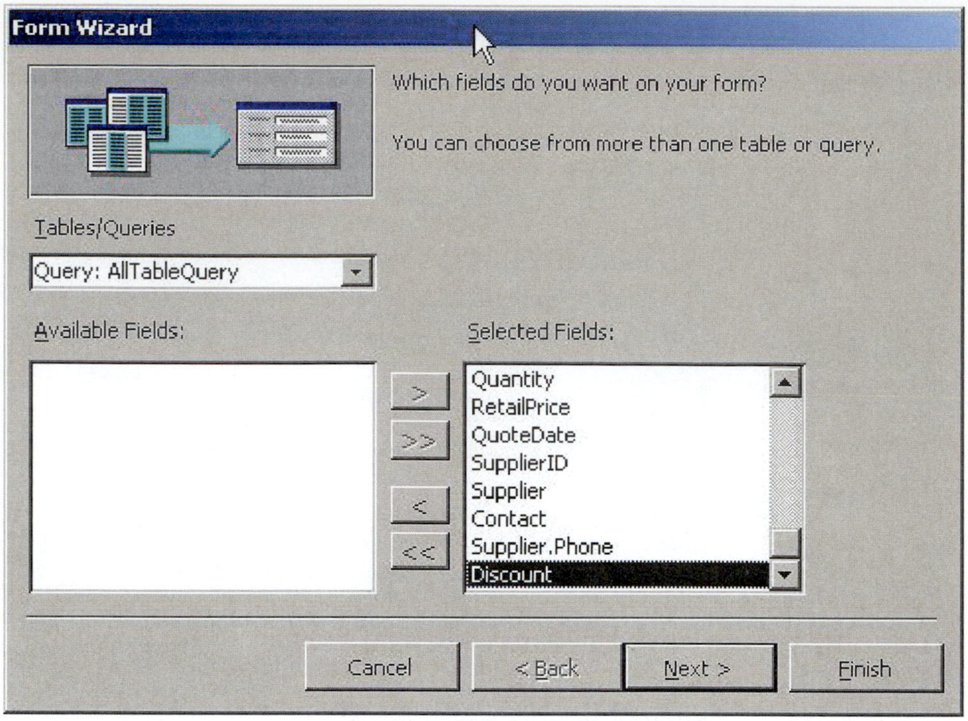

is a spreadsheet that lists the results of the query; in Figure A-28(b), the data have been sorted, grouped, and arranged in a report.

Specifically, in Figure A-28(b) the result of the query was sorted by PROJECT.Name, SUPPLIER.Supplier within PROJECT.Name, and ITEM.Description within SUPPLIER.Supplier. Then repeating values within a group such as PROJECT.Name were suppressed. For example, PROJECT.Name is printed only once for the group of quotations within that project and is suppressed on the remainder of the lines for that project.

Report writers that generate reports in this format are called **banded report writers**. If you examine Figure A-29, you will see why that name is applied. The structure of the report is divided into a series of horizontal bands, each of which consists of a header and a footer. A band called the report band encloses the entire report; this band consists of the Report Header and the Report Footer. Items in the Report Header are printed only once, at the top of the report; similarly, items in the Report Footer are printed only once, at the end of the report.

The next band is the page band, which consists of the Page Header and the Page Footer. Items in the Page Header are printed at the top of each page; those in the Page Footer are printed at the bottom of each page. For this report, column headings are contained in the Page Header, and the date and page number are contained in the Page Footer.

FIGURE A-27

Sample Query for
Carbon River Database

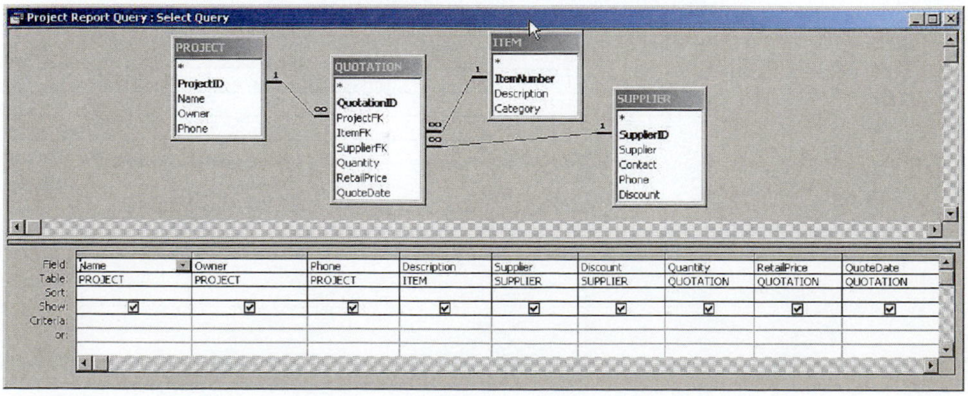

FIGURE A-28(a)

Spreadsheet Display of Query in Figure A-27

Project Report Query : Select Query

Name	Owner	Phone	Description	Supplier	Discount	Quantity	RetailPrice	QuoteDate
Highland House	Elizabeth Barnaby	(555) 444-8899	200 amp Panel	NW Electric	25	1	$170.00	07-Aug-01
Highland House	Elizabeth Barnaby	(555) 444-8899	50 watt breaker	NW Electric	25	3	$60.00	07-Aug-01
Highland House	Elizabeth Barnaby	(555) 444-8899	20 watt breaker	NW Electric	25	0	$35.00	07-Aug-01
Highland House	Elizabeth Barnaby	(555) 444-8899	15 watt breaker	NW Electric	25	15	$35.00	07-Aug-01
Highland House	Elizabeth Barnaby	(555) 444-8899	12 ga, 3 wire, per foot	EB Supplies	15	200	$1.50	07-Aug-01
Highland House	Elizabeth Barnaby	(555) 444-8899	14 ga, 3 wire, per foot	EB Supplies	15	300	$1.25	07-Aug-01
Baker Remodel	John Stanley	(555) 787-8392	siding, 4x8	Contractor, Inc.	35	35	$22.50	11-Aug-01
Highland House	Elizabeth Barnaby	(555) 444-8899	15 watt breaker	EB Supplies	15	10	$35.00	17-Aug-01
Baker Remodel	John Stanley	(555) 787-8392	1x4x8	Contractor, Inc.	35	28	$4.75	07-Sep-01
Baker Remodel	John Stanley	(555) 787-8392	Cedar shingles, bundle	Contractor, Inc.	35	100	$45.00	07-Sep-01
Highland House	Elizabeth Barnaby	(555) 444-8899	Door handle set	Interior, Inc.	18	15	$52.50	07-Sep-01
Highland House	Elizabeth Barnaby	(555) 444-8899	Door hinge set	Interior, Inc.	18	15	$29.95	07-Sep-01
Highland House	Elizabeth Barnaby	(555) 444-8899	Door	Interior, Inc.	18	15	$275.00	11-Oct-01
Hew Remodel	Ralph & Geri Hew	(555) 298-4244	200 amp Panel	NW Electric	25	1	$170.00	12-Oct-01
Hew Remodel	Ralph & Geri Hew	(555) 298-4244	50 watt breaker	NW Electric	25	2	$60.00	02-Nov-01
Hew Remodel	Ralph & Geri Hew	(555) 298-4244	20 watt breaker	NW Electric	25	5	$35.00	07-Nov-01
Hew Remodel	Ralph & Geri Hew	(555) 298-4244	15 watt breaker	NW Electric	25	20	$35.00	07-Nov-01
Hew Remodel	Ralph & Geri Hew	(555) 298-4244	12 ga, 3 wire, per foot	NW Electric	25	150	$1.50	11-Nov-01
Hew Remodel	Ralph & Geri Hew	(555) 298-4244	14 ga, 3 wire, per foot	Interior, Inc.	18	300	$1.25	11-Nov-01

Record: 1 of 19

The remaining bands represent groups within the data. This report has a PROJECT Name band (called Name in this figure because the group is based on the Name column of PROJECT) with a Name Header and a Name Footer, and a SUPPLIER band with a Supplier Header and a Supplier Footer. Finally, the Detail section has item and quotation data.

When constructing a banded report, all of the data from a table should appear in the same band. For example, all columns from the PROJECT table should appear in the Name band, along with Name. All columns from the SUPPLIER table should appear in the Supplier band. Placing columns from the same table in different bands creates confusing and misleading reports. Placing Discount, for example, in the Detail section would imply that discounts vary with an item or quote rather than with a supplier.

Computations in Reports

With Access, it is possible to perform calculations either in queries or in reports. Generally, it is best to perform calculations that do not depend on report structure in a query; that way, those calculations need be defined only once and can be used in all of

FIGURE A-28(b)

Formatted Report of Query in Figure A-27

QUOTATIONS BY PROJECT

Name	*Owner*	*Supplier*	*Discount*	*Description*	*Quantity*	*RetailPrice*	*Date*
Baker Remodel	**John Stanley**						
		Contractor, Inc.	*35*				
				1x4x8	28	$4.75	7-Sep-01
				Cedar shingles, bundle	100	$45.00	7-Sep-01
				siding, 4x8	35	$22.50	1-Aug-01
Hew Remodel	**Ralph & Geri Hew**						
		Interior, Inc.	*18*				
				14 ga, 3 wire, per foot	300	$1.25	1-Nov-01
		NW Electric	*25*				
				12 ga, 3 wire, per foot	150	$1.50	1-Nov-01
				15 watt breaker	20	$35.00	7-Nov-01
				20 watt breaker	5	$35.00	7-Nov-01
				200 amp Panel	1	$170.00	2-Oct-01
				50 watt breaker	2	$60.00	2-Nov-01
				Door handle set	1	$52.50	2-Aug-01

Friday, November 21, 2003 *Page 1 of 2*

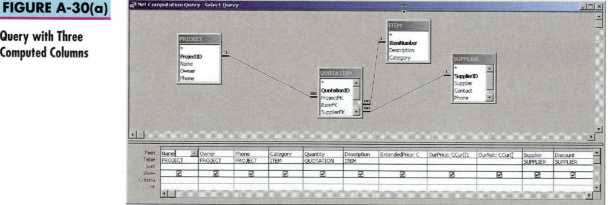

FIGURE A-29

Example Banded Report Writer

the reports that are based on the query. Calculations that depend on groups and pages must be done in the report.

Figure A-30(a) shows the structure of a query that includes three computed columns: ExtendedPrice, OurPrice, and OurNet. The SQL code for this query and these computations is shown in Figure A-30(b). CCur, which stands for "convert to currency," is a function that converts the results of a numeric computation to a string in currency format. Within the CCur parentheses, you can see the algebraic expressions that compute ExtendedPrice, OurPrice, and OurNet.

The result of this query is shown in Figure A-30(c). Note that the values in the ExtendedPrice, OurPrice, and OurNet columns have been computed correctly and appear in currency format.

FIGURE A-30(a)

Query with Three Computed Columns

FIGURE A-30(b)

SQL View of Query in Figure A-30(a)

```
SELECT PROJECT.Name, PROJECT.Owner, PROJECT.Phone, ITEM.Category, QUOTATION.Quantity, ITEM.Description,

CCur([RetailPrice]*[Quantity]) AS ExtendedPrice,
CCur((100-[Discount])*[Quantity]*[RetailPrice]/100) AS OurPrice,
CCur([ExtendedPrice]-[OurPrice]) AS OurNet,

SUPPLIER.Supplier, SUPPLIER.Discount
FROM SUPPLIER INNER JOIN (PROJECT INNER JOIN(ITEM INNER JOIN QUOTATION ON ITEM.ItemNumber = QUOTATION.ItemFK)
ON PROJECT.ProjectID = QUOTATION.ProjectFK)
ON SUPPLIER.SupplierID = QUOTATION.SupplierFK;
```

FIGURE A-30(c)

Results of Query in
Figure A-30(a)

Name	Owner	Phone	Category	Quantity	Description	ExtendedPrice	OurPrice	OurNet	Supplier	Discount
Highland House	Elizabeth Barnaby	(555) 444-8899	Electrical	1	200 amp Panel	$170.00	$127.50	$42.50	NW Electric	25
Highland House	Elizabeth Barnaby	(555) 444-8899	Electrical	3	50 watt breaker	$180.00	$135.00	$45.00	NW Electric	25
Highland House	Elizabeth Barnaby	(555) 444-8899	Electrical	7	20 watt breaker	$245.00	$183.75	$61.25	NW Electric	25
Highland House	Elizabeth Barnaby	(555) 444-8899	Electrical	15	15 watt breaker	$525.00	$393.75	$131.25	NW Electric	25
Highland House	Elizabeth Barnaby	(555) 444-8899	Electrical	200	12 ga, 3 wire, per foot	$300.00	$255.00	$45.00	EB Supplies	15
Highland House	Elizabeth Barnaby	(555) 444-8899	Electrical	300	14 ga, 3 wire, per foot	$375.00	$318.75	$56.25	EB Supplies	15
Baker Remodel	John Stanley	(555) 787-8392	Exterior	35	siding, 4x8	$787.50	$511.88	$275.63	Contractor, Inc	35
Highland House	Elizabeth Barnaby	(555) 444-8899	Electrical	10	15 watt breaker	$350.00	$297.50	$52.50	EB Supplies	15
Baker Remodel	John Stanley	(555) 787-8392	Exterior	28	1x4x8	$133.00	$86.45	$46.55	Contractor, Inc	35
Baker Remodel	John Stanley	(555) 787-8392	Exterior	100	Cedar shingles, bundle	$4,500.00	$2,925.00	$1,575.00	Contractor, Inc	35
Highland House	Elizabeth Barnaby	(555) 444-8899	Interior	15	Door handle set	$787.50	$645.75	$141.75	Interior, Inc.	18
Highland House	Elizabeth Barnaby	(555) 444-8899	Interior	15	Door hinge set	$449.25	$368.39	$80.87	Interior, Inc.	18
Highland House	Elizabeth Barnaby	(555) 444-8899	Interior	15	Door	$4,125.00	$3,382.50	$742.50	Interior, Inc.	18
Hew Remodel	Ralph & Geri Hew	(555) 298-4244	Electrical	1	200 amp Panel	$170.00	$127.50	$42.50	NW Electric	25
Hew Remodel	Ralph & Geri Hew	(555) 298-4244	Electrical	2	50 watt breaker	$120.00	$90.00	$30.00	NW Electric	25
Hew Remodel	Ralph & Geri Hew	(555) 298-4244	Electrical	5	20 watt breaker	$175.00	$131.25	$43.75	NW Electric	25
Hew Remodel	Ralph & Geri Hew	(555) 298-4244	Electrical	20	15 watt breaker	$700.00	$525.00	$175.00	NW Electric	25
Hew Remodel	Ralph & Geri Hew	(555) 298-4244	Electrical	150	12 ga, 3 wire, per foot	$225.00	$168.75	$56.25	NW Electric	25
Hew Remodel	Ralph & Geri Hew	(555) 298-4244	Electrical	300	14 ga, 3 wire, per foot	$375.00	$307.50	$67.50	Interior, Inc.	18

Record: 1 of 19

This query can now be used as the basis of any number of reports. The report in Figure A-31(a) displays the results of these computations. This report includes computations from the query and also makes its own computations that depend on the report structure. As you can see in Figure A-31(b), the sum of OurNet has been placed in the Name Footer and also in the Report Footer.

Parameterized Reports

With Access, it is possible to construct queries that prompt the user for values that will be used in the WHERE clauses of the queries. Figure A-32(a) (see page 210) shows the design of the query in Figure A-30(a) with such a prompt.

The expression

Like [Enter the first letter of the Project Name:] & "*"

FIGURE A-31(a)

Report Using Query
with Computed
Columns

Part Net by Project

Name	Baker Remodel		Owner	John Stanley	Phone	(555) 787-8392
	Description	Category	Quantity	ExtendedPrice	OurPrice	OurNet
	1x4x8	Exterior	28	$133.00	$86.45	$46.55
	Cedar shingles, bundle	Exterior	100	$4,500.00	$2,925.00	$1,575.00
	siding, 4x8	Exterior	35	$787.50	$511.88	$275.63

Total Net for Project: $1,897.18

Name	Hew Remodel		Owner	Ralph & Geri Hew	Phone	(555) 298-4244
	Description	Category	Quantity	ExtendedPrice	OurPrice	OurNet
	12 ga, 3 wire, per foot	Electrical	150	$225.00	$168.75	$56.25
	14 ga, 3 wire, per foot	Electrical	300	$375.00	$307.50	$67.50
	15 watt breaker	Electrical	20	$700.00	$525.00	$175.00
	20 watt breaker	Electrical	5	$175.00	$131.25	$43.75
	200 amp Panel	Electrical	1	$170.00	$127.50	$42.50
	50 watt breaker	Electrical	2	$120.00	$90.00	$30.00
	Door handle set	Interior	1	$52.50	$39.38	$13.13

Total Net for Project: $428.13

Name	Highland House		Owner	Elizabeth Barnaby	Phone	(555) 444-8899
	Description	Category	Quantity	ExtendedPrice	OurPrice	OurNet

Page 1 of 2

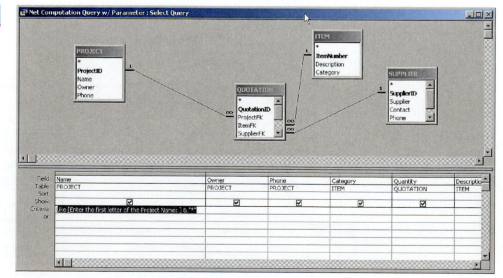

has been entered in the Criteria row of the Name column. Expressions entered in the Criteria row are added after the equal sign in the WHERE clause of the underlying query. Here, the expression

WHERE PROJECT.Name Like [Enter the first letter of the Project Name:] *

will be added to the query. When Access's query processor encounters [please run in] the expression in the brackets, it displays a dialog box like the one in Figure A-32(b). When the user enters a letter, such as *H* in this figure, Access completes the WHERE clause by adding the letter as follows.

WHERE PROJECT.Name Like 'H*'

As explained in Chapter 3, the asterisk is the notation for a wildcard of any number of characters. In this case, the query will search for projects starting with the letter *H*. Figure A-32(c) shows the result.

When a parameterized query is used as the data source for a report, Access will present the dialog box in the same way before printing the report. This has been done for the report in Figure A-33. Here, the user entered the letter B, and the report was generated using only data for projects having a Name value starting with B.

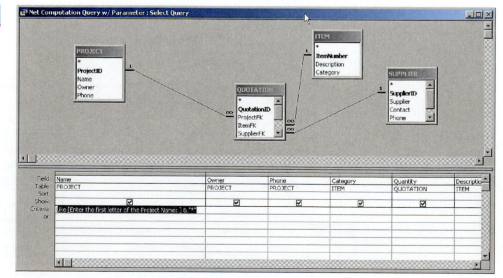

FIGURE A-32(b)

Dialog Box Resulting from Query in Figure 1-32(a)

FIGURE A-32(c)

Query Results from Query in Figures A-32(a) and A-32(b)

FIGURE A-33

Report Using Query from Figure A-32(a) and Letter B

SUMMARY

A database schema is the design of tables, relationships, and constraints. A data structure diagram shows tables and their columns and represents relationships among the tables. In data structure diagrams, a crow's foot at the end of a line signifies the "many" side of a relationship. An oval over a relationship line means that the relationship is optional, and a hash mark indicates that at least one record must participate in the relationship.

In Access, tables are defined using a graphical window in which the name, data type, and properties of each column of the table are defined. Important properties of columns are Field Size, Input Mask, Default Value, and Required. The primary key column(s) are defined by highlighting the column(s) and clicking the key symbol on the toolbar.

Relationships are defined by dragging a primary key over a foreign key in the Relationships window. Relationships can be defined so that Access will enforce referential integrity. If so, Access can be used to cascade updates when primary key values are changed and to cascade deletes when a parent row is deleted. If cascading updates or deletes are not selected but enforcement of referential integrity is selected, Access will disallow updates or deletes on records that are linked to other records in the relationship. If enforcement of referential integrity is selected for a relationship, the foreign key value will be required. Hence, with Access it is not possible to enforce referential integrity on optional relationships.

After the database tables and relationships have been defined, queries, forms, and reports can be created. For each of these, the developer can either start from scratch with the design window or use a wizard to create a query, form, or report. In most cases, it is useful to use the wizard, if only to create a starting point for subsequent modification and customization.

When creating a query with the design tool, the developer can work in the query design window or can enter SQL statements in the SQL View window. Unfortunately, Microsoft created its own version of SQL syntax for joins in Access. For this and other reasons, it is usually best to use the query design window to create a basic SQL statement and then modify that statement as necessary in the SQL View window.

Access refers to any query that makes data changes as an action query. Queries that modify and delete data are action queries, as are those that append rows to tables and that make tables. For modify and delete queries, the developer can first develop the query as a SELECT query with the query design tool and then change the query into either an update or delete query.

A form is a graphical display for adding, updating, viewing, and deleting data. Simple forms can be created using the form generation wizard. Combo boxes can be used to look up data to supply foreign key values. That technique can be extended to look up nonkey columns from parent tables as well, as shown in Figure A-25.

A report is a formatted display of data. Access generates reports using a banded report writer. This tool has report and page bands, as well as other bands defined by the developer. The lowest-level data in the report are displayed in the detail band.

Computations for reports can be made in the query that underlies the report, as well as in the report itself. Generally, it is best to perform calculations that do not depend on report structure in a query; calculations that depend on groups and pages must be done in a report.

A parameterized query is one that dynamically obtains WHERE clause data values from the user. The value obtained is used to constrain query results. A report based on a parameterized query will ask the user for a data value and produce the report using the constraining data.

REVIEW QUESTIONS

The following database design is used to track players, teams, and positions in a softball league. Use it for responding to the following questions.

PLAYER (<u>PlayerID</u>, Name, EmailAddress, Phone)

TEAM (<u>TeamName</u>, HomeField, JerseyColor)

POSITION (*<u>PlayerID</u>*, *<u>TeamName</u>*, Position, <u>Season</u>)

A.1 Examine the column definitions for this design. Do you agree with the data types and lengths assigned? Do you think the required fields are correct? Make any changes that you think are appropriate, and justify your changes.

A.2 Examine the relationship characteristics of this design. Explain the referential integrity checking and the cascading deletion and update behavior specified.

Do you agree with the specifications that are given? If not, change them and justify your changes.

A.3 Create a data structure diagram for this design.

A.4 Create the table structures for this design (with your modifications, if any) in Access.

A.5 Create relationships for this design (with your modifications, if any).

A.6 Use the Access form wizard to create a data entry form for the PLAYER relation and a second data entry form for the TEAM relation. Do not include any POSITION data in these forms.

A.7 Using the forms from your answer to question A.6, enter data for at least seven players and at least five teams. Ensure that at least two teams have a jersey color of purple.

A.8 Use the Access form wizard to create a data entry form for POSITION. Use the same format as shown in Figure A-21.

A.9 Using the form from your answer to question A.8, enter data for at least 10 positions. Assume that a player can have several positions, either on the same team or on different teams. Ensure that at least three players have the position of catcher.

For the following questions, use the Access query design tool unless otherwise instructed.

A.10 Create a query to display all teams.

A.11 Create a query to display all teams having a jersey color of purple.

A.12 Create a query to display the names, e-mail addresses, and positions of all players.

A.13 Create a query to display the names, e-mail addresses, and positions of all players who play catcher. Present your list in ascending order of name.

A.14 Create a query to display the names, e-mail addresses, positions, and team names of all players on teams having a jersey color of purple. Present your list in descending order of position.

A.15 Create a query to display the jersey color of all teams.

A.16 Create an update query to modify the jersey color to purple of all teams having a jersey color of pink. Create this query by first creating a SELECT query using the Access query design tool and then changing your query into an update query. Run your query.

A.17 Add a team with a jersey color of dark puce and a second team with a jersey color of light puce.

A.18 Create a delete query to delete all teams with a jersey color of light puce. Create your query by first creating a SELECT query in the Access query design tool and then changing your query into a delete query.

A.19 Modify the table design of POSITION so that the default value for Season is 2002.

A.20 Create a data entry form for POSITION that replaces PlayerID and TeamName with combo boxes. Use Figure A-24(c) as an example.

A.21 Create a query that has all columns from all tables in the database. Name this query AllTableQuery.

A.22 Using the query AllTableQuery, create a form that looks up nonkey data and displays it on the form. Use Figure A-25 as an example.

A.23 Create a report based on AllTableQuery that shows team rosters. The report should have a TEAM band. List the name, position, and e-mail of players in the detail band. Show the name and jersey color of the team on the TEAM band.

A.24 Open the TEAM table in design view and add two columns: GamesWon and GamesLost. Set the data type of each column to Number (Integer). Open the table in datasheet view and add sample data for each team.

A.25 Copy AllTableQuery and paste it back using the name Query Computations. Add the columns GamesWon and GamesLost to QueryComputations. Modify the query to compute a new column called TotalGamesPlayed that is the sum of GamesWon and GamesLost, and a second new column called PercentWon as a percentage of GamesWon divided by TotalGamesPlayed.

A.26 Create a report based on QueryComputations. Create a Player band; within this band, list the values for Position, TeamName, and GamesWon on the detail line. Add a field to the Player Footer that displays the total of games won by all teams on which that person played.

A.27 Create a copy of QueryComputations under the name Player QueryComputations. Add a parameter to this query to ask for the first letter of the name of a player. Use Figure A-32(a) as an example.

A.28 Modify your report from question A.26 to use the query you created for question A.27.

EXERCISES

A.29 Open AllTableQuery and from View select SQL View. Examine the syntax for a join that is used by Access. Compare and contrast this syntax with the SQL-92 standard syntax you learned in Chapter 3. In your opinion, is the Access syntax better, worse, or the same as the SQL-92 standard syntax?

A.30 Using your database for the softball league, add a new row PLAYER but do not assign that player a position on a team. Run AllTableQuery and verify that the new player you added does not appear in the result. Now, open AllTableQuery in design mode and double-click the relationship line between PLAYER and POSITION. Select the option necessary to cause the new row in PLAYER to appear in your query. Run the query to verify that the player now appears. Open the modified query in SQL View and explain the differences in the query syntax from that which you found in exercise A.29.

A.31 Describe the relationship between report bands and functional dependencies. How can functional dependencies be used to constrain the design of a report effectively?

GARDEN GLORY PROJECT QUESTIONS

Use Access to create a database for Garden Glory. Assume the following table and column definitions.

OWNER (<u>OwnerID</u>, Name, Email, Type)

PROPERTY (<u>PropertyID</u>, Street, City, State, Zip, *OwnerID*)

EMPLOYEE (<u>Initials</u>, Name, CellPhone, ExperienceLevel)

SERVICE (*<u>PropertyID</u>*, *<u>Initials</u>*, <u>Date</u>, HoursWorked)

A. Open Access and create a new database named Garden Glory.

B. Create tables according to the specifications given.

C. Specify relationships and relationship properties. (Use Figure A-9 as an example.)

D. Create relationships; specify referential integrity constraints in accordance with your answer to question C.

E. Open the OWNER table and add three owner rows.

F. Open the PROPERTY table and add at least five rows. Create data so that at least one owner has three or more properties.

G. Open the EMPLOYEE table and add at least three rows.

H. Open the SERVICE table and add at least five rows. Create data so that one employee has at least three service rows and one property has at least three service rows.

I. Open the query designer and create a query that includes all data from the PROPERTY, EMPLOYEE, and SERVICE tables.

J. Modify the query in your answer to question I to sort the rows by employee, and within employee, by HoursWorked.

K. Create a form to enter a new service. Require the user to enter PropertyID and SERVICE.Initials; use Figure A-21 as an example.

L. Modify your form from question K to allow the user to choose the property and employee from combo boxes; use Figure A-24(a) as an example.

M. Create an owner report that shows all owner data, and within owner, all of the owner's properties.

N. Create an employee report that shows all employee data, and within an employee, all services the employee has performed. Include Street and City from PROPERTY, and Name from OWNER.

JAMES RIVER JEWELRY PROJECT QUESTIONS

Use Access to create a database for James River Jewelry. Assume the following table and column definitions.

CUSTOMER (<u>CustomerID</u>, Name, Phone, Email, CurrentAwardBal, NumPurch)

PURCHASE (<u>InvoiceNumber</u>, Date, PreTaxAmount, *CustomerID*)

AWARD (<u>AwardID</u>, Date, CreditAmount, *CustomerID*)

A. Open Access and create a new database named James River.

B. Create tables according to the aforementioned specifications.

C. Specify relationships and relationship properties. (Use Figure A-9 as an example.)

D. Create relationships; specify referential integrity constraints in accordance with your answer to question C.

E. Open the CUSTOMER table and add five customer rows.

F. Open the PURCHASE table and add PURCHASE rows. Give at least 12 purchases to one of your customers.

G. Open the AWARD table and add AWARD rows as appropriate. Keeping in mind the rule that James River gives an award of 50 percent of the average of the 10 most recent purchases, at least one AWARD row should be allotted for the customer who has at least 12 purchases.

H. Open the query designer and create a query that includes all data from the CUS-TOMER and PURCHASE tables.

I. Modify the query in your answer to question H to sort the rows by customer name, and within name, by PreTaxAmount.

J. Create a form to enter a new purchase. Require the user to enter the CustomerID value for the customer; use Figure A-21 as an example.

K. Modify your form from question J to allow the user to choose the customer from a combo box; use Figure A-24(a) as an example.

L. Create a customer report that shows all customer data, and within customer, all of that customer's purchase data.

M. Create an award report that shows all award data; within an award, all customer data; and within a customer, all purchase data.

N. Something is wrong with the report in your answer to question M. What is it? Can you think of any way to fix this problem?

Glossary

ACID transaction: An acronym that stands for *atomic, consistent, isolated, and durable*. An atomic transaction is one in which all of a set of database changes are committed as a unit; either all of them are completed or none of them are. A consistent transaction is one in which all actions are taken against rows in the same logical state. An isolated transaction is one that is protected from changes by other users. A durable transaction is one that, once committed to a database, is permanent regardless of subsequent failure. There are different levels of consistency and isolation. See Transaction level consistency and Statement level consistency. Also see Transaction isolation level.

Active Server Page (ASP): A combination of HTML and scripting language statements. Any statement included in <%...%> is processed on the server. Used with Internet Information server (IIS).

After-image: A record of a database entity (normally a row or a page) after a change. Used in recovery to perform rollforward.

Anomaly: An undesirable consequence of a data modification; the term is used primarily in discussions of normalization. With an insertion anomaly, facts about two or more different themes must be added to a single row of a relation. With a deletion anomaly, facts about two or more themes are lost when a single row is deleted.

Application metadata: Data dictionary; data concerning the structure and contents of application menus, forms, and reports.

Application program interface (API): The set of objects, methods, and properties that is used to access the functionality of a program such as a DBMS.

Atomic: A set of actions that is completed as a unit. Either all actions are completed or none are.

Atomic transaction: A group of logically related database operations that are performed as a unit. Either all of the operations are performed or none of them are.

Attribute: 1) A value that represents a characteristic of an entity. 2) A column of a relation.

Band: The section of a report definition that contains the format of a report section. Bands normally are included for the report heading and footing, page heading and footing, and the detail line of a report. Bands also are created for group or break points within a report.

Banded report writer: A report writer in which the sections of reports are defined by bands. See Band.

Before-image: A record of a database entity (normally a row or a page) before a change. Used in recovery to perform rollback.

Binary relationship: A relationship between exactly two entities or tables.

Boyce-Codd normal form: A relation in third normal form in which every determinant is a candidate key.

Built-in function: In SQL, any of the functions COUNT, SUM, AVG, MAX, or MIN.

Business rule: A statement of a policy in a business that restricts the ways in which data can be inserted, updated, or deleted in the database.

Candidate key: An attribute or group of attributes that identifies a unique row in a relation. One of the candidate keys is chosen to be the primary key.

Cardinality: In a binary relationship, the maximum or minimum number of elements allowed on each side of the relationship. The maximum cardinality can be 1:1, 1:N, N:1, or N:M. The minimum cardinality can be optional/optional, optional/mandatory, mandatory/optional, or mandatory/mandatory.

Cascading deletion: A property of a relationship that indicates that when one row is deleted, related rows should be deleted, as well.

Checkpoint: The point of synchronization between a database and a transaction log. All buffers are written to external storage. This is the standard definition of checkpoint, but this term is sometimes used in other ways by DBMS vendors.

Child: A row, record, or node on the "many" side of a one-to-many relationship.

Cluster analysis: A form of data mining that uses statistical techniques to identify groups of similar data.

Column: A logical group of bytes in a row of a relation or a table. The meaning of a column is the same for every row of the relation.

Commit: A command issued to the DBMS to make database modifications permanent. After the command has been processed, the changes are written to the database and to a log in such a way that they will survive system crashes and other failures. A commit usually is used at the end of an atomic transaction. Contrast this with *rollback*.

Composite identifier: An identifier of an entity that consists of two or more attributes.

Composite key: A key of a relation that consists of two or more columns.

Computed value: A column of a table that is computed from other column values. Values are not stored but are computed when they are to be displayed.

Concurrency: A condition in which two or more transactions are processed against a database at the same time. In a single CPU system, the changes are interleaved; in a multi-CPU system, the transactions can be processed simultaneously, and the changes on the database server are interleaved.

Concurrent update problem: An error condition in which one user's data changes are overwritten by another user's data changes. Also called lost update problem.

Constraint: A rule concerning the allowed values of attributes whose truth can be evaluated. A constraint usually does not include dynamic rules such as "SalespersonPay can never decrease" or "Salary now must be greater than Salary last quarter."

CRUD: An acronym representing *create, read, update, delete,* which are the four actions that can be performed on a database view.

Cube: In OLAP a set of measures and dimensions normally arranged in the format of a table.

Data administration: The enterprise-wide function that concerns the effective use and control of an organization's data assets. It can be performed by a person but more often is performed by a group. Specific functions include setting data standards and policies, and providing a forum for conflict resolution. See Database administration.

Database: A self-describing collection of integrated records.

Database administration (DBA): The function that concerns the effective use and control of a particular database and its related applications.

Database administrator: The person or group responsible for establishing policies and procedures to control and protect a database. They work within guidelines set by data administration to control the database structure, manage data changes, and maintain DBMS programs.

Database data: The portion of a database that contains data that are of interest and use to the application end users.

Database management system (DBMS): A set of programs used to define, administer, and process a database and its applications.

Database save: A copy of database files that can be used to restore a database to some previous, consistent state.

Data Definition Language (DDL): A language used to describe the structure of a database.

Data dictionary: A user-accessible catalog of database and application metadata. An active data dictionary is a dictionary whose contents are updated automatically by the DBMS whenever changes are made to the database or application structure. A passive data dictionary is one whose contents must be updated manually when changes are made.

Data integrity: The state of a database in which all constraints are fulfilled; usually refers to interrelation constraints in which the value of a foreign key must be present in the table having that foreign key as its primary key.

Data item: (1) A logical group of bytes in a record, usually used with file processing. (2) In the context of the relational model, a synonym for *attribute*.

Data Manipulation Language (DML): A language used to describe the processing of a database.

Data mining: The application of statistical and mathematical techniques to find patterns in database data.

Data model: (1) A model of the users' data requirements, usually expressed in terms of the entity-relationship model. It is sometimes called a users' data model. (2) A language for describing the structure and processing of a database.

Data structure diagram (DSD): A graphical display of tables (files) and their relationships. The tables are shown in rectangles, and the relationships are shown by lines. A "many" relationship is shown with a crow's foot on the end of the line, an "optional" relationship is depicted by an oval, and a "mandatory" relationship is shown with hash marks.

Data sublanguage: A language for defining and processing a database intended to be embedded in programs written in another language—in most cases, a procedural language such as COBOL, C#, or Visual Basic. A data sublanguage is an incomplete programming language, because it contains only constructs for data definition and processing.

Deadlock: A condition that can occur during concurrent processing in which each of two (or more) transactions is waiting to access data that the other transaction has locked. It also is called the deadly embrace.

Deadlock detection: The process of determining whether two or more transactions are in a state of deadlock.

Deadlock prevention: A way of managing transactions so that a deadlock cannot occur.

Deadly embrace: See **Deadlock.**

Degree: For relationships in the entity-relationship model, the number of entities participating in the relationship. In almost all cases, such relationships are of degree 2.

Deletion anomaly: In a relation, the situation in which the removal of one row of a table deletes facts about two or more themes.

Denormalization: The process of intentionally designing a relation that is not normalized. Denormalization is done to improve performance or security.

Determinant: One or more attributes that functionally determine another attribute or attributes. In the functional dependency (A, B) Δ C, the attributes (A, B) are the determinant.

Dimension: In an OLAP cube, a characteristic that is associated with a data measure.

Dirty read: Reading data that have been changed but not yet committed to a database. Such changes may later be rolled back and removed from the database.

Distributed database: A database that is stored and processed on two or more computers.

Distributed two-phase locking: A sophisticated form of record locking that must be used when database transactions are processed on two or more machines.

Domain: (1) The set of all possible values an attribute can have. (2) A description of the format (data type, length) and the semantics (meaning) of an attribute.

Domain key/normal form (DK/NF): A relation in which all constraints are logical consequences of domains and keys. In this text, this definition has been simplified to a relation in which the determinants of all functional dependencies are candidate keys.

Entity: Something of importance to a user that needs to be represented in a database. In an entity-relationship model, entities are restricted to things that can be represented by a single table. See **Existence-dependent entity, Strong entity,** and **Weak entity.**

Entity class: A set of entities of the same type; two examples are EMPLOYEE and DEPARTMENT.

Entity instance: A particular occurrence of an entity; for example, Employee 100 (an EMPLOYEE) and the Accounting Department (a DEPARTMENT).

Entity-relationship diagram (E-R diagram): A graphic used to represent entities and their relationships. Entities normally are shown in squares or rectangles, and relationships are shown in diamonds. The cardinality of the relationship is shown inside the diamond.

Entity-relationship model (E-R model): The constructs and conventions used to create a model of the users' data (see Data model). The things in the users' world are represented by entities, and the associations among those things are represented by relationships. The results usually are documented in an entity-relationship diagram.

Exclusive lock: A lock on a data resource that no other transaction can read or update.

Existence-dependent entity: Same as a weak entity. An entity that cannot appear in a database unless an instance of one or more other entities also appears in the database. A subclass of existence-dependent entities is ID-dependent entities.

Explicit lock: A lock requested by a command from an application program.

Export: A function of a DBMS that writes a file of data in bulk. The file is intended to be read by another DBMS or program.

Extensible Markup Language (XML): A markup language whose tags can be extended by document designers. See also **XML Schema**.

Field: (1) A logical group of bytes in a record used with file processing. (2) In the context of a relational model, a synonym for *attribute*.

First normal form: Any table that fits the definition of a relation.

Foreign key: An attribute that is a key of one or more relations other than the one in which it appears.

Fourth normal form: A relation in Boyce-Codd normal form in which every multivalue dependency is a functional dependency.

Functional dependency: A relationship between attributes in which one attribute or group of attributes determines the value of another. The expressions X∆Y, "X determines Y," and "Y is functionally dependent on X" mean that given a value of X, we can determine the value of Y.

Granularity: The size of a database resource that can be locked. Locking the entire database is large granularity; locking a column of a particular row is small granularity.

Horizontal security: Limiting access to certain rows of a table or join.

ID-dependent entity: An entity that cannot logically exist without the existence of another entity. An APPOINTMENT, for example, cannot exist without a CLIENT to make the appointment. To be an ID-dependent entity, the identifier of the entity must contain the identifier of the entity on which it depends. Such entities are a subset of a weak entity. See also Strong entity and Weak entity.

Identifier: In an entity, a group of one or more attributes that determines entity instances. A unique identifier determines exactly one entity instance. A nonunique identifier determines a group of entity instances.

Implicit lock: A lock that is placed automatically by a DBMS.

Inconsistent backup: A backup file that contains uncommitted changes.

Inconsistent read problem: An anomaly that occurs in concurrent processing in which transactions execute a series of reads that are inconsistent with one another. It can be prevented by two-phase locking and other strategies.

Index: Overhead data used to improve access and sorting performance. Indexes can be constructed for a single column or groups of columns. They are especially useful for columns used for control breaks in reports and to specify conditions in joins.

Inner join: Synonym for *join*.

Insertion anomaly: In a relation, the condition that exists when, to add a complete row to a table, one must add facts about two or more logically different themes.

Internet Information Server (IIS): A Windows Web server that processes Active Server Pages (ASPs).

Intersection relation: A relation used to represent a many-to-many relationship. It contains the keys of the relations in the relationship. When used to represent entities having a many-to-many relationship, it may have nonkey data if the relationship contains data.

Isolation level: See **Transaction isolation level**.

Java Server Page (JSP): A combination of HTML and Java that is compiled into a servlet.

JDBC: A standard means for accessing DBMS products from Java. Using JDBC, the unique API of a DBMS is hidden and the programmer writes to the standard JDBC interface.

Join: A relational algebra operation on two relations, A and B, that produces a third relation, C. A row of A is concatenated with a row of B to form a new row in C if the rows in A and B meet restrictions concerning their values. For example, A1 is an attribute in A, and B1 is an attribute in B. The join of A with B in which A1, B1 will result in a relation C having the concatenation of rows in A and B in which the value of A1 is less than the value of B1. See **Natural join**.

Key: (1) A group of one or more attributes identifying a unique row in a relation. Because relations may not have duplicate rows, every relation must have at least one key that is the composite of all of the attributes in the relation. A key is sometimes called a logical key. A unique key identifies a single row in the relation. A nonunique key identifies a group of rows in the relation. (2) With some relational DBMS products, a key is an index on a column used to improve access and sorting speed. It is sometimes called a physical key.

Lock: The process of allocating a database resource to a particular transaction in a concurrent-processing system. The size of the resource locked is known as the lock granularity. With an exclusive lock, no other transaction can read or write the resource. With a shared lock, other transactions can read the resource, but no other transaction can write it.

Lock granularity: The size of a lock.

Log: A file containing a record of database changes. The log contains before-images and after-images.

Maximum cardinality: (1) The maximum number of values that an attribute may have within a semantic object. (2) In a relationship between tables, the maximum number of rows to which a row of one table may relate in the other table.

Measure: In OLAP, a data value that is summed, averaged, or processed in some other simple arithmetic manner.

Metadata: Data concerning the structure of data in a database stored in the data dictionary. Metadata are used to describe tables, columns, constraints, indexes, and so forth. Compare this with **Application metadata.**

Minimum cardinality: In a relationship between tables, the minimum number of rows to which a row of one table may relate in the other table.

Modification anomaly: The situation that exists when the storing of one row in a table records facts about two themes, or the deletion of a row removes facts about two themes, or when a data change must be made in multiple rows for consistency.

Multivalue dependency: A condition in a relation with three or more attributes in which independent attributes appear to have relationships they do not have. Formally, in a relation R (A, B, C), having key (A, B, C) where A is matched with multiple values of B (or of C or of both), B does not determine C and C does not determine B. An example is the relation EMPLOYEE (EmpNumber, Emp-skill, Dependent-name), where an employee can have multiple values of Emp-skill and Dependent-name. Emp-skill and Dependent-name do not have any relationship, but they do appear to in the relation.

Natural join: A join of a relation A having attribute A1 with relation B having attribute B1 where A1 equals B1. The joined relation, C, contains either column A1 or B1 but not both.

N:M: An abbreviation for a many-to-many relationship between the rows of two tables.

Nonrepeatable reads: The situation that occurs when a transaction reads data it has previously read and finds modifications or deletions caused by a committed transaction.

Nonunique key: A key that potentially identifies more than one row.

Normal form: A rule or set of rules governing the allowed structure of relations. The rules apply to attributes, functional dependencies, multivalue dependencies, domains, and constraints. The most important normal forms are 1NF, 2NF, 3NF, Boyce-Codd NF, 4NF, 5NF, and domain/key normal form.

Normalization: The process of evaluating a relation to determine whether it is in a specified normal form and, if necessary, of converting it to relations in that specified normal form.

Null value: An attribute value that has never been supplied. Such values are ambiguous and can mean (a) the value is unknown, (b) the value is not appropriate, or (c) the value is known to be blank.

Object-oriented DBMS (OODBMS): A type of DBMS that provides object persistence; has not received commercial acceptance.

Object-relational DBMS: A DBMS that provides a relational model interface as well as structures for object persistence. Oracle is the leading object-relational DBMS.

Object persistence: The process of storing object data values.

OLAP cube: In OLAP, a set of measures and dimensions arranged, normally, in the format of a table.

1:1: An abbreviation for a one-to-one relationship between the rows of two tables.

1:N: An abbreviation for a one-to-many relationship between the rows of two tables.

OnLine Analytical Processing (OLAP): A technique for analyzing data values, called measures, against characteristics associated with those data values, called dimensions.

Open Database Connectivity (ODBC): A standard means for accessing DBMS products. Using ODBC, the unique API of a DBMS is hidden, and the programmer writes to the standard ODBC interface.

Optimistic locking: A locking strategy that assumes no conflict will occur, processes a transaction, and then checks to determine if conflict did occur. If so, the transaction is aborted. See Pessimistic locking and Deadlock.

Outer join: A join in which all the rows of a table appear in the resulting relation regardless of whether they have a match in the join condition. In a left outer join, all the rows in the left-hand relation appear; in a right outer join, all the rows in the right-hand relation appear.

Overhead data: Metadata created by a DBMS to improve performance; for example, indexes and linked lists.

Owner: In data administration, the department or other organizational unit in charge of the management of a particular data item. An owner also can be called a data proponent.

Parent: A row, record, or node on the "one" side of a one-to-many relationship.

Partitioned database: A database in which portions of the database are distributed to two or more computers.

Pessimistic locking: A locking strategy that prevents conflict by placing locks before processing database read and write requests. See Optimistic locking and Deadlock.

Phantom read: The situation that occurs when a transaction reads data it has previously read and then finds new rows that were inserted by a committed transaction.

Physical key: A column that has an index or other data structure created for it; a synonym for *index.* Such structures are created to improve searching and sorting on the column values.

Primary key: A candidate key selected to be the key of a relation.

Processing rights and responsibilities: Organizational policies regarding which groups can take which actions on specified data items or other collections of data.

Program/data independence: The condition existing when the structure of the data is not defined in application programs. Rather, it is defined in the database, and the application programs obtain it from the DBMS. In this way, changes can be made in the data structures that might not necessarily be made in the application programs.

Query by Example (QBE): A style of query interface, first developed by IBM but now used by other vendors, that enables users to express queries by providing examples of the results they seek.

Query/update language: A language that can be employed by end users to query a database and make changes to the database data.

Read committed: A level of transaction isolation that prohibits dirty reads but allows nonrepeatable reads and phantom reads.

Read uncommitted: A level of transaction isolation that allows dirty reads, nonrepeatable reads, and phantom reads to occur.

Record: (1) A group of fields pertaining to the same entity; used in file-processing systems. (2) In a relational model, a synonym for *row* and *tuple*.

Recursive relationship: A relationship among entities, objects, or rows of the same type. For example, if CUSTOMERs refer other CUSTOMERs, the relationship is recursive.

Referential integrity constraint: A relationship constraint on foreign key values. A referential integrity constraint specifies that the values of a foreign key must be a proper subset of the values of the primary key to which it refers.

Relation: A two-dimensional array containing single-value entries and no duplicate rows. The meaning of the columns is the same in every row. The order of the rows and columns is immaterial. See Figure 2-1.

Relational database: A database consisting of relations. In practice, relational databases contain relations with duplicate rows. Most DBMS products include a feature that removes duplicate rows when necessary and appropriate. Such a removal is not done as a matter of course because it can be time-consuming and expensive.

Relational data model: A data model in which data are stored in relations, and relationships between rows are represented by data values.

Relational schema: A set of relations with referential integrity constraints.

Relationship: An association between two entities, objects, or rows of relations.

Relationship cardinality constraint: A constraint on the number of rows that can participate in a relationship. Minimum cardinality constraints determine the number of rows that must participate; maximum cardinality constraints specify the largest number of rows that can participate.

Repeatable read: A level of transaction isolation that disallows dirty reads and nonrepeatable reads. Phantom reads can occur.

Replicated database: A database in which portions of the database are copied to two or more computers.

Report: An extraction of data from a database. Reports can be printed, displayed on a computer screen, or stored as a file. A report is part of a database application. Compare this with a form.

Report band: See **Band.**

Resource locking: See **Lock.**

Rollback: The process of recovering a database in which before-images are applied to the database to return to an earlier checkpoint or other point at which the database is logically consistent.

Rollforward: The process of recovering a database by applying after-images to a saved copy of the database to bring it to a checkpoint or other point at which the database is logically consistent.

Row: A group of columns in a table. All the columns in a row pertain to the same entity. A row is the same as a tuple and a record.

Schema: A complete logical view of a database.

Schema-valid document: An XML document that conforms to its XML Schema.

Second normal form: A relation in first normal form in which all nonkey attributes are dependent on all of the keys.

Selection: A relational algebra operation performed on a relation, A, producing a relation, B, with B containing only the rows in A that meet the restrictions specified in the selection.

Serializable: A level of transaction isolation that disallows dirty reads, nonrepeatable reads, and phantom reads.

Servlet: A module of application logic that runs on a Web server, normally used in conjunction with the Java language.

Shared lock: A lock against a data resource in which only one transaction can update the data but many transactions can concurrently read those data.

Sibling: A record or node that has the same parent as does another record or node.

Simple network: (1) A set of three relations and two relationships in which one of the relations, R, has a many-to-one relationship with the other two relations. The rows in R have two parents, and the parents are of different types. (2) Any set of tables and relationships containing the structure defined in (1).

Statement level consistency: All rows impacted by a single SQL statement are protected from changes made by other users during the execution of the statement. Contrast with *transaction level consistency*.

Stored procedure: A collection of SQL statements stored as a file that can be invoked by a single command. Usually, DBMS products provide a language for creating stored procedures that augments SQL with programming language constructs. Oracle provides PL/SQL for this purpose; SQL Server provides TRANSACT-SQL. With some products, stored procedures can be written in a standard language such as Java. Stored procedures are often stored within the database itself.

Strong entity: In an entity-relationship model, any entity whose existence in the database does not depend on the existence of any other entity. See ID-dependent entity and Weak entity.

Structured Query Language (SQL): A language for defining the structure and processing of a relational database. It can be used as a stand-alone query language, or it can be embedded in application programs. SQL is accepted as a national standard by the American National Standards Institute. It was developed by IBM.

Subquery: A SELECT statement that appears in the WHERE clause of a SQL statement. Subqueries can be nested within each other.

Surrogate key: A unique, system-supplied identifier used as the primary key of a relation. The values of a surrogate key have no meaning to the users and usually are hidden on forms and reports.

Third normal form: A relation in second normal form that has no transitive dependencies.

Three-tier: A Web database processing architecture in which the DBMS and the Web server reside on separate computers.

Transaction: (1) An atomic transaction. (2) The record of an event in the business world.

Transaction boundary: The group of database commands that must be committed or aborted as a unit.

Transaction isolation level: The degree to which a database transaction is protected from actions by other transactions. The 1992 SQL standard specified four isolation levels: read uncommitted, read committed, repeatable reads, and serializable.

Transaction level consistency: All rows impacted by any of the SQL statements in a transaction are protected from changes during the entire transaction. This level of consistency is expensive to enforce and probably will reduce throughput. It also might mean that a transaction cannot see its own changes. Contrast with *statement level consistency*.

Transform-oriented language: A data sublanguage such as SQL that provides commands and capabilities to transform a set of relations into a new relation.

Transitive dependency: In a relation having at least three attributes, such as R (A, B, C), the situation in which A determines B and B determines C, but B does not determine A.

Tree: A collection of records, entities, or other data structures in which each element has at most one parent, except for the top element, which has no parent.

Trigger: A special type of stored procedure that is invoked by the DBMS when a specified condition occurs. BEFORE triggers are executed before a specified database action, AFTER triggers are executed after a specified database action, and INSTEAD OF triggers are executed in place of a specified database action. INSTEAD OF triggers normally are used to update data in SQL views.

Tuple: Same as Row.

Two-phase locking: The procedure by which locks are obtained and released in two phases. During the growing phase, the locks are obtained; during the shrinking phase, the locks are released. After a lock is released, no other lock will be granted that transaction. Such a procedure ensures consistency in database updates in a concurrent-processing environment.

Two-tier: A Web database processing architecture in which the DBMS and the Web server reside on the same computer.

Unified Modeling Language (UML): A set of structures and techniques for modeling and designing object-oriented programs and applications. It is a methodology and a set of tools for such development. UML incorporates the entity-relationship model for data modeling.

Unique key: A key that identifies a unique row.

Vertical security: Limiting access to certain columns of a table or join.

Weak entity: In an entity-relationship model, an entity whose logical existence in the database depends on the existence of another entity. See ID-dependent entity and Strong entity.

XML Schema Document: An XML document that describes the structure of a class of XML documents by defining the tags and the valid relationship of those tags.

XML Web Services: A set of standards that enable applications to consume each other's services using Internet technology.

Index